WHY PUPILS FAIL IN READING

A STUDY OF CAUSES AND REMEDIAL TREATMENT

WHY PUPILS
FAIL IN READING

By

HELEN MANSFIELD ROBINSON

Director of the Reading Clinics
The University of Chicago

THE UNIVERSITY OF CHICAGO PRESS
CHICAGO · ILLINOIS

THE UNIVERSITY OF CHICAGO PRESS, CHICAGO 37
Cambridge University Press, London, N.W. 1, England
W. J. Gage & Co., Limited, Toronto 2B, Canada

PREFACE

WHY *Pupils Fail in Reading* is a noteworthy volume for at least two reasons: the study which it reports represents a significant milepost in the progress of research concerning the causes of reading retardation; the findings and conclusions are of great practical value both to classroom teachers and to reading clinicians in their efforts to deal intelligently with poor readers. In order to describe clearly the unique contributions of this study, the history of research relating to reading retardation will be reviewed briefly.

Research in this field was begun in the eighties and nineties by surgeons and neurologists, who made detailed examinations of seriously retarded readers and of others who had "lost" ability to read. On the basis of objective evidence in some cases and through reasoning by analogy in other cases, they concluded that brain lesions of one form or another were largely responsible for failure to learn to read and for loss of ability to read. Their findings influenced to a large extent the thinking of teachers and specialists in reading during the next two decades, when the view prevailed that reading disability was due to a highly specialized deficiency in ability to learn.

In 1918, Hollingworth published a study of spelling, which marked a second milepost in the progress of research in the remedial field. The explanation suggested by her findings was that ability to spell is a complex trait "which distributes itself over a normal distribution curve" and that the poorest spellers form "the fag end" of this curve of distribution. She rejected the assumption that inability to learn to spell is due to damage to the visual word center or to "congenital localized neural lesions," and she argued that poor spelling and poor reading resulted from the operation of the laws of heredity and variation, "but for which the child in question would have normal ability." This explanation greatly modified the attitude of teachers toward poor readers and stimulated effort all over the country to discover better ways of teaching pupils who encountered serious difficulty in learning to read.

Dr. Hollingworth's findings and interpretations exerted a strong influence on subsequent research activities. During the twenties and thirties, scores of important studies of poor readers were carried on, which sought, among other things, to identify the causal factors underlying reading retardation. Dr. Marion Monroe's study, entitled *Children Who Cannot Read*, is an excellent representative of this group. The evidence which was secured justified the assumption that both mild and extreme cases of reading retardation may be due to any one, or more, of many causes, for example, limited learning capacity, congenital or acquired neurological defects, conflicting cerebral tendencies, poor perceptual habits, ill-health, improper glandular functioning, poor vision or hearing, abnormal emotional reactions, poor environment, inappropriate teaching, etc. Whereas this conclusion seemed at first to increase the difficulty of the problems faced by teachers and clinicians, it proved in the long run to make them more intriguing and challenging.

The establishment of the fact that severe reading retardation may be due to various causes paved the way and created a demand for the type of study reported in this volume. Most of the previous studies of poor readers had been made, on the one hand, by highly trained specialists, such as surgeons, neurologists, ophthalmologists, psychologists, psychiatrists, or doctors, or, on the other hand, by reading specialists, who had little or no technical training in the special areas referred to. It was natural, in the former case, that the scope of the investigations, the techniques of diagnosis used, and the interpretations of findings, should be dictated by and limited to the special interests and experiences of those making the studies. In the latter case the techniques used were often inadequate or inappropriate to identify the causal factors involved.

In the investigation reported in this volume, Dr. Robinson has attempted the Herculean task of enlisting the interest and securing the co-operation of a group of specialists over a five-year period in the individual study of thirty poor readers and in group interpretation of findings. As diagnosis proceeded, an effort was made to reach agreement concerning the possible causal factors and needed therapy or remedial training. If any pathological condition or physical defect was discovered, steps were taken to correct or eliminate it, if possible. Such corrections were usually made prior to any remedial work in reading, in order to determine their effect, if any, on the reading interests and habits of the subject. If several corrective measures were recommended, they were administered in controlled sequence in order to determine the effect of each.

As implied by the foregoing comments, this is the first comprehensive survey and appraisal of the significance of various possible causal factors in the case of each of several seriously retarded readers. Use was made of the highly specialized skills and insights of experts and of their combined judgments and interpretations concerning the pertinence of the various anomalies identified. The co-operating group also utilized, to a much larger extent than did previous studies, the principle of providing therapy and remedial training in controlled sequence to determine the effect of each. The use of this procedure not only insured valid findings concerning the specific issues studied but also illustrated a technique which may be used to distinct advantage in further research in this field.

The findings of the study are no less significant than the techniques used. They justify three conclusions that form a broad conceptual framework both for future research concerning reading retardation and for the guidance of teachers who face the practical problems presented by poor readers. The first is that pupils who are seriously retarded in reading exhibit many anomalies, that is, physical, mental, social, and emotional deficiencies or disturbances. The second is that, as a rule, the number of anomalies is greater, the more serious the retardation in reading. The third is that many of the anomalies exhibited have little or no relation to reading retardation. These findings emphasize the importance of great care on the part of classroom and remedial teachers, clinicians, and research specialists, in reaching conclusions concerning the specific causes of reading retardation in individual cases. The practice which has often been adopted in the past of accepting the first anomaly observed as the cause of retardation in individual cases is quite inadequate. The findings lend striking support to the assumption that various conditions which influence the reader should be considered in seeking to determine why he is failing in reading.

Of special significance is the fact that a large proportion of the causes of reading retardation on the part of the subjects studied were attributed to home conditions, environmental factors, and previous inappropriate teaching procedures. These are conditions which lend themselves readily to study by classroom teachers. Observations and constructive work with poor readers may well begin in these areas in which the likelihood is great that causes of poor reading can be identified and corrected. The alert teacher, however, will continue her study in other areas and will enlist the co-operation of specialists in the school system or community in identifying other possible causes of slow progress in reading by individual pupils. As a guide in this connection teachers are referred to the comprehensive summary of causal factors in reading presented in the final section of Part II of this book.

In conclusion, Dr. Robinson's report represents a significant milepost in the progress of research in reading retardation. It provides a wealth of illuminating information that may be read to advantage by various types of specialists who are concerned with the physical, mental, social, and emotional conditions of poor readers. It is equally valuable to clinicians, reading specialists, school officers, classroom teachers, and parents who are interested in finding out why certain pupils are failing in reading and the steps that may be taken to eliminate handicaps and to improve reading competence.

WILLIAM S. GRAY
Professor of Education

UNIVERSITY OF CHICAGO

ACKNOWLEDGMENTS

THIS book would not have been completed without the co-operation of many persons. To each I wish to express my gratitude.

The study was carried out with the co-operation of the staff of the Orthogenic School at the University of Chicago. Financial aid to cover stenographic services was provided by the Social Science Research Fund.

Dr. Frank Freeman, acting chairman of the Department of Education, and Dr. Arthur Bachmeyer, director of the University Clinics, provided assistance in organizing the specialists to plan the co-operative enterprise.

Specialists from the University of Chicago Clinics were Dr. Douglas Buchanan, Dr. E. V. L. Brown, Dr. Philip Schanedling, Dr. Mary Jane Fowler, Dr. Allan Kenyon, Dr. Gordon Scott, Dr. Arthur Turner, and Mr. Joseph Wepman.

Social service assistance was under the direction of Miss Charlotte Towle and was carried out by Miss Gladys Hall and Mrs. Louise Smith.

Specialists from the Department of Education included Dr. Mandel Sherman, Dr. Karl J. Holzinger, and Dr. William S. Gray.

The specialists read sections of the manuscript and examined the children to secure the experimental data. Each gave of his time generously, and I especially appreciate their enthusiasm for the study.

Guidance and helpful suggestions in preparing this book were provided by Dr. William S. Gray. His encouragement was an inspiration in producing it.

I am deeply indebted to each of these persons mentioned.

HELEN M. ROBINSON

DEPARTMENT OF EDUCATION
UNIVERSITY OF CHICAGO

TABLE OF CONTENTS

LIST OF TABLES

CHAPTER I

INTRODUCTION

THE chief purpose of this study is to extend understanding of the causes of severe forms of reading disability and to consider the nature of appropriate therapeutic procedures. The achievement of this aim involves three significant steps.

First, to summarize and interpret significant research findings and opinions of authorities concerning causes of severe reading retardation and, with the aid of specialists in the particular fields concerned, to evaluate the findings.

Second, to study the various causal factors contributing to severe cases of reading disability and to further understanding of such factors by considering the various causes that operate in each case rather than by studying each factor in isolation. The term "cause," as used here, is interpreted to mean a factor which, on the basis of tangible evidence, is found to be responsible for part or all of the reading deficiency, such that, when the factor is eliminated or compensated for, improvement in reading occurs.

Finally, to present significant conclusions and new problems which the present study has opened up or found to be significant.

It was hoped that the successful completion of such a study would lay the foundation for more intelligent treatment of poor readers and for more penetrating and productive research relating to them.

NEED FOR THE PROPOSED STUDY

Since the publication of the first report of a case of special disability in reading about a half-century ago, the possible causes reported have increased rapidly in number and now include factors relating to many phases of child life. The first half of this period was devoted largely to proving or disproving the presence of word-blindness, or congenital alexia. Since facilities were not available for the satisfactory solution of such an issue, other possible causes began to receive attention. In fact, numerous theories relating to causes of reading disability were proposed, followed by research to establish

1

46339

their authenticity. Unfortunately, most of the studies reported were open to serious limitations.

Of large importance is the fact that previous studies of the causes of reading retardation have been done largely as individual projects. As a result, most of the research reported has reflected the specific lines of interest and the biases of the persons making the diagnoses. Since these investigators included ophthalmologists, neurologists, psychologists, teachers, and others, different approaches to the study of causal factors have been employed. Because the laboratories used in many of these investigations were not equipped for complete analyses of causes of reading disability, only those causal factors which could be studied by the equipment at hand were identified. As a result, previous studies have related to only certain types of causal factors, have not been closely co-ordinated, and have often added confusion rather than clarity to our understanding of contributing factors.

Equally important is the fact that facilities for determining many abnormalities that may affect reading have not yet been developed or perfected. This applies also to the examination techniques used. It appears necessary, therefore, in further studies of reading disability to secure the co-operation of specialists in many different fields to aid in identifying possible causal factors.

Furthermore, the data secured in many previous studies were interpreted by a general diagnostician or by a specialist in a particular field. As a result, it was impossible for him to interpret broadly the various types of data secured—educational, psychological, physical, emotional, social. In fact, similar data have often been interpreted quite differently by different investigators.

The foregoing facts emphasize the need for more refined methods of studying severely retarded readers. Particularly important is the need for co-operation among different specialists in securing and interpreting basic data concerning the causal factors underlying severe forms of reading disability.

Because previous research studies in this area are open to serious limitations in these respects and because the need is urgent for a clearer understanding of problems relating to deficient readers, this book has been designed to provide a critical summary of existing data and to offer new techniques for the solution of the problem.

OUTLINE OF THE PRESENT STUDY

As indicated in the statement of purpose, this study is divided into three major divisions. First, the summary of previous studies, which is based upon a critical review of about one thousand articles, monographs, and books. A preliminary analysis of the literature revealed the fact that the causes of reading disability could be grouped under the following headings: (1) visual difficulties; (2) intellectual and maturational status; (3) neurological and dominance factors; (4) auditory, speech, and language factors; (5) physical difficulties; (6) emotional reactions; and (7) social and environmental conditions. When the summaries in each of these areas had been prepared in preliminary form, they were submitted to one or two specialists in each area for criticism as to completeness of information and correctness of interpretations. Their suggestions were then incorporated in the particular section involved. The final summary was then submitted to each specialist for approval.

Second, the co-ordinated investigation of causal factors of reading disability in each of thirty seriously retarded readers was planned on a comprehensive scale in order to make a complete evaluation of each case.

To accomplish the purposes of such a study, the services of specialists in each of various fields seemed desirable. Thus each child was examined by the following specialists: a social worker, a psychiatrist, a pediatrician, a neurologist, three ophthalmologists, a speech-correction specialist, an otolaryngologist, an endocrinologist, a reading specialist, and the investigator who acted as psychologist and reading technician.

The findings of each specialist were recorded, and tentative recommendations were made. When all the medical data were available concerning a given child, they were summarized and interpreted by the pediatrician. The investigator then summarized all the data concerning this child and attempted to fit them together into a tentative report. At this time a conference of all the specialists was called for the purpose of looking at the child as a whole and evaluating each separate finding in the light of the total picture. Many factors were found which could be causal or merely coincidental, and an attempt was made to identify these factors and to classify them.

Recommendations for treatment were prepared as a result of this conference, and an attempt was made to correct one difficulty at a time and to evaluate the effect of each corrective measure on progress in reading. If the first recommendations were carried out without success, the group reviewed the case again in the light of subsequent developments and recommended a change in treatment or the addition of another type of therapy to those already operating.

Standard record forms were used, and the incidence of each factor was tabulated separately. An attempt was made to determine the significance of each factor as a cause of reading failure by providing the therapy recommended and measuring progress or estimating changes.

Finally, an interpretation of the findings led to tentative conclusions and emphasized problems in need of further study to clarify completely the causes of severe reading retardation.

PART I

A SUMMARY OF THE CAUSES OF SEVERE READING RETARDATION

IT IS the purpose of this section to summarize pertinent opinions and research findings relating to causes of severe reading retardation. The definition of a cause in each case is not the same as the one used in this study but is the definition assumed by the writer of each article. Each section was prepared first by the investigator and then submitted for criticism to the specialist in the field concerned. It may be assumed, therefore, that the interpretations presented are more valid than could be expected if prepared only by a specialist in any given field.

CHAPTER II

VISUAL MALADJUSTMENTS AS A CAUSE OF READING DISABILITY

READING is commonly defined as "the interpretation of printed symbols." Although this definition places emphasis on the central cerebral processes, the impressions or stimuli that give rise to meanings are secured through the visual mechanism. It is necessary, therefore, to consider the ways in which disturbances of visual structure or function might distort the stimuli, so that inappropriate responses would be produced.

Research studies dealing with the function of vision in reading have been of two general types: (1) studies of behavior of the eyes during the process of reading and (2) studies of visual defects associated with reading difficulty.

GENERAL BEHAVIOR OF THE EYE IN READING

As early as 1879, Javal, of the University of Paris, reported the fact that the eyes pass across the page from left to right in a series of discontinuous steps rather than in a continuous sweep. This opened the way for extensive investigations of the meanings of pauses, called "fixations," as well as of their position and duration. Since that time, expensive and elaborate equipment has been constructed to record the behavior of the eyes while reading. The development of this equipment is reviewed at length in a volume by Taylor.[1] Only a brief sketch of this development will be included here.

Eye-movements were first observed directly and were then counted through the use of a telescope, microscope, mirror, or peephole. Between 1890 and 1900, attempts were made to attach a microphone, an ivory cup, or a plaster-of-Paris cup to the eye to measure eye-movements more accurately. At first, records of these eye-movements were made on a kymograph cylinder.

A light thread was attached to the eye later, and a small piece of Chinese white was placed on the cornea so that the whole face could be photographed. Dissatisfaction with the artificiality of these devices

7

led to the photographing of the reflection of light projected on the cornea of the eye. At first, the horizontal movements were recorded on a falling film, and, later, horizontal and vertical movements were recorded simultaneously on two moving films. The perfection of motion-picture film has enabled the workers in this field to record the reflection of light from the cornea of the two eyes simultaneously on the same film and thus determine the behavior of the eyes during the act of reading.

Attention was first focused on determining the function of the fixation pause, and the interfixation movements of the eye in reading. Dodge and his associates believed that there was no reception of visual stimuli while the eyes were in motion; Dearborn concluded that the stimulation time was well below the threshold necessary for creating a distinct visual impression.[2] Greater emphasis was then placed on the number and duration of pauses and their location with reference to words and parts of words. Dearborn came to the conclusion that all those factors varied with individuals.

Judd[3] studied convergence and divergence between two fixed points and found that, in general, divergence seemed to be a much simpler form of adjustment than convergence. In the execution of these movements, it was evident that the paths of the two eyes varied in form and degree of rapidity. He found that fixation did not occur until the slower eye had caught up with the other. Convergent and divergent adjustments required relatively a long time and might account for frequent pauses made by one or both eyes in passing from one fixation to another.

These and similar studies of the behavior of the two eyes stimulated various investigations of visual co-ordination, abnormalities, and pathology as they might be associated with failure to learn to read.

In recent years a moving-picture film, driven by a motor at a uniform speed, has been used for the purpose of recording the horizontal, as well as the vertical, movements of the eyes. This binocular reading graph may serve two purposes: first, to determine the general level of maturity of the habits of reading as indicated by speed of reading, number and types of fixations, and number and pattern of regressions and, second, to indicate symptoms of visual difficulties, such as excessive convergence, or turning of the eyes toward the nose; excessive divergence, or turning of the eyes away from the central line; nystagmus, or constant movement of the eyes; and lack of co-ordinated movements of the two eyes toward the same place at the same time.

Recently a newer method has been reported. It is called an "electromyogram," which is a record of minute changes in electrical potential between two electrodes placed near one eye, as the eyes sweep along one line of print after another during the process of reading. The authors say that these records reveal the brain as ". . . . an uncompromising taskmaster demanding exquisitely accurate responses as well as perfect teamwork from the ocular mechanism."[4]

MATURATION OF THE READING HABIT

Buswell[5] pointed out that the reading habit as recorded by the eye-movement camera appeared to undergo a change as the age of the subject increased. Thus the reading habit appeared to mature. The average number of fixations, for example, in the first half of Grade I was 19 per line, while the average was 7 per line in Grade IV. Supporting evidence for this trend was secured by Taylor, who photographed eye-movements from Grade I to the college level. The changes from level to level are evident from his norms for fixations,[6] regressions or return movements, and speed of reading in words per minute. Typical films taken at successive levels were used.

SYMPTOMS OF VISUAL DIFFICULTIES

In addition to the maturation of the reading habit, the reading graph may show evidences of certain visual disturbances. Although McAllister[7] found that fixation of a point is not constant and steady, nevertheless a great variation as shown on the film is an indication of nystagmus and as such gives the eye specialist objective evidence of such difficulties.

The fixations of the two eyes should be examined for parallelism. The *Manual* for the ophthalmograph[8] says that a

V-shaped inclination of the fixations for the two eyes . . . . indicates that the eyes were overconverging at the start of the fixation and made a divergent adjustment during the fixation. . . . . In rare instances, Λ-shaped adjustments are noted. This condition is just the reverse of that mentioned above.[9]

Any unusual type of behavior of the two eyes in reading, whenever one eye behaves differently from the other, indicates the need for a careful examination to determine whether there is a physical cause for this behavior.

Parkins investigated various visual skills as handicaps to effective reading and concluded that fixation ability was one of the most important skills. He studied various means of recording this skill and finally decided that he should depend entirely upon the first fixation in each line for the diagnosis of defects in fixation ability.[10]

The foregoing statements indicate that eye-movement camera records show symptoms of the way in which the eyes behave in response to stimuli which set off the central cerebral processes involved in reading. Accordingly, eye-movement records reveal symptoms of reading difficulty.

VISUAL DISTURBANCES ASSOCIATED WITH READING DISABILITY

The second type of research studies with which this summary is concerned deals with visual difficulties that affect reading. Since ophthalmologists were among the first to study reading disabilities and since eye-movement photographs pointed to possible visual problems, much emphasis has been placed on visual disturbances as a cause of failure to learn to read. This factor has received much more attention in the literature than any other, and the findings are much more confusing.

The early case studies by ophthalmologists lacked objective evidence of adequate intelligence or measures of progress. Psychologists and educators were therefore stimulated to study reading failure and began to study visual problems in relation to reading disabilities. In most instances they used devices that were very crude but were designed to screen out cases with visual defects. Since investigators did not have sufficient data or background to make complete diagnoses, it is not surprising that they often arrived at different conclusions.

CONTROVERSIAL ISSUES

Some writers maintain that visual disturbances are largely responsible for reading disabilities, while others take the opposite view and maintain that there is no relation between the two. Another group believes that visual disturbances are one of the many factors which may be operative in any case of reading disability. A few writers have implied that visual disturbances and poor reading may have a common cause, while it is inferred by others that certain types of visual anomalies may be produced by a successful reading adaptation.

All the writers agreed that vision should be considered in the individual diagnosis of poor readers. The real issue seems to be a matter of emphasis on the etiology of reading disability.

Betts[11] suggested that the present disparity in findings might be based upon a number of factors which had not been held constant. For example, ages of the subjects differed markedly, and the results achieved at different ages may not be comparable. The readiness to learn to read has not been considered in these cases. Furthermore, the methods and quality of teaching have not been taken into consideration in comparing good and poor readers. Even the policy of the school is important. For example, in a school where reading was delayed until children were ready, 90 per cent of the remedial-reading cases had visual difficulties. In another school where other factors were not so well controlled, only 40 per cent of the remedial-reading cases had visual difficulties, implying that these other uncontrolled factors were much more prevalent in this latter school.

Betts[12] also called attention to the fact that no universal definition of reading disability has been set up. Whereas some writers consider that a child is a reading problem when he is one-half grade retarded, others believe that a pupil should be two or three grades retarded to be so classified. There might be a considerable difference in the findings of pupils with varying amounts of reading retardation.

Differences in methods of measuring visual efficiency have also been mentioned by Betts[13] as a reason for disparity in findings. This explanation seems important, since some findings are based on research done only by educators and with tests meant only to screen out visual problems, while others are done by persons competently trained in visual diagnosis. In spite of training, however, there is little uniformity in diagnostic procedure even among expert refractionists. When minor visual abnormalities are discovered, refractionists do not agree concerning their significance as a cause for reading failure.

For example, many refractionists believe that a subject can com-

pensate for a refractive error of one diopter, but Luckiesh and
Moss reported that an error of one diopter, which was not unusual
among those possessing refractive errors, would produce a decrease
of nearly 50 per cent in relative visability.[14] It is not surprising, then,
to discover that similar findings may have different interpretations.
In order to study these differences, visual disturbances will be considered according to the most frequent classifications.

VISUAL ACUITY

Visual acuity may be defined as sharpness or keenness of vision as
measured by a standard target at a standard distance. The target
usually is the Snellen chart, and the distance is twenty feet. For
children who do not know their letters, there is a chart with the
letter E standing in various positions, which the child must identify.
The sizes of the letter E correspond to the sizes of letters on the
Snellen chart. With either chart, each eye is tested separately while
the other is covered, and then both eyes are tested while working
together. The visual acuity as measured above is usually the same
for each eye. Collins[15] reported a correlation of $+.73 \pm .003$ between
visual acuity in the two eyes of 9,245 cases.

Inadequate visual acuity may be caused by errors of refraction or
by disuse of the eye. Low grades of simple hyperopia, or farsightedness, will not interfere with visual acuity tested at twenty feet, since
the distant vision may be improved by this condition. However,
myopia, or nearsightedness, in any great degree, will influence visual
acuity as measured at twenty feet; high degrees of astigmatism will
produce changes also. The inequality of visual acuity in the two eyes
is most marked when one eye has become less efficient because of
disuse, as in the case of a squint in which the turning eye is sup-
pressed.

The validity of the Snellen chart as a means of testing vision in
school children has been questioned by a number of writers. Spache
used it with two other tests, and his results led him to conclude that
because of its many defects, avoidable by using more recent tests, it
should no longer be employed as a test of the vision of school children.[16]

Betts believed that unequal visual acuity might interfere with
single binocular, or two-eyed vision. He said: "Occasionally an eye

will have only 50 per cent visual acuity while both eyes are seeing, but when the good eye is covered the 'poor' one can be forced to function at a 100 per cent level. . . . .''[17]

Fendrick studied children in Grades II and III who were manifesting retardation in reading and who had no deficiency in general intelligence. A control group was selected so that each child was the same in chronological age, sex, amount of formal schooling, and general intelligence, except that the control group made normal progress in reading. There were 64 cases in each group. A modification of the Snellen chart with the letter *E* was used for monocular and binocular measurements. A measure of visual acuity was also made at the reading distance of 14 or 16 inches. A modified form of the Jaeger chart was used, and tests were given for both monocular and binocular vision. His conclusions were as follows:

A statistically significant difference was isolated favoring good readers that indicated better than normal visual acuity for distant vision in the right eye. Although the difference became much less marked for children taught by the phonetic method, it was even more striking when good and poor readers taught by the non-phonetic method were compared. Differences were found that indicated better acuity in the left eye and in binocular vision for the good readers, but they were not so significant as those for the right eye measurements.[18]

Eames[19] studied 114 reading-disability cases and 143 unselected cases of approximately the same ages and found no statistically reliable difference in the visual acuity of the two groups. He measured the acuity monocularly with the Snellen chart.

Selzer[20] investigated the vision of 100 deficient and 100 normal readers in Grades II–VI. The data concerning deficient readers showed that 44 per cent possessed less than 20/20 visual acuity in both left and right eyes and that 22 per cent had less than 20/30 vision, which, he said, is commonly considered inefficient. In the normal reading group, 27 per cent had less than 20/20 visual acuity in the left eye and 24 per cent less than 20/20 in the right eye. Normal readers with less than 20/30 acuity comprised about 10 per cent of the group. From this finding he concluded that visual acuity is less adequate among poor readers than among normals.

Monroe reported a comparison of 100 reading-defect cases paired with 100 clinical cases who were satisfactory readers. Seventy-seven per cent of the 100 poor readers had visual acuity above eight-tenths in both eyes, as compared with 73 per cent of the good readers.

Her conclusion was that inadequate visual acuity was not a very frequent cause and did not distinguish the groups of poor readers from other groups of children not exhibiting reading difficulties.[21] In spite of this finding, she believed that defects in visual acuity might interfere in learning to read. Should the retinal image be blurred, the child might not distinguish between similar patterns of letters.[22]

Farris studied 1,685 pupils in the seventh grade and found that 44 per cent had eye defects of various kinds. He concluded that his data did not support the hypothesis that children with defective visual acuity of any type were always handicapped in learning to read.[23]

In speaking of causes for reading failure in a school for problem boys in Chicago, Stulken stated that visual acuity, which was the only factor measured adequately by physical examinations, did not seem to be a primary factor in producing reading difficulty among problem boys.[24] He did not explain how it was measured.

At the college Freshman level, Swanson and Tiffin examined 70 poor readers, 63 good readers, 94 unselected cases, and 40 stutterers with the Betts Tests of Visual Sensation and Perception. They concluded that the

uncorrected eyes of the good reader are poorer in general, except in the case of astigmatism, than the uncorrected eyes of the poor reader, and the fact that the corrected eyes of both groups are approximately the same, make it improbable that differences in visual efficiency are causally related to differences in reading ability among college students.[25]

Blake and Dearborn[26] compared 104 college Freshmen who rated below the twentieth percentile on the verbal section of a scholastic aptitude test with those rating above the eightieth percentile and found that, in general, a larger proportion of the lower group exhibited "defective vision" but that no single visual test differentiated the two groups.

Stromberg[27] matched 71 pairs of university students, whose intelligence was above average, for slow and fast reading. Using the Betts Tests of Visual Sensation and Perception and the Ives Screen Grid Test of acuity and ametropia, he found little difference in the mean of acuity of the two groups. He concluded that speed of reading could not be assumed to be associated with visual acuity.

Taylor compared the visual efficiency of 387 normal high-school students with 100 who were failing in high school. He concluded that the tests used showed little relationship between visual acuity, as such, and reading efficiency.[28]

The foregoing research provides evidence that, regardless of age level or tests used, gross measures of visual acuity do not differentiate good readers from poor readers. All investigators, however, concede that, in individual cases, visual acuity should be considered.

REFRACTIVE ERRORS

When the parallel rays of light entering the eye do not converge properly, the condition is known as a "refractive error." These refractive errors include, first, hyperopia, or farsightedness, in which the parallel rays are focused behind the retina; second, myopia, or nearsightedness, in which the parallel rays are focused in front of the retina; and, third, astigmatism, which is unevenness of focus of rays of light, which results in blurring of a part of the image.

The refractive error may be the same or different in each eye. The term "anisometropia" refers to inequality of refractive error in the two eyes. One eye may even be myopic and the other eye hyperopic.

HYPEROPIA

Cole said that among visual defects affecting reading the most frequent was farsightedness. She reported that among all children of school age, about 60 per cent were farsighted. She emphasized symptoms of ocular defects and stated that generally the symptoms of inadequate vision were similar for all the defects.[29] She said that the eyes watered, appeared swollen and red, or the child rubbed them. There might also be peculiarities of posture and facial expressions. A child might recognize words on the board but not on the printed page or vice versa. The child might appear to see "spots," the page might "jump," or the words look "foggy." Headache, dizziness, or pain might be the complaint, but this was not usual.

She believed that a child with visual difficulties might refuse or fail to read or might become nervous, irritable, and fatigued. The child might read well at first and do increasingly poorer reading. After resting, he might do well again. The brighter children might refuse to subject themselves to the discomfort, thus failing to learn to read, while the duller ones would keep right on trying, thus showing their discomfort.

Eames compared the visual handicaps of 100 reading cases with 143 unselected cases. He found that hypermetropia, or farsightedness, existed with much greater frequency in both eyes of the reading-disability cases, with 43.4 per cent for the right eye and 42.4 per cent for the left eye, as compared with 27.8 per cent and 25.9 per cent, respectively, for the unselected group. His interpretation was as follows:

> Farsightedness operates as a factor in poor reading by causing fatigue which is followed by either blurred vision or discomfort ranging from a tired feeling to sharp ocular and frontal pain with nausea and vomiting. The low and medium grades of farsightedness are more troublesome to poor readers than the high grades of the defect because a rather unsuccessful muscular compensation can be made for the lower degrees. If kept up long enough, this upsets the accommodation-convergence reflex, produces early fatigue in reading, and results in inattention followed by pain and later by gastro-intestinal disturbances. Distant vision is usually normal, particularly when the child is rested, hence the ordinary school eye tests do not demonstrate the presence of any but the extreme cases.[30]

Concerning the ocular condition of 350 poor readers, Eames found that over 50 per cent of the cases had more than $\frac{1}{2}$ diopter of refractive error and that more than one-third had greater than 1.00 diopter. He said: "It is noteworthy that there was a greater incidence of markedly defective right eyes with a relatively good left eye than in the reverse condition."[31] The method of determining refractive errors was not described.

Farris matched 384 visually defective pupils in Grade VII with the same number who had no visual defects. He concluded that hyperopia and strabismus, which is turning of the eyes so that the image of an object cannot fall on the same part of the two retinas, were related to less-than-normal progress in reading.[32] He found that in hyperopic cases corrective lenses were aids to achievement.

In his book on controlled reading, Taylor compared 387 so-called "normal" high-school students with 100 failures, using the Betts tests. He concluded that failures included more cases of hyperopia than did normal subjects. Blurred retinal image at the near point resulted unless the pupil was able to compensate with excessive accommodation.[33]

Betts[34] reported that 80 out of 183 first-grade entrants were farsighted in both eyes and suggested that this was not surprising, since nearly all children are born with slightly hyperopic eyes.

At the college level, Blake and Dearborn[35] found a higher proportion of students of lower scholastic standing to be farsighted.

From the data presented in these reports it would appear that there was a high incidence of hyperopia among reading-disability cases. There was also an indication from at least one report that improvement in reading resulted from the correction of hyperopia by lenses. Surely, then, hyperopia should be considered in cases of reading disability and might be a fruitful field for further research in the prevention of reading failure.

MYOPIA

An interesting description of the relation of myopia to the reading process was produced by May and Perera, who stated:

> Myopia is rarely congenital; there is, however, a *strong hereditary tendency;* it commences at an *early* age and often *progresses;* it is definitely related to a *developmental* factor; there is evidence of a constitutional factor; endocrine disturbances and various dietary deficiencies are said to play a role.
>
> Myopia is more prevalent among the *highly educated* but is found in all classes. Among the *exciting causes* favoring its development and progress in those who are predisposed are the following: Excessive study or close work especially when associated with insufficient outdoor exercise or relaxation, indistinct print, poor illumination, opacities of the cornea and other lesions causing imperfect vision, faulty posture, faulty construction of desks and poor health.[36]

A recent statement by Luckiesh and Moss adds:

> It is not necessary to assume that all, or even a large part of this tendency toward myopia is "natural" or unpreventable. At any rate, prudence demands that consideration be given to the possible artificial causes such as enforced slavery to more and more prolonged tasks of near-vision and to the commonplace sub-optimal conditions for easiest seeing.[37]

Eames[38] found that myopia occurred more frequently in the unselected cases than among poor readers and was considered to be less important in poor reading. He even thought that myopia might be favorable for reading, since it was unnecessary for the child to exert the usual amount of accommodative effort. He also found[39] that 3 per cent of 114 children with educational difficulties were nearsighted, while 7 per cent of the general population were nearsighted.

Farris[40] concluded that myopia and myopic astigmatism were both associated with more than normal progress in reading. His data showed that no improvement in reading occurred when lenses were fitted to correct myopia.

In his book, Taylor reported that 51.16 per cent of the 387 normals were classified as myopic, in contrast with only 28 per cent of the 100 reading failures. In explanation he stated:

> The fact that the normal subjects are more myopic than the failing subjects indicates that myopia alone, especially in low degrees, does not influence reading efficiency at the near point. The high percentage of myopia in the older classes, however, suggests that the continued use of the eyes in near-point work tends to accelerate the development of this defect.[41]

The study by Blake and Dearborn concluded:

> The evidence of this study is convincing that visual defects, the effects of which are sometimes uncorrected even after ocular examination, are a contributing, if not a primary cause, of difficulty in reading. When the compensatory action of the focusing muscles is continued during long periods of close study, often a condition known as pseudo-myopia arises. The ciliary (focusing) muscles of the eyes develop a state of hypertension, or permanent cramp, which is not relaxed easily by lenses placed before the eyes, so that objects beyond 10 or 15 feet cannot be brought into clear focus.[42]

This condition was found in 26 per cent of the poorer readers and in only 2 per cent of the better ones.

The research cited indicates that myopia is probably not a cause of poor reading and may be an asset to good reading. However, there is a possibility that myopia may be a result of our demands placed on young children to do prolonged reading, although this view is not universally accepted. If present in high degrees, myopia should be considered, especially when blackboard or chart-work is important in the educative program.

ASTIGMATISM

Betts found that among 183 first-grade entrants, 67 had astigmatism in both eyes, 25 in the right eye, and 12 in the left eye. He also observed that many of his severe cases of reading disability had been traced to astigmatism as one of the contributing causes,[43] but he failed to state the amount present in these cases. He reported that, up to 1934, 90 per cent of the poor readers he examined had faulty binocular co-ordination and astigmatism.

Fendrick tested for ametropia, or refractive errors associated with astigmatism, and for myopia or hyperopia with the Betts Telebinocular, as reported earlier. He found that 58 per cent of the experimental group and 77 per cent of the control group showed evidence of ametropia. He said: "Although ametropia exists among pupils not manifesting reading disability, its existence cannot be condoned as its presence unnecessarily handicaps the child even though immediate effects may not be evident."[44] Further, 50 experimental cases and their controls were examined by optometrists. Recommendations for corrections were made for 16 per cent of the experimental group and for 6 per cent of the control group.

Less astigmatism in the reading-disability group was found by Eames, and he explained that in clinical work few nonreaders were found to have astigmatism but, on these occasions, the disability was severe.[45]

The studies made by Swanson and Tiffin,[46] Stromberg,[47] and Witty and Kopel[48] indicated that myopia, hyperopia, and astigmatism were not differentiating factors between good and poor readers All these studies employed the Betts tests with the Telebinocular rather than reporting the findings of eye specialists.

It would appear from these studies that astigmatism is not closely associated with poor reading. In some instances it may even be associated with better-than-average reading. However, Betts and Eames believed that it might be a serious handicap, in individual cases, especially when present in higher degrees.

BINOCULAR CO-ORDINATION

The term "binocular co-ordination" refers to the ability to direct the two eyes on the same object at the same time, so that a single impression is obtained. Inability to see the object singly results in, first, blurring; second, double vision, known as diplopia; third, suppression, or lack of function of one eye; or, fourth, alternating the use of the two eyes. Betts stated:

If we were a one-eyed race, our reading difficulties from the point of vision would probably be fewer. A person using only one eye which has normal visual acuity usually has fewer visual troubles but cannot enjoy true depth perception. An individual with normal visual acuity in both eyes presents a different problem; not only must the dominant eye fix on a word or phrase, but its companion also must fix on the same target simultaneously and with as much precision and speed. In addition to this, he must fuse (unify or combine) the right- and left-eye images into one for normal interpretation. Some reading problems appear to be traceable to a lack of co-ordination between the two eyes and to the probable failure to combine the right-eye and left-eye images for correct interpretation.[49]

This belief of Betts was tested by Farris,[50] who concluded from his matched pairs of reading cases that pupils whose visual perception was monocular made better progress in reading than those who lacked correct co-ordination of the two eyes.

Many writers believed that this binocular inco-ordination was due to a lack of muscular balance, as did Whipple, who stated:

> Under normal conditions, the balance and the innervation of these (six pairs of extrinsic eye) muscles are such that both eyes move in concert, i.e., the eye movements are automatically co-ordinated for purposes of single vision. . . . . In some individuals, however, there exists more or less "imbalance" or asymmetry of eye movement, so that the two eyes fail to "track," as it were.[51]

This failure may be one of two types: the eyes may tend to turn out from the desired position, thus creating a condition known as "exophoria"; or they may tend to turn in, which is called "esophoria."

Eames found a greater degree of exophoria among reading-disability cases, which was statistically reliable and significant. In explanation he stated:

> This tendency is carried over when the eyes are in use and results in imperfect convergence, fixation, etc. When the eyes deviate, the retinal images no longer fall on corresponding points of the two retinae, and the resulting mental picture is blurred and confused. Double vision may result and the visual image caused by the stimulation of one eye may be imperfectly superimposed on that of the other.[52]

As a result of this, Eames concluded that fatigue was evidenced by improper eye-movement habits:

> The superimposition of images of words and letters that often occurs in exophoria creates mental impressions of a composite word or letter form, which may be quite unfamiliar, or may blend into a familiar looking symbol. This can be demonstrated by looking through a stereoscope at a stereograph with the letter F on the left and the letter L on the right. When the retinal images of these two letters are made to fall on corresponding retinal points, and the two visual impressions are correctly superimposed, the mental picture is E. It results from the fusion of the letters F and L. . . . . Combinations of letters such as W and S, for example, appear as an unfamiliar form.[53]

He further found that if the exophoria is 3^Δ or over at reading distance, it was nearly always troublesome in reading cases, although the poor readers might not be conscious of the discomfort. Fatigue was a characteristic and was evidenced by inattention.

Selzer[54] found that 90 per cent of his reading-disability cases examined in the laboratory had muscle imbalance. He then examined 100 unselected cases and found that 9 per cent had muscle imbalance and that 5 of these were poor readers. Two of these 5 cases were fitted with prisms, and their reading improved.

Crider[55] studied eye-muscle imbalance and alternating vision, which he called "suspenopsia." He selected 105 cases which he described as "left-eye muscle imbalance" and 38 "with right-eye imbalance." The eye-muscle imbalance was determined monocularly with techniques described by Wells[56] and Mills.[57] Crider found that 75 per cent of the cases "with left-eye imbalance" read the digits with the left eye. He concluded that digits were read by the eye exhibiting best musculature.[58]

Referring to eye-muscle imbalance, visual fusion, alternating vision, and ocular dominance, he stated:

> The fundamental nature of this relation is not clear, but it is the writer's belief that all four factors are in some way connected with the general problem of hemispheric dominance. However, for immediate attack on the reading problem it is suggested that the two eyes be photographed simultaneously on a high-speed film during the reading of ordinary material. Characteristic differences in the movement of the two eyes will probably be revealed and these will give a clue to certain disabilities in reading, such as omissions and reversals, that have not heretofore been explained satisfactorily.[59]

Clark photographed eye-movements of six subjects who had exophoria of 16^Δ–24^Δ at the near point. He concluded that the group who were exophoric made greater divergent movements when starting the lines of print. These divergent movements could cause considerable fatigue, hence would be important in remedial reading.[60] This study is based on too few cases for great reliability but indicates a field for future study.

Farris[61] made a study of refractive errors and binocular imbalances and found that there was greater improvement in reading among students with lens corrections supplied than for those without. Lenses were likewise supplied to correct hyperopia and strabismus, although the types of lenses were not described.

Taylor emphasized the importance of binocular co-ordination when he recommended that every teacher of reading should have available means of facilitating reading and at the same time developing binocular fixations, which he believed necessary for quick perception in reading.[62] He described a method, using rotary prisms and the

Metron-O-Scope, whereby binocular co-ordination might be improved. He used ductions, which he defined as the "power of the extrinsic muscles of the eyes to maintain binocular single vision under stress,"[63] as a measure of binocular co-ordination. He set as his goal training ". . . . the interni recti muscles to give four times the reaction, in prism diopters, of the externi recti muscles, or to condition a $10^\Delta/40^\Delta$ reading-ratio."[64]

After studying thirty experimental, and an equal number of control, cases, Good says: "One is forced to conclude from the scope of this research that adduction and abduction weaknesses definitely accompany difficulty in learning to read. Retests following corrective ocular treatment for increasing duction strength show marked improvement in reading."[65]

Davis suggested that ". . . . the pupil of one eye is not on the same plane as the pupil of the other. Prisms have been used for this particular student with considerable comfort to him."[66] She also pointed to children who ". . . . turn their eyes in too far toward the nose as they make the return sweep to the new line of print. This constant over-convergence could result in fatigue."[67]

Fendrick's[68] study tended to show that muscle imbalance in reading disability had been overemphasized. He found no significant difference between poor readers and control groups in fusion at far and near points, or muscle imbalance.

Witty and Kopel[69] made a study of two groups of children. The poor readers were the 100 poorest among 1,000 children in Grades III–VI, with I.Q.'s above 80. The normal readers were 100 children who rated up to grade or above on the Metropolitan Achievement Test. They found that 29 per cent of poor readers and 1 per cent of good readers exhibited slow fusion. The authors did not interpret this finding as important etiologically. They further stated that analysis of the data caused them to conclude that poor readers exhibited no greater incidence of visual defects and anomalies than did good readers.[70]

In her recent book, Fernald takes the position that reading may increase the efficiency of eye co-ordination. She says:

No other activity requires the exceedingly complex eye adjustments necessary for successful reading. Consequently, unless the individual has learned to read, he does not develop the reading adjustments and so fails to show certain eye co-ordinations. This lack of the finer eye adjustments was characteristic of all our cases at the start. In all our cases of partial disability, eye fatigue accompanied efforts to read, because of the inadequacy of the eye adjustments. As reading skill developed, the eye adjustments became normal and all evidence of fatigue disappeared.[71]

FIXATION ABILITY

Parkins studied fixation ability in relation to reading achievement and concluded that ". . . . fixation ability, which proved to be the all-important visual skill, being responsible, if defective, for handicapping the student over 50 per cent in attaining academic knowledge."[72] This seems to be based on slowing up reading speed and some tests of comprehension.

Furthermore, he suggested that fixation ability be tested by having the patient fixate on a distant object, and then on a pencil placed midway between the eyes at reading distance. As the subject looks at the near object, the examiner observes closely the corneal reflex to see if it reacts easily and rapidly. He suggests the following four manifestations:

1. An efficient fixation ability. The eyes converge rapidly and smoothly for near, each fixing the new object at the same time with exactness.

2. Defective fixation ability. The operator notes that one eye moves in sluggishly or by a jerky motion. This is one of the frequently encountered fixation defects.

3. When attention is called to the near objects, one or both eyes converge or turn in too far and a corrective movement is required to attain an accurate fixation. This is the most commonly encountered fixation defect.

4. The subject makes a smooth speedy fixation but finds it difficult to maintain that fixation, the eyes continually making a slight nystagmoid movement. This is one of the less frequently encountered defects in the fixation ability.[73]

This investigation suggests that fixation ability may be a fruitful field for further research.

FUSION

When the binocular co-ordination of the eyes is precise and accurate, there is a "merging in the brain centers of the neural impulses coming from the stimulation of both retinas in such a way that, although an image is recorded on each retina, we are aware of only one object,"[74] which is called "fusion." Also required for this fusion is precision of accommodation or focus, so that the object is seen clearly as well as singly. Taylor found that 12.40 per cent of "normal" and 25 per cent of reading "failures" had difficulty in fusing retinal images, as measured by the telebinocular at near point.

Eames[75] reported that 35 per cent of 114 children with educational difficulties had fusion difficulty, while 18 per cent of the general population experienced the same trouble. In another article[76] he suggested that fusion varied with the size of type. Again he explained that "in reading, it [low fusion] produces confusions, mixing of letters and small words, jumbling of words, loss of place, and some inability to follow lines across the page."[77] He found that 44 per cent of the poor readers and 18 per cent of the control group exhibited this condition.

Witty and Kopel[78] examined 100 poor readers and 80 controls and found that 29 per cent of the first group and 1 per cent of the latter group exhibited slow fusion. In spite of this, they concluded that it had doubtful effect in producing poor reading.

The evidence in this area is confusing, but it indicates that defective fusion may be associated with reading failure and should be studied in each case.

STEREOPSIS

Stereopsis, or depth perception, is another result of precise binocular co-ordination. It is ". . . . brought about by the disparity, or unlikeness, of the image received by each eye viewing the object from different angles,"[79] according to Betts. Concerning its relation to reading difficulty, he believed: "Although depth perception per se is not required for reading on the usual flat surface, the degree of visual fusion possessed by individuals with the two-eyed vision required to pass this test appears to contribute to the mechanics of rapid reading habits."[80]

Taylor[81] and Witty and Kopel[82] found that stereopsis did not differentiate the good and the poor readers. In fact, stereopsis had not been emphasized by any writers in the field as a cause of poor reading.

In summarizing the importance of binocular co-ordination to reading, we can only conclude that the evidence is very conflicting. The reason may be that the cause of inefficient binocular co-ordination, as well as of fusion and stereopsis, is not clearly understood. Furthermore, methods of measurement used in the studies reported varied among the investigators. It is probable, therefore, that binocular co-ordination can be studied properly only in relation to errors of refraction and general ocular factors. It is apparent that this should be done by a refractionist, in co-operation with a reading specialist.

VISUAL FIELDS

Hinshelwood[83] first recorded changes in visual fields in his extreme cases of reading disability. He found loss of half of the field of vision and attributed the difficulty to neurological changes. Hincks[84] found no such losses, only limited peripheral vision, which she thought might be related to span of visual perception.

Eames[85] explained that the fovea, which is the area of most distinct vision, is capable of reacting to about $\frac{3}{10}$ inch of line or column at reading distance. Since many fixations take in more than this length, he concluded that the extra-foveal area was also utilized. Thus any limitations in the visual fields would limit fixation span. He used a campimeter with black and white targets and studied 85 cases of reading disability, 40 unselected cases, and 12 normals. The latter were selected because they had no educational, visual, or physical difficulties. Among his conclusions were the following:

1. Educational disability cases present *smaller* fields than "normal" or unselected cases.

2. There is a tendency for differences to be greater among left eyes.

3. Restrictions in visual fields can be decreased in size by treatment directed to the underlying cause.

4. The greater increase in field following treatment is in the non-dominant eye.

5. There is a relationship between increment in visual fields and improvement in school work.

In these conclusions, he did not consider the possible effect of practice or closer co-operation on the part of the pupil.

Eames proceeded further to caution educators that every case of restricted visual fields should be under the care of an eye doctor, even if remedial-reading drill is employed.

Spache aptly summarized the results of these studies when he said:

Collectively the evidence indicates that limitations in the visual field may influence reading and spelling by narrowing the span of visual apprehension. This condition may be a partial explanation of the smaller visual memory spans frequently observed among poor readers and spellers.[86]

One can but conclude that more evidence is needed to determine the validity of this relationship.

BLIND SPOTS

Blind spots may be defined as small, regular-shaped areas of the retina which are insensitive to stimulation by light. Brombach charted the size and location of blind spots in poor readers and reported some cases of relationship between enlarged blind spots and poor reading. He even went so far as to suggest a technique which teachers could use for making a rough measurement of the blind spots. He stated that in some instances enlarged blind spots are symptoms

resulting from transitory visual aphasia, the apparent reason appearing to be a desire to eliminate double vision or abnormalities in binocular perception. There is no doubt in my mind that many young people present reading problems as a result of the reduced usable area between the blind spots and the fixation point.[87]

His case studies included no records of intelligence and no reading scores, so that the amount of improvement could not be evaluated. However, blind spots should be investigated further in careful visual examination of poor readers.

ANISEIKONIA

The Psycho-educational Clinic at Harvard University in 1935 directed attention to the nature of the stimulus pattern projected on the retina and its relation to reading failure. This deficiency was called "aniseikonia" and was said to be present when

ocular images are unequal either in size or shape, so that during binocular vision conflicting excitations arrive at the visual centers in the occipital cortex and present difficulties in the ability of the individual to fuse the incongruent images aroused.[88]

Dearborn and Comfort[89] reported on 164 cases, 117 of which were handicapped in school. At that time no controls were available, but they tentatively concluded that 78 per cent of the clinic cases had significant amounts of it. They found five cases of pronounced dyslexia, who had received training in remedial reading without improvement but who made striking progress after correction for aniseikonia. Such cases also reported greater enjoyment in the use of their eyes. They concluded that this was a lead which should have further study.

Dearborn and Anderson[90] carried this study further by matching 100 retarded readers with 100 unselected cases. The matching was made on the basis of mental age and not chronological age. Using more than 1.00 per cent of aniseikonia as significant, they found that 51 per cent of poor readers and 23 per cent of controls were troubled by aniseikonia. It should be noted that the difference between these findings was not due to chance samplings, hence they were statistically significant. The retarded readers also had a higher percentage of aniseikonia.

A more careful study of 38 pairs of these cases at reading distance and at 20 feet, showed that 56 per cent of retarded reading cases and 22 per cent of controls were affected at the near point, while 40 per cent of reading cases and 24 per cent of controls were affected at 20 feet. This difference is significant statistically at the near point but not at 20 feet. Of this group of poor readers, 71 per cent had a higher percentage of aniseikonia at reading distance than at 20 feet. From these data they concluded:

> The greater frequency with which the larger amounts of aniseikonia occurred among the experimental than control cases and the fact that the measurements secured at reading distance differentiated the groups more significantly than did those obtained at 20 feet justify the conclusion that aniseikonia is one of the many factors that may contribute to the causation and persistence of disability in reading.[91]

The high percentage of aniseikonia in poor readers was not borne out by the study of Imus, Rothney, and Bear, who studied a large number of college Freshmen for various ocular defects, including aniseikonia, and concluded that, according to their diagnosis of ocular defects, no significant differences in performance on reading tests, eye-movement camera records, or academic points were evident.[92] Neither did they find improvement in reading during the school year to be associated with ocular defects. They did find that 60 per cent of the cases of aniseikonia examined reported headache, car-, train-, seasickness, or difficulty in reading, or combinations of these.

The subjects may not be aware of small amounts of aniseikonia, since they learn to ignore or adjust to them; but these small degrees affect binocular vision by causing difficulty in fusion, whereas fusion cannot be obtained in over 5 per cent of difference in retinal image.[93] This affects reading by causing early fatigue and interferes with the peripheral visual process.

The difference in findings of these studies may be attributed to selection of cases, since Dearborn and his co-workers studied reading problems that were found in younger people and were probably more severe than those of the Dartmouth study. Perhaps the cases whose counterpoise is not sufficient to compensate for various degrees of aniseikonia would not reach the college level. The evidence available justifies the conclusion that aniseikonia, especially over 1.00 per cent, should be considered in seriously deficient readers, although most clinics are not equipped to give tests for it.

UNDEFINED VISUAL DEFECTS

Some writers do not define the visual difficulties studied, yet reach conclusions concerning relationships. For instance, Clowes[94] found 18 out of 44 children, admitted to the reading clinic at Western Reserve University, to have defective vision.

Wagner gave the Betts tests to about 850 pupils in kindergarten and Grades I–IV. He concluded:

> The differences in visual functioning between good and poor readers are small, and in some cases, perhaps, due to chance. However, the fact that in almost every case the difference favors the good readers supports the general hypothesis that visual inefficiencies, as revealed by the Betts battery, are basically associated with poor reading at the age levels considered in this study.[95]

Kanarik and Manwiller, who studied poor readers with the Betts Telebinocular and Ophthalm-O-Graph, point out that their data supply clear evidence that visual defects are prominent among poor readers. Significant among the difficulties are fusion problems, inadequate visual acuity, lateral imbalance, and loss of sharpness of image.[96]

Gates and Bennett[97] studied reversal tendencies among poor readers and observed the number of children wearing glasses and for whom they were prescribed. Known visual defects existed with twice the frequency in the reversal group as compared with the non-reversal group. They assert that unclear vision calls for prolonged study, necessitating frequent fixations. These back-and-forth refixations may be expected to produce more reversal errors than normal.

SUMMARY

In summarizing the relationship between visual difficulties and ability to learn to read, several points seem clear.

1. Research workers do not agree as to the amount of importance, etiologically, to attach to visual difficulties.

2. The reports, many of them conflicting, are often based on individuals varying in ages from seven to twenty-one years and in reading achievement from Grade I to college level. It is probable that the most seriously retarded readers do not reach these upper levels.

3. Among the visual difficulties most frequently linked with reading inability and apparently in need of more careful investigation are hyperopia, hyperopic astigmatism, binocular inco-ordination, visual fields, and aniseikonia if younger children are being studied.

4. Many of the studies of visual difficulties have not been made by refractionists. Since, in most instances, the eye specialist is not qualified to conduct reading tests, co-operative research between refractionists and specialists in reading diagnosis is needed. It is also essential to consider all other causative factors in an evaluation of the relation of visual inefficiencies to reading, because, as Monroe has said, "the reading defect may result in those cases in which the number or strength of the impeding factors is greater than the number or strength of the facilitating factors."[98] Concerning visual results Eames stated: "Every finding must be weighted in relation to *the child as a whole;* his physical and mental make-up, his health, state of nutrition, habits of life, and the demands made on him by the life that he is required to lead."[99]

Gray has summed up this need in relation to the work of the child in reading by saying that ". . . . many pupils read well in spite of visual defects and that they might read better or with less discomfort if such defects were corrected or eliminated. In any event, the fact is now widely accepted that visual examinations are essential as a part of an individual diagnosis."[100] And, according to Imus, Rothney, and Bear: "Since ocular defects can be readily measured and corrected, it is advisable to look for these conditions before attempting long and somewhat costly remedial measures."[101]

NOTES

1. Earl A. Taylor, *Controlled Reading* (Chicago: University of Chicago Press, 1937).

2. Walter F. Dearborn, *The Psychology of Reading* ("Columbia University Contributions to Philosophy, Psychology, and Education," Vol. XIV, No. 1 [New York: Columbia University Press, 1906]), p. 47.

3. Charles H. Judd, "Photographic Records of Convergence and Divergence" ("Yale Psychological Studies," New Series, Vol. I, No. 2), *Psychological Review, Monograph Supplements*, VIII, No. 3 (1907), 370–423.

4. Matthew Luckiesh and Frank K. Moss, *Reading as a Visual Task* (New York: D. Van Nostrand Co., Inc., 1942), p. 15.

5. Guy T. Buswell, *Fundamental Reading Habits: A Study of Their Development* ("Supplementary Educational Monographs," No. 21 [Chicago: University of Chicago, 1922]), pp. 26–36.

6. *Op. cit.*, pp. 126, 128.

7. C. N. McAllister, "The Fixation of Points in the Visual Field," *Psychological Review Monograph Supplements*, VII (March, 1905), 17–53.

8. *The Ophthalmograph, the Metron-O-Scope: Manual for Controlled Reading* (Southbridge, Mass.: Bureau of Visual Science, American Optical Co., 1937–38).

9. *Ibid.*, pp. 30–31.

10. George A. Parkins, *The Diagnosis and Elimination of Visual Handicaps Preventing Efficient Reading* (Rutland, Vt.: Tuttle Pub. Co., 1941), p. 13.

11. Emmett A. Betts, "Visual Aids in Remedial Reading," *Educational Screen*, XV (April, 1936), 108–10.

12. *Ibid.*

13. *Ibid.*

14. *Op. cit.*, p. 278.

15. S. D. Collins, *Eyesight of the School Child as Determined by the Snellen Test* ("Public Health Reports," reprint No. 975 [Washington, D.C.: Government Printing Office, November, 1924]). Pp. 37.

16. George Spache, "Testing Vision," *Education*, LIX (June, 1939), 623.

17. *Op. cit.*, p. 109.

18. Paul Fendrick, *Visual Characteristics of Poor Readers* ("Teachers College Contributions to Education," No. 656 [New York: Teachers College, Columbia University, 1935]), p. 47.

19. Thomas H. Eames, "A Comparison of the Ocular Characteristics of Unselected and Reading Disability Groups," *Journal of Educational Research*, XXV (March, 1932), 211–15.

20. Charles A. Selzer, *Lateral Dominance and Visual Fusion: The Application to Difficulties in Reading, Writing, Spelling, and Speech* ("Harvard Monographs in Education," No. 12 [Cambridge: Harvard University Press, 1933]).

21. Marion Monroe, *Children Who Cannot Read* (Chicago: University of Chicago Press, 1932), p. 80.

22. *Ibid.*

23. L. P. Farris, "Visual Defects as Factors Influencing Achievement in Reading," *Journal of Experimental Education*, V (September, 1936), 59.

24. Edward H. Stullken, "Retardation in Reading and the Problem Boy in School," *Elementary English Review*, XIV, No. 5 (May, 1937), 180.

25. Donald E. Swanson and Joseph Tiffin, "Betts' Physiological Approach to the Analysis of Reading Disabilities as Applied to the College Level " *Journal of Educational Research*, XXIX (February, 1936), 447–48.

26. Mabelle B. Blake and Walter F. Dearborn, "The Improvement of Reading Habits," *Journal of Higher Education*, VI (February, 1935), 83–88.

27. Eleroy L. Stromberg, "The Relationship of Measures of Visual Acuity and Ametropia to Reading Speed," *Journal of Applied Psychology*, XXII (February, 1938), 70–78.

28. *Op. cit.*, p. 182.

29. Luella Cole, *The Improvement of Reading* (New York: Farrar & Rinehart, 1938), p. 28.

30. Thomas H. Eames, "A Frequency Study of Physical Handicaps in Reading Disability and Unselected Groups," *Journal of Educational Research*, XXIX (September 1935), 2.

31. Thomas H. Eames, "The Ocular Conditions of 350 Poor Readers," *Journal of Educational Research*, XXXII (September, 1938), 16.

32. L. P. Farris, "Visual Defects as Factors Influencing Achievement in Reading," *California Journal of Secondary Education*, X (October, 1934), 51.

33. *Op. cit.*, p. 183.

34. Emmett A. Betts, "A Physiological Approach to the Analysis of Reading Disabilities," *Educational Research Bulletin* (Ohio State University), XIII (September and October, 1934), 135–40, 163–74.

35. *Op. cit.*

36. Charles H. May and Charles A. Perea, *Manual of the Diseases of the Eye* (18th ed., rev.; New York: William Wood & Co., 1943), p. 375.

37. *Op. cit.*, p. 37.

38. Thomas H. Eames, "A Frequency Study of Physical Handicaps in Reading Disability and Unselected Groups," *op. cit.*

39. Thomas H. Eames, "Improvement of School Eye Testing," *Education*, LVI (September, 1935), 14–17.

40. *Op. cit.*

41. *Op. cit.*, p. 183.

42. *Op. cit.*, p. 85.

43. Emmett Betts, *The Prevention and Correction of Reading Difficulties* (Evanston, Ill.: Row, Peterson & Co., 1936), p. 156.

44. *Op. cit.*, p. 51.

45. "A Frequency Study of Physical Handicaps in Reading Disability and Unselected Cases," *op. cit.*, p. 3.

46. *Op. cit.*

47. *Op. cit.*

48. Paul Witty and David Kopel, "Factors Associated with the Etiology of Reading Disability," *Journal of Educational Research,* XXIX (February, 1936), 449–59.

49. *The Prevention and Correction of Reading Difficulties,* p. 157.

50. Farris, "Visual Defects as Factors Influencing Achievement in Reading," *op. cit.*

51. G. M. Whipple, *Manual of Mental and Physical Tests* (Baltimore, Md.: Warwick & York, 1910), I, 175.

52. "A Comparison of the Ocular Characteristics of Unselected and Reading Disability Groups," *op. cit.,* p. 214.

53. *Ibid.,* pp. 214 and 215.

54. *Op. cit.,* p. 296.

55. Blake Crider, "Certain Visual Functions in Relation to Reading Disabilities," *Elementary School Journal,* XXV (December, 1934), 295–97.

56. David W. Wells, *The Stereoscope in Ophthalmology* (rev. ed.; Boston: E. F. Mahady Co., 1926), pp. 28–29.

57. Lloyd Mills, "Eyedness and Handedness," *American Journal of Ophthalmology,* VIII (December, 1925), 933–41.

58. *Op. cit.,* p. 296.

59. *Ibid.,* p. 297.

60. Brant Clark, "Additional Data on Binocular Imbalance and Reading," *Journal of Educational Psychology,* XXVII (September, 1936), 475.

61. "Visual Defects as Factors Influencing Achievement in Reading," *op. cit.*

62. *Op. cit.,* p. 326.

63. *Ibid.,* p. 234.

64. *Ibid.,* p. 246.

65. G. H. Good, "Relationship of Fusion Weakness to Reading Disability," *Journal of Experimental Education,* VIII (September, 1939), 115–21.

66. Louise Farwell Davis, "Visual Difficulties and Reading Disabilities," in William S. Gray (ed.), *Recent Trends in Reading* ("Supplementary Educational Monographs," No. 49 [Chicago: University of Chicago, 1939]), p. 140.

67. *Ibid.*

68. *Op. cit.*

69. "Factors Associated with the Etiology of Reading Disability," *op. cit.*

70. *Ibid.,* p. 457.

71. Grace Fernald, *Remedial Techniques in Basic School Subjects* (New York: McGraw-Hill Book Co., Inc., 1943), p. 177.

72. *Op. cit.,* p. 12.

73. *Ibid.,* p. 13.

74. Taylor, *op. cit.,* p. 234.

75. "Improvement of School Eye Testing," *op. cit.*

76. "The Ocular Conditions of 350 Poor Readers," *op. cit.*

77. "A Frequency Study of Physical Handicaps in Reading Disability and Unselected Cases," *op. cit.,* p. 3.

78. "Factors Associated with the Etiology of Reading Disability," *op. cit.,* p. 457.

79. Betts, *The Prevention and Correction of Reading Difficulties,* p. 158.

80. *Ibid.,* p. 158.

81. *Op. cit.*

82. "Factors Associated with the Etiology of Reading Disability," *op. cit.*

83. James Hinshelwood, *Congenital Word-Blindness* (London: H. K. Lewis, Ltd., 1917).

84. Elizabeth M. Hincks, *Disability in Reading and Its Relation to Personality* ("Harvard Monographs in Education," No. 7 [Cambridge: Harvard University Press, 1926]).

85. Thomas H. Eames, "Restrictions of the Visual Field as Handicaps to Learning," *Journal of Educational Research*, XXIX (February, 1936), 460–65.

86. George Spache, "The Role of Visual Defects in Spelling and Reading Disabilities," *American Journal of Orthopsychiatry*, X (April, 1940), 236.

87. T. A. Brombach, "Blind Spot Measurements and Remedial Reading Problems" (mimeographed by American Optical Co., 1936), pp. 7–8.

88. Walter F. Dearborn and Irving Anderson, "Aniseikonia as Related to Disability in Reading," *Journal of Experimental Psychology*, XXIII (December, 1938), 560.

89. Walter F. Dearborn and Forrest D. Comfort, "Differences in the Size and Shape of Ocular Images as Related to Defects in Reading reported by Emmett A. Betts," "Reading Disabilities and Their Correction," *Elementary English Review*, XII (May, 1935), 131–32.

90. *Op. cit.*

91. *Ibid.*, p. 577.

92. H. A. Imus, J. W. M. Rothney, and R. M. Bear, *An Evaluation of Visual Factors in Reading* (Hanover, N.H.: Dartmouth College Publication, 1938), p. 121.

93. Dearborn and Anderson, *op. cit.*

94. Helen Clowes, "The Reading Clinic," *Elementary English Review*, VII (April, 1930), 98–101, 111.

95. Guy W. Wagner, "The Maturation of Certain Visual Functions and the Relationship between These Functions and Success in Reading and Arithmetic" ("Studies in Psychology of Reading," Vol. I; "University of Iowa Studies in Psychology," No. 21), *Psychological Monographs*, XLVIII. No. 3 (Princeton, N.J.: Psychological Review Co., 1937), 146.

96. Rosella Kanarik and C. E. Manwiller, "How a High School Attacks Its Learning Difficulties in Reading and Arithmetic," *Pittsburgh Schools*, XI (January, February, 1937), 115.

97. A. I. Gates and Chester C. Bennett, *Reversal Tendencies in Reading: Causes, Diagnosis, Prevention, and Correction* (New York: Bureau of Publications, Teachers College, Columbia University, 1933).

98. *Op. cit.*, p. 110.

99. "The Ocular Conditions of 350 Poor Readers," *op. cit.*, p. 10.

100. William S. Gray, with the co-operation of Donald D. Durrell, Arthur I. Gates, Ernest Horn, and Paul McKee, "Reading," *Review of Educational Research*, VII (December, 1937), 505.

101. *Op. cit.*, p. 35.

CHAPTER III

NEUROLOGICAL BASIS FOR READING DISABILITY

NEUROLOGICAL difficulties include, first, damage to or lack of development or function of any part of the brain and, second, dominance, or the inconsistent preference of one cerebral hemisphere over the other for activities of the body and, in addition, the control of language factors.

Various theories of the relation between the brain and the body have been propounded since the beginning of the history of medicine. About 1800, according to Head,[1] however, it was first suggested that a local brain injury could disturb the use of language.

Weisenburg and McBride say that later, Gall attempted to localize six different forms of memory in "centres." They were called memory for things, locality, names, verbal, grammar, and numbers. He thought all these "organs" were in those portions of the brain which were related to the posterior part of the orbital cavity. Head[3] says that Bouillard carried this work further and developed the theory that certain functions were dependent on certain areas of the brain. He attempted to check his theories by post-mortem examination. Many of his findings were accurate, but he made an error in assuming that the speech area lay in the anterior lobes.

According to Weisenburg and McBride,[4] Broca discovered that destruction of the brain in the posterior part of the second and third convolutions, the inferior portion of the Rolandic area, and the first temporal convolution when he performed an autopsy on a case of "aphasia." He divided speech affectations into "aphemia" and "amnesia verbalis." The former was characterized by reduced vocabulary, while the latter was described as a loss of association between ideas and words. He was confused as to the site of the lesion in these cases. They[5] also reported that Marie then disputed the whole theory of the seat of origin, insisting that the real lesion lay in Wernicke's zone.

They[6] said that Bastian propounded the theory that, since we think in words, the mental activities in amnesia are almost propor-

34

tionally impaired. Thus he decided that all aphasia and amnesia could be attributed to lesions of a "motor," "auditory," or "visual word centre," or of the fibers which connect them.

Attempts to explain this vital process in terms of anatomy failed. All the manifestations are more or less transitory and cannot be associated with the severity of the lesion. Damages to the same region have resulted in widely varied clinical manifestations.

In 1896 when Morgan,[7] an English physician, discovered a fourteen-year-old boy with good ability in arithmetic and algebra but with extreme difficulty in reading even the simplest words, he assigned the cause as congenital word-blindness, implying neurological disorder.

DEFINITION OF WORD-BLINDNESS

Word-blindness is of two types: first, acquired word-blindness, which is a loss of ability to read because of injury to the brain and, second, congenital word-blindness, which is a lack of ability to learn to read by ordinary methods, when all other factors are favorable.

Word-blindness, according to Hinshelwood, occurs when difficulty in interpretation of written and printed language is not caused by ocular defects, but by disorder of the visual centers of the brain.[8] He stated, further, that he interpreted congenital word-blindness as a defect of children possessing normal and undamaged brains. It is characterized by difficulty in learning to read, manifestly due to a pathological condition. Ordinary methods of teaching the child to read have failed completely.[9] It is interesting to note that he emphasized, first, the seriousness of the defect in reading and, second, the fact that it is not complicated by other signs of cerebral defect or by visual disorders.[10] He further qualified his definition when he said that general intelligence, powers of observation, and reasoning are not affected in true cases of word-blindness and that auditory memory is average or even above that of other pupils.[11] This definition was widely accepted and, except for minor changes, is used even today.

In 1918, Schmitt preferred to apply the term "developmental alexia" to these poor readers, although she stated:

Congenital word-blindness, inability to learn to read, or dyslexia, has been defined as an extreme difficulty to learn to recognize printed or written language on the part of persons otherwise normally endowed mentally and without defect of vision or other physical defect of such gravity as to constitute an interference of the process of learning to read.[12]

Wallin emphasized interpretation rather than "seeing," when he pointed out that congenital word-blindness referred

not to inability to *see* printed or written characters, but to the inability to *understand* or interpret them..... Word-blindness is only an instance of mind-blindness, or psychic blindness. Word-blindness may affect only letters, or Arabic numerals, or certain groups of letters or figures, or certain syllables, or whole words or certain groups of words, or certain languages but not others .....[13]

Fildes investigated the psychological characteristics of word-blindness and mentioned that, in addition to extreme difficulty in reading or complete failure in learning to read, the condition seems very similar to that known as "acquired alexia," caused by brain injury in later life.[14] She used the term "alexia" as synonymous with word-blindness.

From these definitions it appears that word-blindness is a term applied to individuals who lose their ability to read, usually coincidental with brain injury. In all cases, most of which were adults, post-mortems showed the site of the lesion in the brain. Thus the symptoms of children who failed to learn to read appear to resemble those of adults who have lost their abilities in reading. Therefore, congenital word-blindness has come to be recognized as a condition existing in children who are seriously retarded in reading without other explainable causes.

BASIS FOR CONGENITAL WORD-BLINDNESS

The ways in which the brain might be responsible for congenital word-blindness and reading failure were explained by different investigators. Hinshelwood succeeded in having a post-mortem examination on one case, and the results convinced him of the fact that underdevelopment or injury of part of the brain might lead to reading failure. He concluded that any abnormality in the angular and supramarginal gyri of the left side of the brain of a right-handed person might cause failure in reading. Such abnormality might be due to disease, birth-injury, or faulty development. In fact, any condition which might diminish the number of cortical cells in this area or interfere with the blood supply would diminish the activity of the center. Varying degrees of brain damage or interference might account for varying degrees of reading deficiency.[15]

Bronner[16] noted in 1909 that McCready reported 41 cases of congenital alexia and a year later noted that there was a distinct hereditary factor. In addition, she stated that defective intra-uterine developments, injuries at birth, acute infections, diseases in infancy, and defective postnatal development might be responsible.

Most neurologists up to the present time have accepted pathological changes in the brain as a basis for word-blindness. However, attempts to localize any seat of difficulty in the brain have been unsuccessful. Herrick stated:

> The general conclusion to be drawn from the entire series of physiological and pathological studies of the cortex is that specific mental entities are not resident in particular cortical areas, but that cortical functions involve the discharge of nervous energy from one or more sensory centers to various near and remote regions, each of which, in turn, may serve as a point of departure for new nervous discharges, and so on until the complexity of action and interaction of part upon part becomes too intricate for the mind to conceive. The resultant effect of all these nervous activities which reverberate from one cortical field to another will be the establishment of some sort of a neural equilibrium which finds its expression in a definite motor act or idea. The nature of this physiological process is still unknown.[17]

Schmitt pointed out in 1918 that, since children who are presumed to have a neurological defect do learn to read, then something has happened to the brain lesion. Connections with some other group of brain cells have been made by the stimulus-receiving center involved, and the new center then has taken over the specialized function of storing word images, or the biological center set aside for such a purpose has developed or changed in some way.[18] This point seems very pertinent, since it has been quoted many times in the subsequent literature.

There being no pathological proof of the theory that reading is represented by a definite area in the brain, Lord suggested another explanation:

> If our conclusions have been correctly drawn, so-called congenital word-blindness is not a pathological condition of a visual memory center for words and letters, but is due to a defect in the association fibers; to insufficient associations between the sense areas and to lack of co-ordination in the motor response to visual and auditory stimuli.[19]

Relationship between word-blindness and intelligence, visual discrimination, visual memory, and auditory memory were ruled out by Fildes[20] and Wallin.[21]

Orton summarized views on word-blindness up to 1928 and stated: "Such criterion is obviously unsound. No pathological condition of the visual memory centre has yet been demonstrated, and ordinary methods of school instruction may cover a multitude of sins."[22] Furthermore, he pointed out the fact that no necropsy reports of congenitally word-blind cases had been made.

He suggested the parallelism between adults who have word-blindness and children who fail to learn to read, but warned that children are in the plastic stages of speech development, so other areas should take over that function.

Fernald found that poor readers resembled cases of alexia caused by brain lesion or injury, and she suggested that the condition was "due to certain variations in the integrated brain functioning involving the same region as that in which the lesion is found in acquired alexia."[23] In spite of this, she stated that her cases learned to read merely by changing methods of teaching.

METHODS OF INVESTIGATION

Neurological investigation may be either direct or indirect. The direct investigation would involve sectioning and studying the brain. This is rarely possible, since most severely retarded readers, who have been recognized as such, are still living. Even if post-mortem examinations were possible, perhaps the methods of investigation would not be adequate to note every change in the brain.

The indirect methods of investigation have been used in the study of most reported cases of alexia, or word-blindness. The neurologists apparently have noted the symptoms, ruled out all other causes, and made a diagnosis of alexia or word-blindness, since no other cause could be located. Differences of opinion may exist and may not be proved correct or incorrect because the direct approach is not possible.

SUMMARY

Hinshelwood, who was one of the first to recognize reading disability in children, believed this failure in learning to be due to a congenital defect in the brain, because the symptoms of exceedingly poor readers were similar to those of word-blind adults. His theory has never been proved or disproved, because methods of verification have not yet been established. Post-mortems have rarely been performed, and scant findings on children are available.

No localized areas in the brain can be found, since so little is known of localization of the higher mental processes. In general, it is believed that the seat of reading is in the left hemisphere in persons preferring the right side and in the right hemisphere in persons preferring the left side.

Some accept a more neutral statement, such as that of Eames, who said:

Defects or diseases of the retina, optic nerves, chiasm, and tracts or the lack of appropriate elimination from them of waste products may restrict or slow the process as the neural discharge passes through these structures. This may apply equally well to the mid-brain, the occipital lobes (vision), and the area in which memory and recognition of words appears to be located. Regardless of the reader's opinion as to localization, he must admit that the process of seeing and recognizing takes time, and if it takes time to see and recognize letters and words, slowness in doing so must affect the ability to read.[24]

This, again, is only a theory which appears to explain certain characteristics of poor readers and is without logical proof.

There is need for a more careful evaluation of other causative factors among children on whom a diagnosis of congenital word-blindness or alexia has been made, to see if they can be taught to read by special methods and also if they may become normal readers.

Other methods of investigation, such as electroencephalographic studies, may be helpful in the indirect evaluation of some of these characteristics.

DOMINANCE

"Dominance" is the term applied to the consistent choice of one hand, one eye, one ear, one foot, or one side. The dominant cerebral hemisphere is on the opposite side from the dominant hand or foot. Thus, in right-sided individuals, the left hemisphere is dominant, and in left-sided, the right hemisphere is dominant. Dominant cerebral hemisphere, eye, and hand have been linked with both readng and speech. However, this summary will consider dominance in relation to reading only.

One of the first investigators placing great emphasis on dominance in reading problems was Orton.[25] First, Orton objected to the term "word-blindness" and offered as a substitute "strephosymbolia," which means "twisted symbols."

Orton believed that the two cerebral hemispheres are of about equal size and that the gyri of the dominant hemisphere correspond to those in the nondominant one. The latter are called "silent areas," since injury to this nondominant hemisphere does not destroy language. Since they correspond and are about equally developed in size, nerve cells, and fibers, the assumption is made that they receive and register nerve impulses with almost identical freedom.[26] Since both hemispheres receive and record these impulses but both are not active at the same time, it follows that the impressions in the nondominant hemisphere are elided or unused. He called the record of the impulse in the brain the "engram." Thus:

.... engrams must be formed in the non-dominant as well as in the dominant hemisphere. To account then for the difference in effect of damage in the two sides we must assume that the engrams of one side become the controlling pattern through establishment of a physiological habit of use of that set and that the other set of recorded engrams is latent or elided. Variation in the completeness of this physiological selection, i.e., failure of elision of the non-dominant engrams, forms the kernel of my conception of the reading disability. Such a theory conforms nicely to our observations that these cases are not to be divided into two categories, that is, cases of word-blindness and cases of slow acquisition of reading, but that they form a series graded in severity according to the degree of confusion which exists in choice of engrams and it also offers an explanation of certain errors and peculiarities which characterize their performance.

The two halves of the body are strictly antitropic, that is, reversed or mirrored copies of each other. .... Thus the movements of sinistrad (mirror) writing with the left hand are exactly comparable to those of dextrad writing with the right hand and it seems therefore highly probable that the engrams which are stored in the silent areas of the non-dominant hemisphere are opposite in sign, i.e., mirrored copies of those in the dominant. If then these opposite engrams are not elided through establishment of consistent selection from one hemisphere we would expect them to evince themselves by errors or confusion in direction and orientation and this is exactly what we find in cases of delayed reading.[27]

He also postulated three levels of cortical activity as: perception, recognition, and elaboration. He thought that the destruction of either hemisphere did not affect the first two levels, but the third is the "level at which the written or printed symbol is linked with its meaning and hence it is variously described as the associative, concept, or symbolic level."[28]

In evaluating these neurological factors, Jastak[29] said that Orton's theory was deduced outside rather than induced from the facts. Thus it would appear that Orton saw a group of symptoms and was explaining them neurologically, just as Hinshelwood and others have done, using theory rather than research findings as a basis for conclusions.

However, some investigators have found evidence favoring the theory. For example, Eames[30] examined 100 cases of reading disability and compared their lateral-dominance anomalies with 100 unselected cases and found that such anomalies occur much more frequently in children with reading problems than in the unselected cases. Furthermore, Tinker stated that in cases in which cerebral dominance is marked the child usually has no difficulty in learning to read.[31]

Stanger and Donahue[32] suggested a battery of tests to be used to determine dominance and recommended that the dominant hand chosen by these tests be trained for writing. By following this choice with the kinaesthetic and phonetic methods of teaching reading, they reported excellent success in remedial work, but they failed to consider the number of cases treated successfully by these methods without establishing dominance.

In summarizing these opinions, Dearborn stated:

It appears that in the development of speech and writing one of the cerebral hemispheres is primarily concerned or dominant in the coordinations or associations made. It has long been held that in the case of right-handed individuals, it is the left hemisphere and in left-handed the right hemisphere. This implies a lateral dominance of one side of the body which may be best described objectively in terms of the relative valence of hand and eye, the two organs primarily concerned in (silent) reading and writing. To put the matter in a nutshell, it appears that in order to avoid difficulties in reading and writing one should be either left-eyed and left-handed, or right-eyed and right-handed, and preferably the latter.[33]

He then went on to explain that "in writing and reading (in our language) the movements of the hand and eye are dextrad. . . . . This is the natural and easiest movement of the right-handed—away from the center of the body. Left-handed and left-eyed children have a preference for the other direction, i.e., sinistrad."[34] Dearborn pointed out that reversals were characteristic of these severely retarded readers and might develop because of this difference in directional tendency, since "the result is that faulty word images with letters interchanged are stored up in the mind which later make the prompt and precise recognition of words difficult or almost impossible."[35]

He obtained experimental evidence to support his theory by studying 100 cases of reading disability and comparing them with unselected cases. He found that one-half the unselected group were right-handed and right-eyed, while one-fifth of the cases of dyslexia, or reading problems, were so classified. Eighty-one per cent of the dyslexia cases were either left-dominant, crossed in dominance, or of mixed dominance, as compared to $51\frac{1}{2}$ per cent of the unselected group. Some of these cases, Dearborn[36] believed, were children whose lateral dominance had been changed deliberately or had been changed by accident.

Crider stated that both Dearborn and Orton derived their theory solely from clinical cases, and "the opinions advanced by Orton and Dearborn are commendable as hypotheses but they are not theories and even less are they facts."[37] He felt that any physiological theory seemed to be an oversimplification, and he did not consider many factors, such as intelligence and visual and personality factors. He also felt that there was no evidence that eye preference, as commonly determined, was related to cerebral dominance or even to handedness. He pointed out, too, that there was a tendency for neurologists to veer away from localization of functions, such as "reading level."

In another study Crider[38] pointed to a factor often neglected in considering dominance. The nerve paths from the hands and feet to the brain completely cross, so that the cortical center for each side lies in the opposite side of the brain. The nerve fibers for the eyes do not follow this pattern. The nerve fibers from the nasal side decussate at the optic chiasma and terminate in the opposite hemisphere, while the nerve fibers from the temporal sides remain on the same side with no decussation. Moreover, he found that in right-handed persons the right sides of the retinas are more sensitive than the left. Since the fibers of the right side of the retinas end in the right hemisphere, if it were dominant the individual would be left-handed. So for neurological expediency, one should be right-handed and left-eyed, or vice versa. Actually, the low correlation between the two types of dominance substantiates this theory. He holds that the theory is only tentative, since enough is not yet known about the course of the nerve fibers related to visual function or cerebral dominance.

In a more recent summary, Dearborn[39] reported findings on 200 cases referred to the Harvard Psycho-educational Clinic. In comparing 76 severely retarded readers with the 124 others, he found 14 per cent more of left-eyedness and 17 per cent more of crossed-dominance among the reading cases.

Crosland examined 31 superior readers and 34 inferior readers with his letter-position range of attention tachistoscopic test and several dominance tests. He said: "The tachistoscopic tests reveal that the superior readers excel the defective readers in the left visual field. The inferior readers excel the superior children in the extreme right visual field. . . . ."[40] He also found a majority of poor readers to be left-eyed and a greater majority of superior readers to be right-eyed. From this evidence he concluded that there was a relationship between left-eye dominance and reading failure.

This substantiated Dearborn's conclusion that the left-eyed readers are somewhat more likely to catch the end letters of words than are the right-eyed. Thus Dearborn concluded that it is not yet possible to rule out lateral dominance as a possible etiological factor in producing reading difficulties.[41]

Jenkins, Brown, and Elmendorf[42] reported findings on two pairs of identical twins, one of whom presented difficulty in reading, whereas the other did not. Both of the left-handed twins had difficulty with reading, whereas the right-handed twins had none. However, the left-handed twins were also handicapped, in one case by a lower I.Q. and in the other case by a visual defect. They conclude from this study that mixed dominance is not an "over-shadowing" cause of specific reading disability.

Tinker summarized the information on dominance when he said that "one is justified in inferring that both left-eyedness and tendencies to sinistra sequences in the perception of words and letters are due to cerebral dominance."[43]

Teegarden studied 50 children of Grade I, ranging in reversals from few to many, and concluded that "consistent right dominance or left dominance, or ambidexterity with use of the right eye or the left eye are the conditions of lateral dominance most favorable to success in reading."[44] The conditions least favorable to success, as she found them, were "ambidexterity with use of either eye, and use of right hand with left eye or vice versa. . . . ."[45]

Hildreth[46] used the Van Riper method and had children copy figures. She tested for hand preference and eye preference as well. She found no relation between eye preference and reversals of these figures. She concluded that bilateral tests prove that unilateral orientation comes about as a result of mental development and maturity. It results from practice, learning, and conscious effort as well. She thinks that confusion due to change of preferred hand may prolong the tendency to reverse figures.

Bennett made careful dominance tests of 50 cases of reading disability. In interpreting his findings concerning both poor readers and 50 control cases of good readers, he concluded that there was evidence that children of mixed dominance had a tendency to be poorer readers than those of consistent dominance, although the difference was not statistically significant.[47] His study of reversal errors failed to show any relationship to dominance.

Several investigated dominance and found no evidence of its relation to reading as a whole or to specific types of reading errors, such as reversals. Among these were Hildreth, who used word pronunciation, three oral-reading paragraphs, and a set of flash cards with forms, numbers, and words. She concluded that left-handed and right-handed children appeared to make almost the same number of reversal errors.[48]

Gates and Bond studied hand and eye dominance and visual acuity and their results led them to conclude that

the data obtained from groups of first grade pupils, older normal readers, and older reading problem cases, show no consistent tendency for eye dominance, single eye superiority in acuity, hand dominance, or any combination of these to be related to achievement in reading, word pronunciation, reversal errors, or visual perception of various items.[49]

Woody and Phillips examined 136 pairs of right-handed and left-handed children, matched in as many factors as possible, to determine whether reversals were more common among left-handed children in the first three grades. They reported that their

one outstanding conclusion derived from the numerous types of comparisons made of the responses given to situations in this battery of tests involving reading or activities closely related to the mental reaction in the act of reading is that handedness *per se* with the two groups under consideration had little or no influence on the type of reading response made. Left-handed pupils reacted to the various reading situations just as right-handed pupils did.[50]

Wolfe studied two matched groups of boys. The experimental group was one year or more retarded in reading achievement. Her conclusion was that "the findings of the entire study indicate that eye dominance, hand dominance, and hand versus eye dominance are not related in a primary way to reading disability of the degree represented here."[51]

An extensive investigation was made by Witty and Kopel into the literature concerning dominance and reading, and a study was also made of 100 of the worst reading cases selected from 2,000 children in Grades III–VI. They used a twenty-two-item questionnaire to determine dominance and concluded that their finding tended "to negate the assertions of various writers that reading disability is frequently associated with left-handedness."[52] Concerning eye preference, they concluded that, "therefore, if left-eye dominance is a source of difficulty in reading, as is suggested by Dearborn, Gates and Bennett, Monroe, and Stromberg, then this factor operates to an apparently equal extent in groups of poor and of good readers."[53] And, finally, the relationship of mixed hand-eye dominance is negated by the finding that no association with reading disability was determined by the use of standardized tests and as shown by the tendency to make reversals.

Fernald believed that lack of dominance as it affects learning to read may be subject to training. Her explanation follows:

If it is an essential condition, then to say that unilateral cerebral dominance has not been established with reference to any activity is simply to state in physiological terms that the person has not learned that thing. . . . . It would seem that there must be some fundamental traits that explain the failure on the part of intelligent individuals to develop the brain condition, whatever it may be, that is essential for learning in connection with quite limited subject matter.[54]

She found 62 cases of total disability who learned to read by the kinaesthetic method, regardless of dominance. In the last 50 cases she reports, 40 had corresponding eye and hand dominance, 6 had mixed eye and hand dominance, and 4 were ambidextrous. All the cases were similar and learned by the same methods and were successful readers. Furthermore, as a result of learning to read, there was no change of dominance in "mixed" cases. She points out that many very good readers have mixed dominance.

Selzer contends that cross-dominance was an important factor, although his explanation of the manner in which it affected reading was somewhat different. A summary of his explanation follows:

> These conditions of muscle imbalance and alternating of vision, in addition to a lack of fusion, the writer believes account for such reading disability as are not accounted for by general mental disability. The lack of visual fusion is due to muscle imbalance that has existed from birth or early injury. The optic nerves through a process of branching, connect corresponding parts of the two retinae with corresponding parts of the brain. Thus an image falling upon the fovea of one retina would transmit a stimulus to corresponding parts in both hemispheres, and the image would be interpreted simultaneously and identically by the two hemispheres. The two images would thus appear as one. Through the simultaneous stimulation of identical points in the two hemispheres, they probably become connected by the process of neuro-biotaxis. The engrams established in the two hemispheres thus become connected and function as one ever afterward.
>
> If, however, there is muscle imbalance so that the image of an object falls on the fovea of one retina and on the peripheral area of the other retina, there would thus be two sets of impulses sent to the brain. One set would go to the part of each hemisphere corresponding to the foveal area and the other to an area anatomically removed from the foveal area. In individuals where one eye and the corresponding hemispheres were strongly dominant, only one of these sets of engrams would function in the recognition process. Where, however, there is approximately equal dominance of retinas and hemispheres, the pair of engrams established by the two retinas both strive to function. As the alternating process takes place, first one set out-rivals, then the other.[55]

Here is just another theory without basis which tends further to complicate, rather than to clarify, the thinking in this field. For example, there are a number of persons with congenital nystagmus whose eyes move constantly and whose two eyes do not synchronize. Thus an image of an object does not fall on both maculae simultaneously, and, in addition, all parts of the peripheral retinas have to substitute for the macula. Such subjects often do not have confusion of forms, and, in addition, they learn to read normally.

Concerning visual preference and performance, Spache stated that it was not true that the eye indicated as preferred in monocular tests was always the eye preferred in a binocular situation.[56] Furthermore, he found out that 68 per cent of the population showed no decided eye preference in binocular situations.

In evaluating these studies of dominance, it seemed pertinent to consider the findings of Twitmyer and Nathanson, who tested 200 cases and agreed that "there is an indication that a consistent dominance does not exist and that eye, ear, and body dominance does not necessarily follow to establish a theory of complete cortical dominance."[57] The unreliability of dominance tests, which has not been considered by these investigators, may account for some of the disagreement. Also, the same kinds of functions were not measured by all the experimenters.

Traxler considered a number of such studies and reached what seemed to be a sound conclusion that, "although some persons hold very definite opinions on the subject [referring to relationship between dominance and reading], the sum total of the research literature to date does not warrant these opinions."[58]

SUMMARY

Various theories of dominance and preference have been propounded to explain reading disability. None of them have been proved; and, since there is no general agreement, it appears that dominance can be recognized only as one of several possible causes. In studying every aspect of a child's problem, therefore, dominance should be included.

NOTES

1. Henry Head, *Aphasia and Kindred Disorders of Speech*, Vol. I (New York: Macmillan Co., 1926).

2. Theodore Weisenburg and Katherine E. McBride, *Aphasia* (New York: Commonwealth Fund, 1935), p. 7.

3. Head, *op. cit.*, p. 12.

4. Weisenburg and McBride, *op. cit.*, pp. 8–9.

5. *Ibid.*, pp. 20–24.

6. *Ibid.*, pp. 9–10.

7. W. P. Morgan, "A Case of Congenital Word-Blindness," *British Medical Journal*, II (November 7, 1896), 1378.

8. James Hinshelwood, *Congenital Word-Blindness* (London: H. K. Lewis, Ltd., 1917), p. 15.

9. *Ibid.*, p. 40.

10. *Ibid.*, p. 82.

11. *Ibid.*, p. 83.

12. Clara Schmitt, "Developmental Alexia," *Elementary School Journal*, XVIII (May, 1918), 680.

13. J. E. W. Wallin, "Congenital Word-Blindness—Some Analyses of Cases," *Training School Bulletin* (Vineland, New Jersey), September, 1920, p. 77.

14. Lucy G. Fïldes, "A Psychological Inquiry into the Nature of the Condition Known as Congenital Word-Blindness," *Brain*, XLIV (1921), 287–307.

15. *Op. cit.*, p. 53.

16. Augusta F. Bronner, *The Psychology of Special Abilities and Disabilities* (Boston: Little, Brown, & Co., 1917), p. 85.

17. C. Judson Herrick, *An Introduction to Neurology* (5th ed.; Philadelphia and London: W. B. Saunders Co., 1931), p. 351.

18. *Op. cit.*, p. 765.

19. Elizabeth E. Lord, Leonard Carmichael, and Walter F. Dearborn, *Special Disabilities in Learning To Read and Write* ("Harvard Monographs in Education," Ser. I, Vol. II, No. 1 [June, 1925]), p. 28.

20. *Op. cit.*

21. *Op. cit.*

22. Samuel T. Orton, "Specific Reading Disability—Strephosymbolia," *Journal of American Medical Association*, XC (April, 1928), 1096.

23. *Op. cit.*, p. 164.

24. Thomas H. Eames, "A Study of the Speed of Word Recognition," *Journal of Educational Research*, XXXI (November, 1937), 181.

25. "Specific Reading Disability—Strephosymbolia," *op. cit.*

26. Samuel T. Orton, *Reading, Writing, and Speech Problems in Children* (New York: W. W. Norton Co., 1937), p. 152.

27. Samuel T. Orton, "The 'Sight-reading' Method of Teaching Reading, as a Source of Reading Disability," *Journal of Educational Psychology*, XX (February, 1929), 139–40.

28. *Ibid.*, p. 139.

29. Joseph Jastak, "Interferences in Reading," *Psychological Bulletin*, XXXI (April, 1934), 244–72.

30. Thomas H. Eames, "The Anatomical Basis of Lateral Dominance Anomalies," *American Journal of Orthopsychiatry*, IV (October, 1934), 524–28.

31. Miles A. Tinker, "Diagnostic and Remedial Reading. II," *Elementary School Journal*, XXXIII (January, 1933), 346–57.

32. Margaret A. Stanger and Ellen K. Donohue, *Prediction and Prevention of Reading Difficulties* (New York: Oxford University Press, 1937).

33. Walter F. Dearborn, "The Nature of Special Abilities and Disabilities," *School and Society*, XXXI (May 10, 1930), 633.

34. *Ibid.*, p. 633.

35. *Ibid.*, pp. 633–34.

36. Walter F. Dearborn, "Structural Factors Which Condition Special Disability in Reading," *Proceedings and Addresses of the Fifty-seventh Annual Session of the American Association on Mental Deficiency*, XXXVIII (June, 1932—June, 1933), 268–83.

37. Blake Crider, "The Lack of Cerebral Dominance as a Cause of Reading Disabilities," *Childhood Education*, X (February, 1934), 270.

38. Blake Crider, "Ocular Dominance: Its Nature, Measurement, and Development" (unpublished Doctor's thesis, Department of Psychology, Western Reserve University, 1934).

39. Walter F. Dearborn, "The Nature and Causation of Disabilities in Reading," in William S. Gray (ed.), *Recent Trends in Reading* ("Supplementary Educational Monographs," No. 49 [Chicago: University of Chicago, 1939]).

40. H. R. Crosland, "Superior Elementary-School Readers Contrasted with Inferior Readers in Letter-Position, 'Range of Attention' Scores," *Journal of Educational Research*, XXXII (February, 1939), 426.

41. "The Nature and Causation of Disabilities in Reading," *op. cit.*, p. 108.

42. D. L. Jenkins, Andrew W. Brown, and Laura Elmendorf, "Mixed Dominance and Reading Disability," *American Journal of Orthopsychiatry*, VII (January, 1937), 72–81.

43. "Diagnostic and Remedial Reading. II," *op. cit.*, p. 348.

44. Lorene Teegarden, "Clinical Identification of the Prospective Non-reader," *Child Development*, III (1932), 357.

45. *Ibid.*, p. 358.

46. Gertrude Hildreth, "Bilateral Manual Performance: Eye-Dominance and Reading Achievement," *Child Development*, XI (1940), 311–17.

47. Chester C. Bennett, *An Inquiry into the Genesis of Poor Reading* ("Teachers College Contributions to Education," No. 755 [New York: Bureau of Publication, Teachers College, Columbia University, 1938]), p. 84.

48. Gertrude Hildreth, "Reversals in Reading and Writing," *Journal of Educational Psychology*, XXV (January, 1934), 19.

49. Arthur I. Gates and Guy L. Bond, "Relation of Handedness, Eye-sighting, and Acuity Dominance to Reading," *Journal of Educational Psychology*, XXVII (September, 1936), 455–56.

50. Clifford Woody and Albert J. Phillips, "The Effects of Handedness on Reversals in Reading," *Journal of Educational Research*, XXVII (1934), 662.

51. Lillian S. Wolfe, "Differential Factors in Specific Reading Disability. I. Laterality of Function," *Journal of Genetic Psychology*, LVIII (1941), 56.

52. Paul A. Witty and David Kopel, "Sinistrad and Mixed Manual-Ocular Behavior in Reading Disability," *Journal of Educational Psychology*, XXVII (February, 1936), 126.

53. *Ibid.*, p. 128.

54. *Op. cit.*, pp. 159–60.

55. Charles A. Selzer, *Lateral Dominance and Visual Fusion: Their Application to Difficulties in Reading, Writing, Spelling, and Speech* ("Harvard Monographs in Education," No. 12 [Cambridge: Harvard University Press, 1933]), p. 85.

56. George Spache, "Eye Preference, Visual Acuity, and Reading Ability," *Elementary School Journal*, XLIII (May, 1943), 539.

57. E. B. Twitmyer and Y. Nathanson, "The Determination of Laterality," *Psychological Clinic*, XXII (1933), 142.

58. Arthur E. Traxler, *Summary and Selected Bibliography of Research Relating to the Diagnosis and Teaching of Reading, 1930–1937* (New York: Educational Records Bureau, October, 1937), p. 14.

CHAPTER IV

AUDITORY AND SPEECH DIFFICULTIES
OF SEVERELY RETARDED READERS

IN ORDER to secure meaning from symbols, an adequate speaking
vocabulary with clear and distinct speech is usually considered
desirable. Yet the fact remains that nonhearing and mute children
learn to read, although usually only when special help is given to aid
them in compensating for this handicap. This chapter is designed to
summarize findings relative to auditory, speech, and language functions as they are related to reading failure.

AUDITORY DIFFICULTIES

As early as 1922, Gray and others recognized the effect of auditory
limitations on reading, when they said that some pupils are unable
to hear, so they must be taught by methods suitable for deaf children.
Others who hear indistinctly frequently fail in reading because they
are not properly seated so as to hear words clearly.[1]

Stullken felt that, while there was an insignificant number of partially deaf children in remedial-reading classes in the special school,
"in the regular schools, this factor may have been of more importance than suspected, since the small reading classes and highly individualized type of work of the special school cares for this type of
case automatically."[2]

Some children are unable to hear sounds, which is called "lack of
auditory acuity"; others hear very well but are unable to discriminate between sounds which are similar, designated by the term "difficulty in auditory discrimination"; still other children hear and discriminate but fail to remember the sounds, and these are said to
have "short auditory memory spans" for sounds.

AUDITORY ACUITY

The term "auditory acuity" refers to keenness of hearing and is
best measured by a standard audiometer, used in a soundproof room
by a trained operator. The importance of auditory acuity to academ-

ic learning in general, of which reading is a great part, was summarized by Howes, who concluded that a relatively small amount of hearing loss, if undiscovered, might become almost as serious a handicap to educational attainment as congenital total loss.[3] To get an idea of the handicap of those born deaf, she showed that 67 per cent retardation was found in these children. If her findings are an indication of the importance of hearing losses, then auditory acuity would appear to be an important factor in reading failures.

Bond[4] made audiometric studies of 64 matched pairs of cases, one of each pair being a good reader and the other a poor reader. He found that the mean hearing loss of the good readers was 7.1 per cent and the mean loss of the poor readers was 10.6 per cent. The critical ratio of 2.6 indicated that the difference was significant.

Defects of hearing were considered a major contributing cause of reading difficulties by Gates, who further stated that his studies showed that teachers were often unaware of serious hearing deficiencies such that pupils were unable to understand what was said or read to them.[5]

In studying reading readiness, Gates and Bond found a low correlation between hearing loss and final reading achievement, but the pupils in the near-failing group showed a greater amount of hearing loss than the whole group.[6]

Kennedy tested children in the grades and in high school, and found no significant correlation between auditory acuity and reading level. However, she reported a somewhat greater tendency for good hearers to become good readers and for pupils somewhat handicapped in hearing to read less well.[7] She also found that those with a high-frequency hearing loss, above 2,048 d.v., tended to become very good or very poor readers. The group with high-frequency loss was not sufficiently large to establish this as a fact.

In direct contradiction to these findings were the results of experiments by Wallin,[8] and White and Poull,[9] neither of whom found the poor reader inferior in auditory acuity to the good reader. Jastak pointed out that the literature had cited no instances in which reading defect was ascribed to lack of auditory acuity. These findings were summarized by Witty and Kopel,[10] who concluded that auditory factors appear to be related to reading only in individual cases where the defect was great, or under special conditions.

It is possible for children to have good auditory acuity within certain ranges, while having considerable loss at others. Gates hinted at this when he observed that certain children exhibit tonal deficiencies within a certain range only.[11] Betts was more specific in his conclusion that some children are unable to hear low- and high-frequency sounds.[12]

Some children who lack auditory acuity may be impeded in reading progress, according to Monroe.[13] She gave as a symptom the omission of endings of words and nonstressed syllables, as well as confusion of certain consonant and vowel sounds.

AUDITORY DISCRIMINATION

Speaking of auditory factors in reading, Betts stated:

Obviously no analysis of the auditory functions should be terminated with the testing of auditory acuity. In the Shaker Heights clinic, tests of auditory span, auditory fusion, and auditory discrimination have been developed and are used as a part of the routine for the most serious problem cases.[14]

Monroe[15] felt that lack of precision in discrimination of speech sounds might impede progress in reading and was often associated with articulatory speech disorders. She thought that it might be due to a defect in the auditory mechanism for some ranges of pitches and sound qualities. The result was confusion of certain similar words, such as "sand" and "send," "bit" and "bet," etc. In preparing her reading-aptitude test, Monroe included a test of auditory discrimination because it was designed to measure a difficulty which was frequent among poor readers and prevented the adequate mastery of phonetics as an aid in learning to read.[16]

Some children experience difficulty in blending sounds into words, as Ridenour explained:

This difficulty is characteristic of many children who have been unable to learn to read by the regular school methods and it seems to be connected with weakness in auditory discrimination as well as with inability to grasp large visual units such as words or phrases.[17]

A difference in auditory discrimination between experimental and control groups was found by Bond,[18] whose study was described earlier. This difference was more pronounced where phonics were taught.

Wolfe studied two matched groups of boys, with 18 cases in each group. Concerning auditory factors, she found: "On tests of auditory acuity, discrimination, and memory span, the experimental group was consistently inferior to the control group. The difference was not significant statistically save in word discrimination."[19]

The conclusion justified by these references is that auditory discrimination has not been considered by many investigators, although the results of the few investigations reported indicate a relationship between ability to discriminate sounds and success in reading. Few tests were available, and some of these were regarded as phonetically inaccurate.

AUDITORY MEMORY SPAN

In 1922, Gray and others reported that "a somewhat more subtle difficulty is failure to remember what has been heard. This frequently results in inability to remember the sounds of words and consequently in confusion or even complete failure in reading."[20]

Auditory memory span, according to Blankenship,[21] has been measured by a variety of methods. Monroe made use of a story and stated: "Children who are taught to read from sentences and stories as units must be able to retain the stories in order to associate them accurately with the words of the text."[22]

Bond[23] chose to use digits to measure auditory memory span and found a significant difference between the control and the experimental groups in memory for digits.

Digits, consonants, and nonsense syllables were used by Saunders,[24] who found that children who talked late, with normal age of walking and dentition, often had poor auditory memory. These children had speech defects earlier in life and were generally slow in acquiring facility with language. She stated that these children were not musical and had difficulty in learning to read. They struggled with phonics and were poor spellers. It is interesting to note that she found these children had a particular kind of personality, being shy and retiring and emotionally dependent on parents. Her conclusion was that, "while it cannot be stated that all reading disabilities are allied with poor memory spans, yet it can be stated with certainty that all poor memory spans are allied with difficulty in reading and spelling."[25]

Anderson criticized the use of these tests to measure auditory memory, because he felt that anything the child could visualize might also involve visual memory, even though it was introduced orally. So he concluded that "isolated speech sounds were selected as being the most difficult material to visualize and the most free from possible meaningful associations."[26] With 132 college students, he found a mean memory span for consonants to be 4.66 and for vowels 5.46. This auditory memory span was unrelated to auditory acuity but showed a significant relationship to college grades earned in foreign language. The results were not compared with English reading scores.

Both Betts and Van Wagenen utilized ascending scales of sentence length to measure auditory memory span in relation to reading readiness. Gates used this technique in his Diagnostic Reading Test. With this test, Lichtenstein[27] found that the auditory memory span of 20 retarded readers was inferior to their learning ability.

From these statements it is evident that a valid measure of auditory memory span should be established through further investigation, and the result of this test might then be applied to severely retarded readers.

SPEECH AND LANGUAGE DIFFICULTIES IN POOR READERS

Speech may be interpreted by some as speaking vocabulary and by others as ability to articulate. Thus speech difficulties might imply inability to express ideas clearly and paucity of meaningful language experience or might mean articulatory disorders or stuttering.

This section will attempt to cover both types of speech defects. The first very briefly because there is general agreement concerning vocabulary needs; and the second very briefly too, chiefly because of the insufficiency of data.

SPEAKING VOCABULARY

In 1922, Gray and others pointed out that foreign-born children and those reared in a home in which a foreign language was spoken frequently failed because of inadequate speaking vocabularies. Some American children, too, were exposed to a limited vocabulary in their homes or communities. They might learn to pronounce words which they did not understand, but they failed to react to them intelligently.

All the studies of poor readers, dating from this period, have considered adequate vocabulary important. Gates, Betts, Monroe,

Witty and Kopel, Durrell, and Dolch likewise agreed as to its importance.

Adams' summary of this relationship was so clear and direct that it is quoted in detail:

Many children are plunged into reading before they have developed vocabularies to express their own ideas clearly, to say nothing of their lack of ability to understand the content to be read. They are expected to read complete sentences with "expression" before they are "expressing" their own ideas. They are supposed to follow consecutive lines of thought through the simple primer stories while they are still in the single idea stage of their own composition experience. Not until children have developed some ability in oral expression can they be expected to comprehend or reproduce through reading the ideas of others.[28]

ARTICULATORY DIFFICULTIES AND STUTTERING

Both inaccurate articulation and stuttering were reported by Gray and others. Bennett[29] reported that one factor which seemed prominent in relation to reading failure was a history of the child's having had a speech defect, although there was no evidence of the defect at the time of examination. Nineteen out of 50 children reported such a history.

Monroe included tests of articulation in her reading-readiness battery because "speech defects occur more frequently among poor readers than among good readers. Regarding reading and speech as language related skills, ability in one might possibly be predicated by the others."[30] She compared 415 reading-defect cases with 101 controls and 5,000 problem children and found that defective speech might be a factor in reading disability, operating either as one cause of the reading difficulty or as a result of a common cause.[31] She believed that inaccurate articulation might confuse the child as to which sounds were meant to be associated with printed symbols. Davis explained:

A normally developing child reads as he speaks as he learns. Maturity of auditory perception precedes speech, and maturity of speech depends largely upon an individual's auditory acuity. Perhaps maturity of speech should antecede any introduction to interpreting from printed symbols, which is reading.[32]

She found that the correlation between the speech ages of first- and second-grade children and their reading ages was small but significant. If other factors were equated, a child with mature articulation might be expected to read more quickly and easily and with more accurate comprehension than one who uses "baby-talk."[33]

Stullken[34] reported that approximately 8 per cent of his cases of reading disability had pronounced speech defects.

Hall's findings did not agree with previous ones, as she concluded that there was no relation between deficiency in speech and silent-reading achievement.[35] It should be noted that she based her findings on 21 speech defectives and 61 controls, but not on defective readers.

However, Bond[36] found no difference in incidence of speech defects among good and poor readers, although it is possible, as Bennett indicated, that such a difference might have been present earlier.

Witty and Kopel offered another explanation for such a relationship when they stated: "Defective speech creates an emotional concomitant which may contribute to reading disability by causing self-consciousness, embarrassment, ..., and antipathy toward all reading-language situations."[37]

SUMMARY

It is known that complete deafness interferes with oral reading, but deaf children learn to read silently. The amount of hearing loss necessary to interfere with learning to read orally is not known. However, in this connection Howes found that a small percentage of hearing loss might be a real handicap.

In comparing the audiometric records of good and poor readers, the difference seems to be in favor of the good reader, although 10.6 per cent hearing loss, which was the mean for the poor readers in one study, is considered well within the normal range.

Auditory discrimination was considered in relation to reading failure by only a few investigators, although a positive relationship was found in these instances. Results merit further investigation and probably with better tests.

No valid measure of auditory memory span has been established. The possibility of a relationship between auditory memory span and reading should be considered.

All investigators agree that an adequate meaning vocabulary is essential to reading, but they differ in opinion as to what constitutes an adequate vocabulary.

Articulatory defects have been associated with reading disability both as a cause and as a concomitant, but there is no conclusive evidence of a relationship between them.

NOTES

1. William Scott Gray, Delia Kibbe, Laura Lucas, and Lawrence W. Miller, *Remedial Cases in Reading: Their Diagnosis and Treatment* ("Supplementary Educational Monographs," No. 22 [Chicago: University of Chicago, 1922]), p. 14.

2. Edward H. Stullken, "Retardation in Reading and the Problem Boy in School," *Elementary English Review*, XIV, No. 5 (May, 1937), 180.

3. Esther Cornelia Howes, "An Analysis of Some of the Determining Factors of Educational Achievement of Deaf Children," (Master's thesis, Department of Education, University of Chicago, 1936), p. 28.

4. Guy L. Bond, *The Auditory and Speech Characteristics of Poor Readers* ("Teachers College Contributions to Education," No. 657 [New York: Teachers College, Columbia University, 1935]), p. 48.

5. Arthur I. Gates, "Diagnosis and Treatment of Extreme Cases of Reading Disability," *Thirty-sixth Yearbook of the National Society for the Study of Education*, Part I: *The Teaching of Reading: A Second Report* (Bloomington, Ill.: Public School Pub. Co., 1937), p. 400.

6. Arthur I. Gates and Guy L. Bond, "Reading Readiness: A Study of Factors Determining Success and Failure in Beginning Reading," *Teachers College Record*, XXXVII (May, 1936), p. 681.

7. Helen Kennedy, "A Study of Children's Hearing as It Relates to Reading," *Journal of Experimental Education*, X (June, 1942), 238–51.

8. J. E. W. Wallin, "Congenital Word Blindness—Some Analyses of Cases," *Training School Bulletin*, September, 1920, pp. 76–84, 93–99.

9. A. White and L. E. Poull, *Reading Ability and Disability with Subnormal Children* (New York: Department of Public Welfare, 1921).

10. Paul Witty and David Kopel, *Reading and the Educative Process* (Boston: Ginn & Co., 1939), p. 214.

11. Gates, "Diagnosis and Treatment of Extreme Cases of Reading Disability," *op. cit.*, p. 400.

12. Emmett A. Betts, *The Prevention and Correction of Reading Difficulties* (Evanston, Ill.: Row, Peterson & Co., 1936), p. 193.

13. Marion Monroe, *Children Who Cannot Read* (Chicago: University of Chicago Press, 1932), p. 106.

14. Emmett A. Betts, "A Physiological Approach to the Analysis of Reading Disabilities," *Educational Research Bulletin*, XIII (September and October, 1934), p. 171.

15. *Op. cit.*, p. 107.

16. Marion Monroe, "Reading Aptitude Tests in Beginning Reading," *Education*, LVI (September, 1935), 9.

17. Nina Ridenour, "The Treatment of Reading Disability," *Mental Hygiene*, XIX (1935), 391.

18. *Op. cit.*, p. 42.

19. Lillian S. Wolfe, "Differential Factors in Specific Reading Disability. II. Audition, Vision, Verbal Association, and Adjustment," *Journal of Genetic Psychology*, LVIII (1941), 69.

20. Gray and others, *op. cit.*, p. 14.

21. Albert B. Blankenship, "Memory Span: A Review of the Literature," *Psychological Bulletin*, XXXV (1938), 1–25.

22. "Reading Aptitude Tests in Beginning Reading," *op. cit.*, p. 9.

23. *Op. cit.*

58 WHY PUPILS FAIL IN READING

24. Mary Jane Saunders, "The Short Auditory Span Disability," *Childhood Education*, VIII (October, 1931), 59–65.

25. *Ibid.*, p. 64.

26. V. A. Anderson, "Auditory Memory Span as Tested by Speech Sounds," *American Journal of Psychology*, LII, No. 1 (January, 1939), 95.

27. Arthur Lichtenstein, "An Investigation of Reading Retardation," *Journal of Genetic Psychology*, LII (1938), 407–23.

28. Olga Adams, "Implications of Language in Beginning Reading," *Childhood Education*, XII (January, 1936), 158.

29. Chester C. Bennett, *An Inquiry into the Genesis of Poor Reading* ("Teachers College Contributions to Education," No. 755 [New York: Bureau of Publication, Teachers College, Columbia University, 1938]), p. 78.

30. "Reading Aptitude Tests in Beginning Reading," *op. cit.*, p. 10.

31. *Children Who Cannot Read*, p. 92.

32. Irene Poole Davis, "The Speech Aspects of Reading Readiness," *National Elementary Principal*, XVII, No. 7 (July, 1938), 282.

33. *Ibid.*, p. 286.

34. Stullken, "Retardation in Reading and the Problem Boy in School," *op. cit.*

35. Margaret E. Hall, "Auditory Factors in Functional Articulatory Speech Defects," *Journal of Experimental Education*, VII, No. 2 (December, 1938), 125.

36. *Op. cit.*

37. *Op. cit.*, p. 216.

CHAPTER V

PHYSICAL DEFICIENCIES IN SEVERELY RETARDED READERS

THE relationship between the physical "well-being" of children and their progress in learning has been an issue for a long time. A large number of experiments in this field have been carried on, and research has been instituted on thousands of cases in large units, under grants such as the McCormick Fund in Chicago.

All the early books on reading mentioned casually or emphasized the need for children to attend school regularly in the early stages of learning and pointed out that absence from school might be caused by physical diseases or difficulties.

As early as 1922, Gray and others[1] noted lack of satisfactory progress in four cases, and among the causes they mentioned malnutrition and extreme nervousness. They made no attempt to establish a relationship among the factors or to locate a physical basis for all these difficulties.

Most of the recent publications on causes of failure to learn to read have mentioned physical factors. In this section an attempt will be made, first, to list symptoms of physical difficulties; second, to note the types of difficulties believed to be related to reading failure; and, third, to determine how these factors affect learning to read.

SYMPTOMS OF PHYSICAL DEFECTS

According to Monroe and Backus:

Physical factors may be suspected and should be determined by examination in children who show the following characteristics:

a). Inability to concentrate on reading
b). Apathetic, listless behavior
c). Yawning, fatigue, sleepiness
d). Irritability, hyperactivity, nervousness[2]

Clowes[3] found that postural slumping and prominent abdomen not caused by lack of food were symptoms of fatigue due to malnutrition in 20 of the 44 children referred to her Reading Clinic.

Eames[4] believed that slow word recognition might be due to physical causes of various kinds.

As pointed out earlier, Gray mentioned malnutrition as related to reading. Clowes[5] found that nearly half of her cases were cases characterized by the presence of malnutrition, although the mode of diagnosis might be questioned. She also found poor dentition, defective hearing, mouth breathing, speech defectiveness, and one case of goiter. Monroe and Backus[6] listed the following debilitating conditions which were present in reading cases: malnutrition with underweight or overweight; infected tonsils, adenoids, poor teeth, etc.; glandular dysfunction; asthmatic and allergic conditions; susceptibility to colds; and aftereffects of children's diseases. They also stressed the importance of poor physical habits, such as inadequate sleep and dietary irregularities.

Eames[7] tabulated the physical defects in 100 cases of reading disability as compared with 143 unselected cases and found that the following general physical factors occurred more frequently among poor readers than among controls: disorders of the lymphatic system, circulatory disorders, gastrointestinal difficulties, and tuberculosis.

Hypothyroidism, delay in descent of testicles, and similar growth retardations were considered important by Olson.[8]

Mateer[9] believed that the reduced function of the pituitary gland might be an important factor. In fact, she brought out that, while not all cases of reading disability indicated pituitary dysfunction, yet 90 per cent of 100 cases of pituitary dysfunction were poor readers. She gave so little evidence of the fact that these were real pituitary deficiencies that her findings might be questioned. However, this report has awakened an interest in endocrine disturbances and has resulted in serious research.

In addition to sensory difficulties Witty and Kopel suggested that children with glandular dysfunction, low vitality, allergies, diseased tonsils and teeth, slight or serious cardiac disturbance, and those who were convalescing from exhausting fevers or protracted illness, or with excessive proclivity to fatigue should have a curriculum adjusted to their particular needs.[10]

According to Gates, "the child whose physical stamina is low, or who is suffering pain or distress from malnutrition, fatigue, lack of sleep, infections, defective glandular activities, and other physical difficulties is certain to be handicapped in reading."[11]

Among other factors, Betts[12] suggested that children might be handicapped by toxic conditions caused by infected tonsils, adenoids, kidneys, and the like and that these might be reflected in visual and hearing difficulties.

Durrell[13] listed low vitality due to malnutrition or internal glandular disturbances as producing inattention. In addition, he reported cases of chorea, rheumatic fever, and low metabolism.

A large list of physical difficulties received attention, but the ones listed most frequently were malnutrition, glandular disturbances, and infections of various kinds.

HOW PHYSICAL CONDITIONS AFFECT READING

In general, there appear to be two ways in which reading may be affected by physical difficulties. First, children seem to fatigue quickly and become irritable and inattentive when their energy is at a low point. This may also render them more susceptible to diseases, which is the second means of affecting reading, namely, by keeping the child away from school. These are only hypotheses, and in the absence of proof many persons agree with Tinker, who said:

Many workers in the field are now coming to believe that physiological deficiency as a cause of reading disability has been much overemphasized. It would seem that sensory deficiencies are probably relatively unimportant in comparison with more generalized habits and other central processes of perception and assimilation. . . . . It merely suggests that emphasis should not be diverted from central processes to peripheral factors which appear relatively unrelated to reading status.[14]

However, Monroe and Backus indicated that there might be a relationship and felt that learning to read might well be a difficult process for children who suffer from some debilitating physical condition. They stated that inadequate physical stamina prevents competition with healthier classmates, and consequently weaker children frequently cannot keep up in their school subjects.[15]

Eames asserted that the effect of these physical difficulties on reading "depends on the nature of the condition or disease but in general they impede learning by a reduction of vitality and impairment of general health."[16]

Both Olson and Mateer advanced the belief that endocrine disturbances might affect reading. It has been recognized that extreme lack of thyroid secretion would cause a condition known as "cretinism," and in this condition the child's general learning is greatly impaired. From this extreme condition, many workers inferred that, in a less serious affection of the gland, known as "hypothyroidism," the learning process might be much slower. In line with this, Olson stated: "It is also interesting to note that we get certain instances of split growth involving reading in cases which are marked by hypothyroidism, delay in descent of testicles and similar growth retardation. The accompanying behavioral and emotional disorders are highly interesting on a clinical basis."[17]

Monroe and Backus reported that "absences from school are more frequent in such children, and disrupt the learning process. Even if the child attends regularly, fatigue may prevent his making an enthusiastic or energetic attack on his school work."[18]

"Loss of school time during the first year is one of the commonest causes of reading difficulties," said Durrell. "At no other time in school is long absence so disastrous. Childhood diseases result in absences of a few weeks, during which a pupil may miss many of the words in a rather limited vocabulary."[19]

Witty and Kopel seemed somewhat more conservative in their conclusion that school absence resulting from poor physical health may result in failure, but not necessarily.[20]

Monroe's study of these physical diseases and disorders led her to state:

There were no significant differences between good and poor readers in number of diseases, operations, and accidents occurring during the school ages, so that any relationship between illness and reading defects probably would not result primarily from disrupted school attendance.[21]

From this disputed evidence and opinion it seems clear that one can only adopt the philosophy of Betts, who said: "Neither good readers nor poor readers should work under physical handicaps which can be corrected."[22] Thus it would appear essential to consider these conditions in making a thorough examination of a case of reading disability.

SUMMARY

Malnutrition, infections, and endocrine disturbances are the three general physical factors mentioned most frequently as possible causes for failure to learn to read. None of the studies gave conclusive evidence that these factors are frequent causes. Eames found that they occur more frequently among poor readers but failed to ascertain their causal relationship.

It is probable, but not proved, that some of these physical conditions may have an indirect influence on absences from school.

Endocrine disturbances were considered, but little conclusive evidence of the relationship was found. Perhaps such studies can be more conclusive when measures of glandular abnormalities can be made more accurately.

NOTES

1. William S. Gray, Delia Kibbe, Laura Lucas, and Lawrence W. Miller, *Remedial Cases in Reading: Their Diagnosis and Treatment* ("Supplementary Educational Monographs," No. 22 [Chicago: University of Chicago, 1922]).

2. Marion Monroe and Bertie Backus, *Remedial Reading: A Monograph in Character Education* (Boston, Mass.: Houghton Mifflin Co., 1937), p. 21.

3. Helen Coe Clowes, "The Reading Clinic," *Elementary English Review*, VI: (April, 1930), 98–101, 111.

4. Thomas H. Eames, "A Frequency Study of Physical Handicaps in Reading Disability and Unselected Groups," *Journal of Educational Research*, XXIX (September, 1935), 1–5.

5. "The Reading Clinic," *op. cit.*

6. *Op. cit.*, p. 21.

7. "A Frequency Study of Physical Handicaps in Reading Disability and Unselected Groups," *op. cit.*

8. Willard C. Olson, "Reading as a Function of the Total Growth of the Child," in William S. Gray (comp. and ed.), *Reading and Pupil Development* ("Supplementary Educational Monographs," No. 51 [Chicago: University of Chicago, 1940]), pp. 233–37.

9. Florence Mateer, "A First Study of Pituitary Dysfunction," *Psychological Bulletins*, XXXII (1935), 736.

10. Paul Witty and David Kopel, *Reading and the Educative Process* (Boston: Ginn & Co., 1939), p. 218.

11. Arthur I. Gates, "Diagnosis and Treatment of Extreme Cases of Reading Disability," *Thirty-sixth Yearbook of the National Society for the Study of Education*, Part I. *The Teaching of Reading: A Second Report* (Bloomington, Ill.: Public School Pub. Co., 1937), p. 398.

12. Emmett A. Betts, *The Prevention and Correction of Reading Difficulties* (Evanston, Ill.: Row, Peterson & Co., 1936).

13. Donald Dewitt Durrell, *Improvement of Basic Reading Abilities* (Yonkers-on-Hudson, N.Y.: World Book Co., 1940).

14. Miles A. Tinker, "Trends in Diagnostic and Remedial Reading as Shown by Recent Publications in This Field," *Journal of Educational Research*, XXXII (December, 1938), 295.

15. *Op. cit.*, p. 20.

16. "A Frequency Study of Physical Handicaps in Reading Disability and Unselected Groups," *op. cit.*, p. 3.

17. *Op. cit.*, p. 236.

18. *Op. cit.*, pp. 20 and 21.

19. Donald Dewitt Durrell, *Improvement of Basic Reading Abilities* (Yonkers-on-Hudson, N.Y.: World Book Co., 1940).

20. *Reading and the Educative Process*, p. 218.

21. Marion Monroe, *Children Who Cannot Read* (Chicago: University of Chicago Press, 1932), p. 83.

22. *Prevention and Correction of Reading Difficulties*, p. 240.

CHAPTER VI

INTELLIGENCE AND READING FAILURE

SINCE reading has been defined as a complex reaction to the printed page, involving cerebral processes, and since intelligence is frequently defined as the outward manifestation of these complex processes, it would appear that the two should be related. On this point, most investigators agree that there is a positive relationship. The degree of this relationship and the identification of one as cause and the other as effect appear to be the only points of difference.

In 1922, McCall[1] listed subnormal intelligence as a cause of failure to learn to read. About the same time, Gray and others stated: "The fact is commonly recognized that many mentally defective children are unable to learn to read. . . . . On the other hand, there are many children of low native intelligence who have sufficient capacity to learn to read effectively, but who fail because they do not receive appropriate instruction."[2] Since the publishing of these early reports, no survey of the causes of failure to learn to read has neglected to mention intelligence as a factor.

For a more complete understanding of severe retardation in reading, several problems must be considered. As indicated by the literature they seem to be: (a) What is the relationship between intelligence and reading ability? (b) What is the mental age and I.Q. range of children who have disabilities in reading? (c) Is the score on an intelligence test a safe predictor of reading capacity? (d) Is mental age or intelligence quotient the better measure of reading expectancy? (e) What should be the minimum mental age for exposure to reading? (f) Are there relationships between specific types of intellectual abilities and reading achievement? An attempt will be made to bring together pertinent findings related to these questions in the remainder of this chapter.

RELATIONSHIP BETWEEN INTELLIGENCE AND READING

Witty and Kopel reported a correlation of about .6 between reading-test and intelligence-test scores, which they asserted was too low to predict one from the other. They pointed to the similarity in types of questions used in group tests of intelligence and reading tests, as an explanation for part of this relationship. It was further stressed that perhaps the low correlation between these tests was because one test measured only reading, while the other included "arithmetical problem solving, memory of digits, perception of absurdities and other relationships, motor performances, and so forth."[3]

The opinion expressed by Gates is as follows:

Although intelligence is by no means the only factor determining reading ability, it is nevertheless still customary to assume that reading age should, and usually could reach approximately the level of mental age and that the need of diagnostic study is indicated when it falls appreciably lower.[4]

Gates and Bond[5] reported a correlation of .25 between mental age according to the Binet and reading achievement tests at the end of the first school year.

In his book, Gates[6] also reported correlation of .71 between reading ability and group verbal intelligence-test scores and a correlation of .49 between mental age and reading ability.

Monroe and Backus said that "reading tests usually show a fairly high, but by no means perfect, correlation with intelligence tests. Children who are retarded in general intelligence are usually similarly retarded in reading."[7]

Correlations between Binet mental age and ability to learn to read of .50–.65 were reported by Morphett and Washburne, and they indicated that the correlation between the scores on the Detroit test and reading were higher.

At the college level, where the group is necessarily more selected, Blake and Dearborn found that the correlation between the reading score of poor readers and the Army Alpha Intelligence Test was $+.50 \pm .05$, and with good readers $+.44 \pm .06$.

The previous studies seem sufficient to indicate that intelligence and reading ability appeared to increase simultaneously in a large number of cases. The fact that they were not more highly correlated was deemed important, as it showed the need for consideration of other factors acting to prevent each child from reading up to the limit of his mental age.

The exact relationship between intelligence and reading was expressed by most writers as follows: First, inadequate intelligence appeared to cause inability to learn in all school subjects, of which reading was but one phase; and, second, in children who had specific reading disabilities, intelligence seemed to be distributed essentially as it is in the general population. In other words, severely retarded readers may be found with low, average, or superior intelligence. Witty and Kopel have stated that "idiots (I.Q. below 25) and imbeciles (I.Q. 25–50) cannot learn to read."[8] They also pointed out that morons (I.Q. 50–70) rarely achieve better than fourth-grade proficiency. However, these groups comprise only 1 or 2 per cent of the whole population[9] and some are institutionalized. Thus the large proportion of reading problems are not seriously mentally retarded.

The dull child (I.Q. 70–85) according to the above reference, was

. . . . poorly equipped to meet the demands of the typical school, because the standards set for all children are unattainable by these youngsters when academic books are first introduced; at a later time, after these youngsters have failed again and again, the same tasks are no longer appropriate in terms of the children's maturing interests and needs.[10]

THE RANGE OF INTELLIGENCE OF SEVERELY RETARDED READERS

Witty and Kopel reported that 90 per cent of poor readers of both elementary- and high-school ages, had I.Q.'s from 80 to 110, with about equal numbers between 80 and 90, 90 and 100, 100 and 110. Thus they concluded that most poor readers have sufficient mental ability to read satisfactorily if appropriate and attainable goals are set up and if there is proper motivation.[11]

The study by Preston[12] showed a distribution of 90–140 in the I.Q.'s of her 100 cases of reading disability but did not report the mental-age range.

Monroe's tables of mental ages showed a possible range of 5-0 to 18-0 for 215 clinic reading cases, and 6-0 to 18-0 for 155 special reading cases. The I.Q.'s for the first group ranged from about 50 to 130, and for the latter group from 60 to 150. Concerning the mental age, she stated that the mean of the special reading cases is about equal to that found by Terman for unselected children.[13]

Likewise, Blanchard[14] found that half of her 73 cases had I.Q.'s between 90 and 109, while one-third rated from 110 to 139, and the rest were between 70 and 89.

Most investigators of serious reading disabilities have agreed that the intelligence measured by individual tests given to retarded readers corresponds closely to the intelligence of children of the same life-ages in the general population. Thus the conclusion that low intelligence is not a predominant cause of most severely retarded readers appears sound. Low intelligence would be a cause of poor reading only in a small proportion of cases.

MEASURES OF INTELLIGENCE FOR THE STUDY OF READING CASES

Intelligence is measured by various kinds of tests. Because of the time involved and the specialized training and equipment required to give individual intelligence tests, most schools employ group tests of intelligence. Betts called attention to a limitation when he said that group tests requiring reading are inadequate measures of the intelligence of poor readers.[15] Attempts to measure intelligence by tests involving reading, when these tests are to be used as a standard of reading expectancy, are exceedingly unfair to the very retarded reader, since they would usually label him as feeble-minded.

Nolan emphasizes this point when she says: "Pupils who cannot read cannot be measured accurately by a test they do not comprehend. What is needed for them is either a group test that screens out reading difficulty, giving a non-language as well as a language factor, or an individual test."[16]

The New Stanford-Binet[17] is recommended by more recent writers, while the old Binet[18] was recommended as the best single measure by writers earlier than 1936. Most of them agreed with Arthur[19] that supplementary tests were found desirable. She recommended the Arthur Point Scale, and on 14 severely retarded readers she found an average difference of thirteen points in comparing I.Q.'s on the two tests. The higher scores were made on the performance tests.

Monroe and Backus[20] secured evidence that mentally retarded children tend to have about equal mental ages on the Binet and Arthur Point Scale, while reading disability cases do not score equally, tending to be superior on the Arthur tests.

The combination of the Binet and Arthur Point Scale, plus a nonverbal test in some instances, was recommended by Whipple,[21] Witty and Kopel,[22] Jameson,[23] and others.

In spite of the desirability of the use of the Binet, its limitations should also be noted. Some of the subtests in the Binet test require the child to read. Durrell[24] studied 134 cases of reading disability and paired them with an equal number of controls. He found that reading tests were not a fair measure of the mental ages of retarded readers. When he re-scored the Binet, omitting certain tests involving reading, the average I.Q. of the reading-disability cases was raised four points while that of the controls remained the same. This method of re-scoring was used frequently on the old form of the Binet, but no such study has indicated the tests to be omitted in re-scoring the revised Binet.

Assuming that the Binet is used, there seems to be some question as to whether the mental age or the I.Q. would be the most reliable means of estimating ability.

In a study of young children, Davidson[25] concluded that brightness, of which the I.Q. is an indication, was the most important factor in reading success yet considered.

The mental age, rather than the I.Q., was favored by Monroe and Backus,[26] Harrison,[27] Morphett and Washburne,[28] and was emphasized by Betts, who believed that the remedial teacher should be concerned with mental age rather than with I.Q.

In another instance Betts suggested that "basal age may be a more reliable criterion for the prediction of reading achievement than mental age. . . . ."[29] This contention was reflected by Durrell,[30] who found that children with special reading disabilities usually have lower Binet basal ages and show wider scatter than do normals.

PREDICTING READING FROM INTELLIGENCE

The lack of highly significant correlations between measures of intelligence and reading achievement definitely indicated that neither could be predicted from the other with any degree of confidence. However, it was assumed that a child's reading grade should correspond with his mental age if *all factors were ideal for his learning to read*.

A mental-age score on the Binet has been assumed by many as the nearest general estimate of expectancy yet discovered. No point-for-point correspondence was expected, and, as Gates pointed out, mental age only indicates the relative position which a pupil should occupy in an average school. He compiled a table[31] to be used as a guide in translating mental age into mental-age-grade expectancy to determine expectancy in reading.

Monroe chose to assume that the child enters school at about six years and gains one grade for each year of chronological age.[32] Thus, to obtain mental age-grade expectancy, subtract 5–0 from the mental age and the result gives the general level of expectancy.

Witty and Kopel were more conservative and said:

> Finally, there is no reason for assuming that every child (or any child) should read in accord with his mental age. Small disparities in reading and mental ages, therefore, are obviously of little significance. Large disparities, usually of one year or more, deserve investigation and some consideration in determination of the goals to be attained by particular children.[33]

Durrell suggested the use of the Durrell-Sullivan Reading Capacity Test as a measure of reading expectancy. The literature contained no evaluation of the test, although it appeared to meet a real need. It would surely be of value as a supplement to other tests.

Thus it would seem that the most satisfactory means of determining reading expectancy is by the use of the Stanford-Binet plus other tests, all of which are evaluated by a careful psychologist. The expectancy can be only relative and must never be considered an exact goal.

MINIMUM MENTAL AGE FOR BEGINNING READING

Recent articles on causes of reading failure have frequently mentioned that reading was introduced too early, probably before the child was ready to learn. One aspect of readiness, namely, mental maturity, was singled out for special attention.

Harrison studied measures which might predict reading success and concluded that a mental age of 6-6 on both the Detroit and the Binet tests was most conducive to reading growth. As a result of her study, she concluded that ". . . . it is safe to state that a mental age of at least six years must be reached before success will be probable, and we can be much more certain of success if mental age is six years and six months."[34] This would apply to reading as it is taught conventionally.

On the basis of the study of 141 first-grade children, Morphett and Washburne concluded that ". . . . it seems safe to state that, by postponing the teaching of reading until children reach a mental level of six and a half years, teachers can greatly decrease the chances of failure and discouragement and can correspondingly increase their efficiency."[35]

Gates and Bond considered children entering Grade I with mental ages ranging from 4-11 to 7-8 years. They concluded that when they studied the range of mental ages from the lowest to the highest and related them to reading achievement, no crucial or critical point above which very few fail and below which a large proportion fail was apparent.[36] Gates went further to declare that "an inspection of these several groups will show that practically all the near-failures fell in the group with a mental-age below five years."[37] Thus he decided that "statements concerning the necessary mental age at which a pupil can be intrusted to learn to read are essentially meaningless."[38]

In summary we might conclude that many studies have indicated the desirability of beginning to read with a mental age of six years. As Durrell so aptly stated: "It is generally agreed that a mental age of six years is necessary to make normal progress in beginning reading. Children who enter first grade with a mental age lower than six may learn to read, but they usually require a greater amount of practice."[39]

MINIMUM I.Q. FOR READING

In 1930, Gates said that it was remarkable to be able to teach any child with an I.Q. less than 65 to read new material without assistance.[40]

A more recent and careful summary of findings by Kirk[41] indicated that older children with I.Q.'s below 50 should be taught only signs and labels for their own safety, as they are incapable of learning to read. He believed that children with I.Q.'s above 50 could be taught to read in proportion to their mental ages, and he outlined methods for teaching them. As a precaution, he emphasized that the child with the lower I.Q. would not begin to read with a life-age of six years, or at least not until he had attained an adequate mental age.

Whipple summarized the thinking in her statement that it is not possible to designate a minimum intelligence quotient which pupils must have to learn to read.[42]

SPECIAL MENTAL CHARACTERISTICS OF POOR READERS

Although the general intelligence of the poor reader may be adequate, many investigators have felt that they have specialized mental weaknesses. Arthur studied the scores on the vocabulary section of the Binet and translated these into I.Q. ratings. This hypothetical verbal I.Q. fell consistently below the Binet I.Q., which led her to the conclusion that one might wonder whether nonreaders are not essentially nonverbalists.[43]

Monroe and Backus listed the following special disabilities:

1. Verbal disabilities
   a) Vocabulary scores on Stanford-Binet below mental age level.
   b) Child is unable to supply unknown words from context in reading; his guesses or substitutions from context are absurd or meaningless.
   c) Brief and fragmentary sentences are used in oral conversation.
   d) Special difficulty in understanding abstract connective words, who, what, that, which, although, etc.
   e) Higher mental ages are earned on the Point Performance test than on the Stanford-Binet test.
2. Peculiarities in modes of thought
   a) The child is unable to succeed with tests involving forms, such as the Binet designs, diamond, square, etc., or performance tests involving forms.
   b) The child is unable to succeed with tests involving auditory memory, such as the digit-repeating tests, sentence-repeating tests, etc., in the Binet examination.
   c) Peculiarities are observed during reading such as tracing over a letter to identify it; roundabout methods of attacking words by writing or spelling the word, or hunting for peculiar mnemonic clues.[44]

CONFUSION OF WORDS IN RELATION TO INTELLIGENCE

Durrell[45] observed confusions, guessing at the flash words, and attempts at memorizing the stories which go with the pictures, which he attributed to starting first-grade reading with a mental age less than five years.

According to Teegarden, a "tendency to confuse symbols is characteristic of mental ages below six years, and is usually eliminated in mental ages above seven."[46]

Leavell and Sterling studied reversals in reading in relation to intelligence. "The coefficient of correlation ($-.87 \pm .11$) in this study indicated that there seemed to be a fairly marked tendency for the less intelligent children to make more regressions than the more intelligent."[47]

SUMMARY

The references covered in this section have led to the following conclusions:

There is a positive relationship between intelligence-test scores and reading-test scores, although the relationship is not perfect, nor is the extent of it known.

Severely retarded readers seem to range in mental ages and I.Q.'s about the same as unselected cases within a public school, where the low-grade feeble-minded are eliminated. The majority have I.Q.'s between 90 and 110.

The Binet intelligence test, supplemented by a performance and a nonverbal test, seems to give the best estimate of reading expectancy. The mental age seems more significant than the I.Q., but the basal age on the Binet and the scatter should be considered.

Most writers agree that a mental age of more than six years is desirable for learning to read successfully. In fact, confusions and reversals sometimes result from insufficient ability at the initial reading levels.

Special mental characteristics were listed by various investigators, but their exact relationship to reading was not determined. It is known that intelligence ratings are obtained by measuring a number of abilities and combining these into one composite score. Consequently, when tests of the primary mental traits are standardized, a profile of intelligence should show factors more closely related to reading than the general score. This, in turn, should lead to more adequate predictions of reading expectancy.

NOTES

1. William A. McCall, *How To Measure in Education* (New York: Macmillan Co., 1922), pp. 109–11.

2. William S. Gray, Delia Kibbe, Laura Lucas, and Lawrence W. Miller, *Remedial Cases in Reading: Their Diagnosis and Treatment* ("Supplementary Educational Monographs," No. 22 [Chicago: University of Chicago, 1922]), p. 12.

3. Paul Witty and David Kopel, *Reading and the Educative Process* (Boston: Ginn & Co., 1939), p. 226.

4. Arthur I. Gates, "The Measurement and Evaluation of Achievement in Reading," *Thirty-sixth Yearbook of the National Society for the Study of Education*, Part I: *The Teaching of Reading: A Second Report* (Bloomington, Ill.: Public School Pub. Co., 1937), p. 142.

5. Arthur I. Gates and Guy L. Bond, "Reading Readiness: A Study of Factors Determining Success and Failure in Beginning Reading," *Teachers College Record*, XXXVII (May, 1936), 679–85.

6. Arthur I. Gates, *The Psychology of Reading and Spelling with Special Reference to Disability* ("Teachers College Contributions to Education," No. 129 [New York: Teachers College, Columbia University, 1922]).

7. Marion Monroe and Bertie Backus, *Remedial Reading: A Monograph in Character Education* (Cambridge, Mass.: Houghton Mifflin Co., 1937), p. 21.

8. *Op. cit.*, p. 227.

9. *Ibid.*, p. 227.

10. *Ibid.*

11. *Ibid.*, p. 228.

12. Mary I. Preston, "The Reaction of Parents to Reading Failures," *Child Development*, X, No. 3 (September, 1939), 173–79.

13. Marion Monroe, *Children Who Cannot Read* (Chicago: University of Chicago Press, 1932), pp. 4–5.

14. Phyllis Blanchard, "Reading Disabilities in Relation to Difficulties of Personality and Emotional Development," *Mental Hygiene*, XX (July, 1936), 384–413.

15. Emmett A. Betts, *The Prevention and Correction of Reading Difficulties* (Evanston, Ill.: Row, Peterson & Co., 1936), p. 299.

16. Esther Grace Nolan, "Reading Difficulty versus Low Mentality," *California Journal of Secondary Education*, XVII (January, 1942), 34.

17. Lewis Terman and Maud Merrill, *Measuring Intelligence—A Guide to the Administration of the New Revised Stanford-Binet Tests of Intelligence* (Boston: Houghton Mifflin Co., 1937).

18. Lewis Terman, *The Measurement of Intelligence* (Boston, Mass.: Houghton Mifflin Co., 1916).

19. Grace Arthur, "An Attempt To Sort Children with Specific Reading Disability from Other Non-readers," *Journal of Applied Psychology*, XI (August, 1927), 251–63.

20. *Op. cit.*

21. Gertrude Whipple, "Causes of Retardation in Reading and Methods of Eliminating Them," *Peabody Journal of Education*, XVI (November, 1938), 191–200.

22. *Op. cit.*

23. Augusta Jameson, "Method and Devices for Remedial Reading," in William S. Gray (ed.), *Recent Trends in Reading* ("Supplementary Educational Monographs," No. 49 [Chicago: University of Chicago, 1939]), pp. 170–78.

24. Donald Dewitt Durrell, "The Effect of Special Disability in Reading in the Stanford Revision of the Binet-Simon Tests (Master's Thesis, College of Education, University of Iowa, August, 1927)," in Emmett A. Betts, "Reading Disabilities and Their Correction," *Elementary English Review*, XII (May, 1933), 133–34.

25. Helen P. Davidson, *An Experimental Study of Bright, Average, and Dull Children at the Four Year Mental Level* ("Genetic Psychology Monographs," Vol. IX, Nos. 3 and 4 [Worcester, Mass.: Clark University Press, 1931]), pp. 119–89.

26. *Op. cit.*

27. M. Lucille Harrison, *Reading Readiness* (Boston, Mass.: Houghton Mifflin Co., 1936).

28. Mabel Vogel Morphett and Carleton Washburne, "When Should Children Begin To Read?" *Elementary School Journal*, XXXI (March, 1931), 496–503.

29. Emmett A. Betts, "Retardation in Reading," *The Role of Research in Educational Progress* (Official Report of the American Educational Research Association) (Washington: American Educational Research Assoc. of N.E.A., 1937), pp. 186–91.

30. Donald Dewitt Durrell, *Improvement of Basic Reading Abilities* (Yonkers-on-Hudson, N.Y.: World Book Co., 1941).

31. Arthur I. Gates, *The Improvement of Reading* (New York: Macmillan Co., 1927), p. 358.

32. *Op. cit.*, pp. 190–91.

33. *Op. cit.*, p. 72.

34. *Op. cit.*, p. 8.

35. "When Should Children Begin To Read?" *op. cit.*, p. 503.

36. Gates and Bond, "Reading Readiness: A Study of Factors Determining Success and Failure in Beginning Reading," *op. cit.*, p. 680.

37. Arthur I. Gates, "The Necessary Mental Age for Beginning Reading," *Elementary School Journal*, XXXVII (March, 1937), 449.

38. *Ibid.*, p. 506.

39. *Improvement of Basic Reading Abilities*, p. 286.

40. Arthur I. Gates, *Interest and Ability in Reading* (New York: MacMillan Co., 1930), p. 14.

41. Samuel A. Kirk, *Teaching Reading to Slow-learning Children* (Boston, Mass.: Houghton Mifflin Co., 1940).

42. "Causes of Retardation in Reading and Methods of Eliminating Them," *op. cit.*, pp. 191–200.

43. "An Attempt To Sort Children with Specific Reading Disability from Other Non-readers," *op. cit.*, p. 225.

44. *Op. cit.*, p. 24.

45. Donald Dewitt Durrell, "Confusions in Learning," *Education*, LII (February, 1932), 330–33.

46. Lorene Teegarden, "Clinical Identification of the Prospective Non-reader," *Child Development*, III (1932), p. 358.

47. Ullin W. Leavell and Helen Sterling, "A Comparison of Basic Factors in Reading Patterns with Intelligence," *Peabody Journal of Education*, XVI (November, 1938), 154.

CHAPTER VII

EMOTIONAL AND PERSONALITY PROBLEMS
OF SEVERELY RETARDED READERS

THE relationship between a child's emotional pattern and his reactions in the learning situation is being studied with increasing frequency by psychologists. These studies have led investigators such as Sherman to say:

> In many instances a given emotional pattern may be a distinct hindrance to learning a specific task or skill, whereas in others the emotionality of an individual may be a motivating force to greater effort. Thus the emotions must be taken into account in evaluating success and failure.[1]

The effects of the emotions on learning and retention have not been studied extensively, nor have the effects on the emotions of failure to learn been adequately considered. Educators, psychologists, and teachers are showing an increased awareness of this problem and the need for more information concerning it.

Sherman continued:

> The emotionality of an individual at the time he is learning a task has a definite influence upon his efficiency in the learning situation. His emotional balance or imbalance also has a definite effect upon his retention of the material that he has learned and upon his ability to recall and put into use that which he may have learned well previously.[2]

Since it is so difficult to measure ease of learning in varying emotional states, the studies in this direction have been few. Carter[3] selected words classified as "pleasant," "indifferent," and "unpleasant" and showed them, with corresponding pictures, to children. He studied the recall of words when pictures were shown later and found that pleasant words were better learned than unpleasant or indifferent words and that unpleasant words tended to be better learned than indifferent ones. He noted a tendency to replace unpleasant and indifferent words with incorrect pleasant ones, indicating that pleasantness of association of words may be directly associated with the rate of learning the words.

Failure to learn what is expected may lead to frustration or fear-conditioning to such an extent that the sight of the material may cause a disorganized emotional response, which further inhibits concentration, perseverance, and motivation.

Shame may result from failure in which there is a feeling of anxiety. Sanohara[4] noted this in his study, and Sherman[5] pointed out that pupils who are ashamed of their failures may develop defensive reactions.

Frustrations and their effect on learning were considered significant by investigators. Frequent irritation and loss of interest were reported by Thorndike and Woodyard[6] when frequent frustrations were introduced. Kendrew[7] concluded that frustration disturbed the rate of work and of learning.

The knowledge of success and failure was found by Sullivan[8] to affect the length of time required to learn nonsense syllables. Gilchrist's[9] experiment induced him to conclude that praise led to improvement, while reproval led to poorer performance on tests.

While the studies were relatively few, they agreed that learning was more rapid when the stimulus was pleasant, when the subject had been successful and had been praised. However, learning was inhibited by indifferent or unpleasant associations and by failure and frequent frustration, with shame and reproval.

EMOTIONAL REACTIONS AND READING FAILURE

During the last twenty years, failure in reading has frequently been attributed to emotional problems, and emotional problems have likewise been said to be created by reading failure. The experimental studies just mentioned would provide a basis for both opinions.

Children come to school with a variety of experiences and therefore different associations with different words. Whereas the child who has had unpleasant or indifferent associations with words may find learning to read a difficult task, the child who has had many pleasant associations may learn more quickly.

Since reading is required of the child who remains in school, the teacher is expected to present it to him over and over, with the result that he may have very frequent frustrations, resulting in loss of interest, lack of application, and lowered motivation. The teacher who discovers that a pupil is failing to progress in reading may reprimand him, thus adding to the difficulties he is already experiencing in learning to read.

It seems evident that emotional difficulties may cause reading disability in the beginning and that this disability may, in turn, result in frustration, which further blocks learning and again intensifies the frustration. The interaction and intensification become a vicious circle, leading to intense emotional maladjustments and complete failure to progress in reading.

The emotional maladjustment seen in a severely retarded reader, then, may be either the cause, the effect, or the result of the interaction of reading failure and emotional maladjustments.

EMOTIONAL AND PERSONALITY MALADJUSTMENTS AS A CAUSE

As early as 1917, some writers expressed the belief that emotionally unstable children were backward at school, their reading being fluent and expressive but full of guesswork and inaccuracy.

Woolley and Ferris listed among their school failures "the psychopathic" children, who frequently revealed "flashes of genius" but were unable to learn as others did.[10]

Hollingworth explained how this might operate to cause reading failure. She said that neurotic children, even though intelligent, were often deficient in reading because the mechanics of reading requires co-operation, following directions, and sustained effort. Neurotic children are characterized by inferiority in these areas, as well as in others. Where negativism, instability, and illusion interfere with learning, these children fail to make progress, except when taught individually.[11]

The view of Fernald is as follows: "The blocking of voluntary action has long been recognized as one of the conditions that result in emotion. . . . . The individual who fails constantly in those undertakings which seem to him of great importance and who is conscious of failure is in a chronic state of emotional upset."[12]

She thinks that every child entering school is eager to learn to read and write and that, as he sees other children learning while he is not, he always becomes an emotional problem because of this blocking of voluntary action. Of 78 cases of extreme reading disability treated in her clinic, all but four entered school with no history of emotional instability, and the upset occurred as the child showed repeated failure. The child learns to hate or fear the reading situation and everything connected with it, such as books, papers, pencils, etc.

If this is his first group experience, he may react the same way to the the social group. Such conditions promote the development of the "solitary" child and the "bombastic" child.

In a more recent report, Sherman stated that

many neurotic conditions are found in children with reading disabilities. These children clearly fall in the therapeutic realm of the psychiatrist, and no reading therapy can be attempted until treatment by a psychiatrist is completed. Neurotic children are especially sensitive to failure, and a reading disability may be a focal point of an individual's final reorientation from a neurosis to a normal condition.[13]

These more severe personality difficulties, such as neurotic and psychotic conditions, and their relationship to reading failure might be more evident than the subtle ones, such as specific emotional blocks and unfavorable attitudes. However, a number of authorities have concurred in the belief that even minor emotional and personality difficulties may cause failure in reading.

A child who comes to school is faced with new problems of adjustment. Prescott enumerated some of these as follows:

. . . . learning to get along with other children of many types; learning to get along with a group of parent surrogates in a variety of situations; establishing membership in a new social group, experiencing many situations where affection does not temper requirements; learning to accept and live with one's own peculiarities of appearance, physical handicaps, racial and religious differences in a group which recognizes and calls attention to them as undesirable differences from the group; learning and accepting new group standards of behavior; learning new games and physical skills necessary to maintain status.[14]

It is little wonder that, with these problems at hand, the child sometimes occupies himself in learning patterns of behavior and developing security with the teacher and social group rather than attending to reading.

Concerning the relation of these problems to reading, Jameson stated:

This period is a difficult one for many children. When children's anxieties about themselves, about their positions in this new competitive group, are sufficient to cause some preoccupation, they often do not have the energy, the confidence, and the motivation to fortify themselves, to equip themselves to learn the complicated task of reading. When added to that situation are . . . . significant organic and functional handicaps . . . . the child fails in learning to read. Generally his failures have been accepted by him long before they are recognized by his parents and teachers, and his observation of the concern of these adults has intensified his awareness of his inadequacy.[15]

Writers on causes of reading disability have recently recognized the effects of frustrating experiences in learning. Thus a child who has been frustrated in learning other tasks might be conditioned against reading. Dolch expressed such an opinion when he stated:

> Probably more deficiency in reading can be traced to discouragement through failure, and the consequent attitude of antagonism toward reading, than to any other cause. Many children hate the reading lesson simply because it compels them to exhibit before their companions their ignorance or lack of skill. A child caught in this situation is very frequently scolded or held up to ridicule. If this condition is allowed to arise, a child may go on from year to year with scarcely any improvement because he never looks at a book unless he has to and then with a distinct aversion. When he is supposed to be reading, his attention wanders, so that very little reading is really done, and consequently no improvement of skill results.[16]

Such frustration very often results in what the teacher frequently describes as the "lazy" child. Usually this child is unmotivated, and, as Ridenour pointed out, one of the first steps to undertake is to recognize his resistance to reading and to prepare him so that he wants to read.[17]

Beyond this, Durrell found that when there were confusions created by exposing an immature child to reading too early, ". . . . mental blocking, additional confusion, discouragement, withdrawal of attention, or meaningless activity induced by fear of failure or ridicule, the child often stays on the learning plateau a long time."[18]

STUDIES

In addition to the opinions expressed by the writers referred to above, there have been a few experimental studies of emotional and behavior reactions. Bird[19] studied 100 children between the ages of four and six years and found that 30 had habitual personality handicaps that interfered with their learning. They were classified as follows: two showed introversion; eight were retarded by shyness, lack of self-confidence, dislike of scrutiny, or fear of the task; eight showed excessive dependence on commendation; two worked only for the instructor; four wished to win distinction by unusual behavior; two were antisocial, as they teased, bullied, and disobeyed; and four had vagrant tendencies, such as flitting from one task to another and leaving unfinished work.

In studying the effect of short auditory span, Saunders[20] discovered that those children who did not learn to read were not aggressive; they played alone and avoided social contacts until they were considered antisocial; and they developed behavior problems. She also observed that these children were emotionally dependent on their parents.

A study of 13 children before and after entrance to Grade I led Castner to list eight traits as significant for reading failure. Two of the traits were instability and excitable personality, and he explained the effects by reporting that "many of these children are of the active, talkative, energetic, excitable type, not necessarily unco-operative in the interviews and examinations, but showing fluctuations of attention and oftener a greater or less degree of instability."[21] Unfortunately, his number of cases was so small that conclusions could be only tentative.

Monroe and Backus have studied a great many retarded readers and have reported the following primary emotional factors as causes:

General emotional immaturity—the child is dependent on the mother and unaccustomed to responsibility; infantile in manner and interests. He may resist reading as a step to growing up.

Excessive timidity—has failed in social adjustment and is too shy to speak or attempt group activities.

Predilection against reading, since he has heard someone say it is "hard" or he identifies himself with some person who does not read.

Predilection against all school activities.[22]

In a recent summary of his studies of emotional and personality problems in relation to reading disability, Gates[23] expresses the opinion that emotional problems are present in about 75 per cent of retarded readers but that in only one-fourth of these is it a cause of the disability.

SUMMARY

The opinions of authorities in the field and the findings of a few experimental studies are agreed that emotional and personality problems might be a cause of reading failure. The severe maladjustments of the neurotic child are most evident; nevertheless, the minor adjustments which the child must make when he enters school are so many that he may not be prepared to devote himself to reading. Even though he is willing to learn, he may be hampered by emotional immaturity, lack of confidence and security, unpleasant or indifferent associations with words, or excessive timidity. Prescott believes that personality needs are so complicated that it is surprising that their frustration does not more seriously interfere with the work of the school.[24]

Failure to make the first steps in adaptation to reading may lead to frustration and all its accompanying reactions, such as inattention, lack of motivation, confusion, and lack of application to the task of learning to read.

EMOTIONAL AND PERSONALITY DIFFICULTIES
AS AN EFFECT OF READING FAILURE

Authorities have agreed that continued failure in reading might create emotional tension due to frustration. Dislike for the subject, as well as everything surrounding it, might follow, and all manner of compensations have been noted. Social maladjustment and even delinquency and crime have been listed as results of the failure to learn to read.

SYMPTOMS

Sherman made psychiatric studies of a number of severely retarded readers and listed their most common symptoms:

Indifference to the problem of failure and emphasis upon some skill or interest as compensation for school inadequacy.

Instances in which even a slight reading defect causes withdrawal from effort and, in some cases, results in emotional disturbances. Some of these children become behavior and disciplinary problems as a result of these emotional upheavals.

Antagonism to academic problems and a defensive reaction to any activity relating to school.

Refusal to improve reading ability, as a bid for attention and as a mark of differentiation. In some instances children who have had reading difficulties have received a great deal of attention, not only from teachers, but also from their parents. In consequence, failure has become synonymous with personal attention, and as the result these children may at times unconsciously refuse to improve their reading level.[25]

Daydreaming, incorrigibility, inattentiveness, shyness, and negativism were listed by Kirk[26] as personality traits which improved with remedial treatment in his high-grade mentally defective cases.

Gates has listed the symptoms of personality maladjustment of 100 random cases of reading disability as follows:

1. Nervous tensions and habits, such as stuttering, nail-biting, restlessness, insomnia, and pathological illness—ten cases.
2. Putting on a bold front as a defense reaction, loud talk, defiant conduct, sullenness—sixteen cases.
3. Retreat reactions such as withdrawal from ordinary associations, joining outside gangs, and truancy—fourteen cases.
4. Counterattack, such as making mischief in school, playing practical jokes, thefts, destructiveness, cruelty, bullying—eighteen cases.
5. Withdrawing reactions, including mind-wandering and daydreaming—twenty-six cases.
6. Extreme self-consciousness; becoming easily injured, blushing, developing peculiar fads and frills and eccentricities, inferiority feelings—thirty-five cases.
7. Give-up or submissive adjustments, as shown by inattentiveness, indifference, apparent laziness—thirty-three cases.[27]

In only eight cases did the child develop a constructive compensation, such as drawing, etc.

Daydreaming, seclusiveness, lack of interest, "laziness," inattention, absent-mindedness, sensitiveness, etc., were listed as causes for referring children with reading disabilities to Blanchard.[28]

Orton[29] reported that his so-called "strephosymbolics" showed a definite frustration reaction, although they might attempt to cover up their deficiency and evade demands for reading. However, some assumed a swaggering, boisterous attitude and insisted that they read well and liked it very much.

Preston made a careful and detailed evaluation of personality characteristics of 100 reading failures. She found that children who were ". . . . bewildered, fearful, full of inhibitions, or 'shut-in' on the one hand and antagonistic, rebellious, or antisocial on the other,"[30] came from homes where they were overprotected and treated as infants until failure in reading caused a sudden change. She found that after reading failure a child might react in these ways:

Following initial bewilderment he would try to gain the limelight at any cost to offset his position in reading.

Adopt attitudes of suspicion and antagonism toward rivals and teacher, sometimes becoming almost hostile in character.

After fourth to ninth year of failure, those of submissive make-up became "shut-in" and moody with feelings of inferiority. The aggressive ones became increasingly antisocial.[31]

Sherman concisely summarized this effect when he wrote:

A child may react with a deep sense of failure, not only because he realizes his inability to develop adequate reading efficiency, but also because he constantly has to face various social pressures. He must deal with the attitudes of his parents, who are greatly disappointed in his inability to learn, as well as those of his fellow-pupils. He must deal also with the attitudes of the teachers, many of whom do not understand the difference between an inherent reading disability and an unwillingness to learn. The child with a reading disability must also deal with the reactions of his playmates, who certainly do not understand the complexity of a reading problem and who frequently tend to categorize the pupil with a reading disability as "dumb" or backward or peculiar. Thus it is not unnatural that frustration and its consequences play an important role in the case of children who have reading difficulties.[32]

He also pointed out that a feeling of anxiety might result from failure, and, as a consequence, defensive reactions might develop.

Blanchard[33] found that when reading failure continued, it resulted in a feeling of failure and that, unless socially acceptable compensations were developed, personality and behavior deviations were liable to arise. However, with substitution of success for failure, these compensations were no longer needed. Newell[34] believed that the presence of emotional tension with anxiety and misunderstanding led to resentment and antagonism toward help.

The unfortunate attitude of parents was, in a measure, responsible for Preston's conclusion:

Placing the blame on the child is rank injustice and is either felt as such by the victims, with the usual reaction of mankind against injustice, or if the burden of guilt is accepted by the child his personality tends to be overwhelmed by guilt feelings with disintegrating effect, as time goes on.[35]

Concerning the effect of threatened home security on the personality adjustment of the child she stated:

Reading failure causes not only a blighting insecurity in the school world which gives rise to serious maladjustments in the personalities of these normal children, but also an embarrassing, belittling insecurity in the social life of these children at school and sometimes in the home; adding to maladjustments which interfere with proper development and constituting a menace to future social adjustment. More serious still, home security, ... is undermined to an unhealthful, sometimes pernicious degree, and brings forth even greater maladjustments in the personalities. . . . .[36]

If reading disability were a cause of emotional and personality maladjustment in certain cases, then it would follow that treatment resulting in improvement of the former might result in improvement of personal relations. Damereau studied 22 cases of reading disability, all of whom were behavior problems. All the cases received reading treatment; but, in addition, four received psychiatric treatment, seven received treatment from a social worker, and six received both psychiatric and social treatment. After following these cases, she concluded that improvement in one area bore little relation to improvement in the other. Changes in behavior occurred when tutoring was supplemented by social or psychiatric assistance or when the child-parent relations were satisfactory.[37] Thus, if reading disability caused behavior maladjustment, the removal of this disability did not seem to improve behavior. From the evidence presented in her study, there is a question as to whether one might say that the reading disability was removed.

SUMMARY

There is no doubt that reading failure has led to frustration, discouragement, disinterest, inattention, and maladjustment, except in cases in which a satisfactory compensation of a socially approved nature has been established. Children's reactions seemed to be of three general types: first, aggressive reactions, in which the child attacked the whole environment associated with reading; second, withdrawal, when the child sought for satisfaction outside the reading environment, which included playmates; and, third, lack of emotional affectivity where the child appeared responsive but evidenced no feeling tone to his responses.

In some instances, at least, the treatment of the reading disability was not sufficient, and it was necessary to give added psychiatric treatment to obtain satisfactory readjustment.

EMOTIONAL AND PERSONALITY MALADJUSTMENT
AS BOTH CAUSE AND EFFECT

If failure can cause emotional maladjustments, then those maladjustments inhibit further learning, which creates more emotional difficulty. The two interact, each making the other more intense. The reciprocal relationship was emphasized in the following statement by Tinker:

Non-readers usually show an emotional reaction to the reading situation. In one type of case a neurotic constitution is the direct cause of the reading

disability. It seems that many neurotics exhibiting impulsive responses, nega-
tivistic attitudes and illusions are unable to give the co-operation and sustained
effort required in learning to read. For such cases prognosis is poor. Until their
emotional adjustments are improved little progress in reading may be expected,
even with individual teaching. It has been shown, however, that emotional maladjustments, especially emotional reaction to the reading situation, may be
caused by reading disability. Lack of success during early attempt to read produces unfortunate emotional conditioning. Feelings of inferiority arise, and personality and behavior deviations may occur.[38]

Bennett summarized some of the more pertinent findings in this
field and pointed out the implications referred to in this summary.
After weighing the evidence, he concluded:

> There seems general agreement, however, that children with certain types of
> undesirable behavior habits or personal characteristics, and children struggling
> with deep emotional conflicts face more than average likelihood that they will
> find the art of reading difficult to master. There seems equal agreement that a
> serious retardation in reading is quite apt to have detrimental effects upon the
> general development of the child's personality. Probably the relationship is
> often reciprocal, and in older and more seriously handicapped children each
> problem may require specific and intensive treatment. The nature of the dif-
> ficulty seems similar if it is cause or effect.[39]

Monroe found evidence of an interaction and intensification in her
study, in which she compared the personality problems of reading-
disability cases and other unselected cases. She concluded:

> Whether the reading defect is caused by unfavorable behavior or personality,
> or vice versa, is sometimes difficult to determine. A child may be resistant to
> learning through negativism and unfavorable emotional attitudes. In such a
> case reading would undoubtedly suffer along with other scholastic achievements.
> On the other hand, and probably more frequently, a child may develop the
> emotional and personality problems as a result of failure in learning to read.
> The emotional attitude may develop through the child's failure and then, in
> turn, may aggravate still further the retardation in reading.[40]

Her implication, that a child whose learning difficulty was not con-
fined to reading might have an emotional basis for the difficulty, was
particularly significant. Tulchin concurred in this belief when he
suggested that ". . . . the more primary the emotional factors, the
greater the stumbling block in treatment. . . . . Also, when the emotional factors seem primary, disability and general lack of progress
in other subjects as well as in reading are more likely to occur."[41]

Monroe and Backus[42] listed as secondary emotional factors those
which resulted from reading disability and which, in turn, further
retarded the child's progress in reading. These were: aggressive op-

position; withdrawal, either direct or truancy or daydreams; compensating mechanisms, such as getting satisfaction from achievement in other school subjects; defeatism, in which the child gave up and suffered from feelings of inadequacy; and hypertension, or development of anxieties, nervous mannerisms, etc.

Studies of the interaction of emotional maladjustment and reading disability seemed quite limited, since most research workers did not consider it desirable to permit a child with severe reading disability to continue untreated while such observations were being made. Hence this section contains only opinions of authorities, without further evidence of the facts on which they based their opinions.

SUMMARY

Expert opinion concurred in the belief that emotional and personality maladjustment might be both a cause and an effect of a severe reading disability. Studies were not available to substantiate these opinions.

A COMMON CAUSE FOR BOTH READING DISABILITY
AND EMOTIONAL MALADJUSTMENT

A number of factors have been suspected as being basic to reading disability and emotional maladjustment. Wells pointed out that sometimes reading difficulties are a means used by children, reacting to difficulties of home adjustment, just as stealing and tantrums may be another.[43]

A common cause for both is suggested by Blanchard, who said:

. . . . the reading disability often arises from the same source of difficulty in emotional development, and in the same manner as the accompanying personality or behavior problems or neurotic symptoms, such as fears, illness without physical basis, infantile regressions, and the like. . . . .

While sex conflicts are evident in many reading disability cases, even more pronounced, in the material produced in treatment interviews, are difficulties in establishing masculine identifications and in handling aggressive impulses, together with excessive anxiety and guilt over destructive, hostile and sadistic feelings.[44]

Witty and Kopel reported that at least 50 per cent of their cases of subject-matter disabilities at the Northwestern Psycho-educational Clinic had "fears and anxieties" sufficiently serious to require therapeutic measures, and they stressed

success rather than failure, regular habits, home co-operation in the development of such character traits as initiative and self-direction, more effective social relationships, and a sense of security. Bad behavior, we find, is generally a reflection of school and home situations which are limited in opportunity for varied experience and which are saturated with tensions resulting from efforts to make all children equally amenable. . . . .[45]

Either a reading disability or a personality problem might be responsible for the other, according to Hardwick, who concluded that if the personality problem is basic to a reading failure, it must be treated before we can expect much gain in reading.[46] However, if reading failure brings about emotional disturbances, the reading pressure must be alleviated before the emotional difficulty can be entirely cleared up.[47]

SUMMARY

A third factor or group of factors might be responsible for both reading failure and personality problems, according to opinions expressed by several writers. The home and family seem to have received major attention as such a cause.

CONCLUSIONS

Authoritative opinions and results of many studies agree, without exception, that a large number of severely retarded readers also evidenced emotional and personality maladjustments. There was likewise a strong implication that more severely retarded readers were subject to more severe personality problems.

Studies also indicated that words with pleasant associations were more easily learned. Thus the emotions might be definitely responsible for reading failure, especially if the child were not emotionally ready to begin the task of reading. Neurotic children should always be considered by the psychiatrist before reading is attempted, or failure might result.

If a child had failed repeatedly in his attempts to learn to read, he might accept failure and lose all confidence in himself, he might rationalize the failure, or he might refuse to accept it. In general, such children seemed to become aggressive, withdrawn, or to lose emotional affectivity.

In many cases, emotional maladjustments and reading failure seemed to interact, each adding to the seriousness of the other. This might become a vicious circle, such that ordinary attempts at reading training would be unsuccessful. According to the opinion of Sherman:

Whatever therapeutic program is instituted, the initial step must be an evaluation of the emotional pattern of the child, first, because no therapeutic plan can be formulated without first recognizing a child emotionally and, second, because consistent motivation for improvement cannot be introduced if the child is distracted by personal problems.[48]

This evaluation would have been equally useful if reading failure had been a symptom of some other basic factor, just as emotional maladjustments might be. Such factors have proved most difficult to locate and evaluate, although home conditions have received major attention.

The complexity of evaluation of human emotions might well be the reason for so many opinions expressed in the literature, with only a few studies to substantiate such views. Hence the psychiatric study of severely retarded readers should aid materially in evaluating these findings.

BEHAVIOR DISORDERS ASSOCIATED WITH
SERIOUS READING RETARDATION

Even beyond the milder personality and behavior difficulties, there are indications that reading failure may cause delinquency. Gates pointed out that Chatfield, Director of Attendance and Child Welfare of New York City, was convinced that ". . . . the continual frustration in school, produced by inability to read efficiently, frequently led to truancy and delinquency."[49]

A study by Fendrick and Bond[50] summarized various opinions, one of which was that of Peyser, who believed school failures are more highly correlated with delinquency than are poverty, broken homes, physical and mental defects, or psychopathic conditions. In the case of 187 delinquents between the ages of sixteen and nineteen years, the writers found that over 90 per cent had been school failures. When the I.Q. was constant between 90 and 110, there was a mean difference of five years between the life-age and the reading status. The amount of school experience and rating in other subjects, such as arithmetic, was not reported.

Stulken,[51] who secured much information concerning his cases, found that about 20 per cent of the boys who were serious behavior problems also had severe reading disabilities. He reported that about 66 per cent were retarded in reading one or more years below the level of their mental ages. After citing more statistical data, he concluded that this evidence indicated that reading disability was an important factor in producing school maladjustment.[52] He added further:

> In approximately 40 per cent of the cases the important factor in reading disability seemed to be related to personality factors such as emotional instability. . . . .[53]

In describing remedial treatment, he stated:

> More important, however, than the progress in reading is the changed attitude of the problem boy toward school when he realizes that he is learning to read. He ceases to play truant and instead becomes interested in his school work. Furthermore, when the problem boy gets a feeling of satisfaction from his school work he is less liable to go outside of school to win his success in antisocial and often delinquent behavior.[54]

SUMMARY

Some evidence has been presented to indicate that reading disability and delinquency are coincidental in some cases; however, no causal relationship has been established. A great deal more should be known about other operative causes before one can be isolated and labeled as the cause of delinquency. Further studies should be made to throw light on the interrelationship.

NOTES

1. Mandel Sherman, "Emotional Disturbances and Reading Disability," in William S. Gray (ed.), *Recent Trends in Reading* ("Supplementary Educational Monographs," No. 49 [Chicago: University of Chicago, 1939]), p. 126.

2. *Ibid.*, p. 129.

3. Harold D. Carter, "Emotional Correlates of Errors in Learning," *Journal of Educational Psychology*, XXVII (January, 1936), 55–67.

4. T. Sanohara, "A Psychological Study of the Feeling of Shame," *Japanese Journal of Psychology*, IX (1934), 847–90.

5. *Op. cit.*, p. 131.

6. E. L. Thorndike and Ella Woodyard, "Influence of the Relative Frequency of Successes and Frustrations," *Journal of Educational Psychology*, XXV (April, 1934), 241–50.

7. E. N. Kendrew, "A Note on the Persistence of Moods," *British Journal of Psychology*, XXVI (1935), 165–73.

8. Ellen B. Sullivan, "Attitude in Relation to Learning," *Psychological Monographs*, XXXVI, No. 169 (1927), 1–149.

9. E. P. Gilchrist, "The Extent to Which Praise and Blame Affect a Pupil's Work," *School and Society*, IV (December, 1916), 872–74.

10. Helen Thompson Woolley and Elizabeth Ferris, *Diagnosis and Treatment of Young School Failures* (Bureau of Education Bull. 1 [Washington: Bureau of Education, 1923]), pp. 8–9.

11. Leta S. Hollingworth, *Special Talents and Defects* (New York: Macmillan Co., 1923), pp. 69–70.

12. Grace Fernald, *Remedial Techniques in Basic School Subjects* (New York: McGraw-Hill Book Co., 1943), p. 7.

13. *Op. cit.*, p. 134.

14. Daniel A. Prescott, *Emotion and the Educative Process* (Washington: American Council on Education, 1938), p. 231.

15. Augusta Jameson, "Methods and Devices for Remedial Reading," in William S. Gray (ed.), *Recent Trends in Reading* ("Supplementary Educational Monographs," No. 49 [Chicago: University of Chicago, 1939]), p. 171.

16. Edward W. Dolch, *The Psychology and Teaching of Reading* (Boston: Ginn & Co., 1931), p. 241.

17. Nina Ridenour, "The Treatment of Reading Disability," *Mental Hygiene*, XIX (1935), 387.

18. Donald Durrell, "Confusions in Learning," *Education*, LII (February, 1932), 330–31.

19. Grace E. Bird, "Personality Factors in Learning," *Personnel Journal*, VI (June, 1927), 56–59.

20. Mary Jane Saunders, "The Short Auditory Span Disability," *Childhood Education*, VIII (October, 1931), 59–65.

21. B. M. Castner, "Prediction of Reading Disability Prior to First Grade Entrance," *American Journal of Orthopsychiatry*, V (October, 1935), 379.

22. Marion Monroe and Bertie Backus, *Remedial Reading: A Monograph in Character Education* (Boston, Mass.: Houghton Mifflin Co., 1937), pp. 25–26.

23. Arthur I. Gates, "The Role of Personality Maladjustment in Reading Disability," *Journal of Genetic Psychology*, LIX (September, 1941), 77–83.

24. *Op. cit.*

25. *Op. cit.*, pp. 132–33.

26. Samuel A. Kirk, "The Effects of Remedial Reading on the Educational Progress and Personality Adjustment of High-Grade Mentally Deficient Children," *Journal of Juvenile Research*, XVIII (July, 1934), 140–62.

27. Arthur I. Gates (with the assistance of Guy L. Bond), "Failure in Reading and Social Maladjustment," *Journal of the National Education Association*, XXV (October, 1936), 205–6.

28. Phyllis Blanchard, "Reading Disability in Relation to Maladjustment," *Mental Hygiene*, XII (October, 1928), 772–88.

29. Orton, *Reading, Writing, and Speech Problems in Children* (New York: W. W. Norton & Co., Inc., 1937).

30. Mary I. Preston, "Reading Failure and the Child's Security," *American Journal of Orthopsychiatry*, X (April, 1940), 240.

31. *Ibid.*, p. 245.

32. *Op. cit.*, p. 130.

33. *Op. cit.*

34. Nancy Newell, "For Non-readers in Distress," *Elementary School Journal*, XXXII (November, 1931), 183–95.

35. Mary I. Preston, "The Reaction of Parents to Reading Failures," *Child Development*, X, No. 3 (September, 1939), p. 179.

36. Preston, "Reading Failure and the Child's Security," *op. cit.*, p. 252.

37. Ruth Damereau, "Influence of Treatment on the Reading Ability and Behavior Disorders of Reading Disability Cases," *Smith College Studies in Social Work*, V (December, 1934), 182.

38. Miles A. Tinker, "Remedial Methods for Non-readers," *School and Society*, XL (October, 1934), 526.

39. Chester C. Bennett, *An Inquiry into the Genesis of Poor Reading* ("Teachers College Contributions to Education," No. 755 [New York: Bureau of Publications, Teachers College, Columbia University, 1938), p. 36.

40. Marion Monroe, *Children Who Cannot Read* (Chicago: University of Chicago Press, 1932), p. 105.

41. Simon H. Tulchin, "Emotional Factors in Reading Disabilities in School Children," *Journal of Educational Psychology*, XXVI (1935), 446.

42. *Op. cit.*

43. F. L. Wells, "A Glossary of Needless Reading Errors," *Journal of Experimental Education*, IV (September, 1935), 35.

44. Phyllis Blanchard, "Reading Disabilities in Relation to Difficulties of Personality and Emotional Development," *Mental Hygiene*, XX (July, 1936), 410.

45. Paul A. Witty and Charles E. Skinner, *Mental Hygiene in Modern Education* (New York: Farrar & Rinehart, Inc., 1939), p. 409.

46. Rose S. Hardwick, "Types of Reading Disability," *Childhood Education*, VIII (April, 1932), 425.

47. *Ibid.*

48. *Op. cit.*, p. 134.

49. Gates (with the assistance of Bond), "Failure in Reading and Social Maladjustment," *op. cit.*, p. 205.

50. Paul Fendrick and Guy Bond, "Delinquency and Reading," *Pedagogical Seminary and Journal of Genetic Psychology*, XLVIII (March, 1936), 236–43.

51. Edward H. Stulken, "Retardation in Reading and the Problem Boy in School," *Elementary English Review*, XIV, No. 5 (May, 1937), 179–82.

52. *Ibid.*, p. 179.

53. *Ibid.*, p. 181.

54. *Ibid.*, p. 182.

CHAPTER VIII

ENVIRONMENTAL AND SOCIAL CHARACTERISTICS OF POOR READERS

M OST students of child growth agree that the home is an important contributing factor to the child's preschool training, so it would determine many of his attitudes and interests.[1] These attitudes may be favorable or unfavorable; the interests may be broad or narrow.

FACTORS IN THE HOME RELATED TO READING FAILURE

A great number of social factors have been studied in relation to reading failure, for example: education, reading ability, physical health, emotional reactions of parents, language spoken at home, economic status, neighborhood conditions, and ordinal position in the family.

Stulken stated: "Other reading disabilities seem to be caused by environmental factors such as foreign language or dialect speaking homes, broken school history, poor economic status of homes, and poor teaching methods."[2] Many of the boys he studied had changed schools three or more times before coming to the school in which this study was made. He considered their homes inadequate, and found evidence of a lack of reading materials at home.

PARENTS

Since the children's preschool experiences are largely in the hands of the parents, some investigations of relationship of characteristics of the parents and home have been made, although the results obtained threw little light on the solution of the problem.

Monroe and Backus[3] found that illiteracy, foreign language in the home, and insufficient background were causes of reading failure.

Of all his cases, Bennett found that 52 per cent came from families who spoke some language other than English, and he concluded that foreign language at home was a handicap in learning to read. He also studied the educational status of parents of reading-problem children and said: "Certainly the present data do not point to the educational advantages of parents as a significant determinant to children's reading progress."[4]

Preston made a study of the parents of 100 children who had failed in reading and concluded: "Evidently neither wealth, intelligence nor education, singly or together, presupposes an atmosphere fit for the upbringing of children."[5] Her methods of determining education and intelligence of parents were not described; consequently, her findings are open to question.

A study by Ladd[6] indicated a tendency for good readers to come from English-speaking homes and poor readers from foreign-speaking homes, although the only foreign language involved was Jewish.

Thus no conclusive evidence has been produced that any characteristic of the parents themselves influences reading failure. A suggestion that broken homes might be responsible for reading failure came from Monroe.[7] Bennett concluded that "indications are, however, that such gross changes in family structure as result from the death or separation of parents do not account for any large proportion of reading handicaps."[8]

Perhaps some of the factors of greatest importance, such as the attitudes of parents, cannot be measured. Bird[9] found, among her learning problems, introverts who came from environments of repression, harshness, and uneven treatment or general misunderstanding, while the extroverts developed through overindulgence by adults.

Preston[10] investigated the attitudes of parents after reading problems had developed and obtained the history of the earlier attitudes by interviews with parents.

She found parents who had indulged their children until the reading problem arose and who then suddenly changed to impatience and scolding. She listed children's attitudes as beginning with bewilderment and progressing to hostile reactions and antisocial behavior. Since insecurity at home and at school increased with failure to progress, both the behavior and the insecurity might have been dependent on the parents' inability to accept reading failure. This point was further emphasized when she stated that a child who failed to read was considered by his parents to be "abnormal, queer, not quite right."[11]

Monroe and Backus[12] believed that the attitudes and interests of parents were reflected by their children and that children, in turn, were more easily motivated when their parents enjoyed reading. They felt that lack of co-operation between home and school might result in antagonism toward school. These attitudes cannot be measured or evaluated but should be considered in individual cases, because they might impede progress.

The socioeconomic rating of the family was studied by Ladd,[13] who found a correlation of +.16 between reading age and score on the Sims Socio-Economic Score Card. With such a correlation, she rightly concluded that the relationship was not very significant.

Anderson and Kelley[14] found more parents of reading problems in the highest and lowest occupational groups.

Estimates of economic status made by Preston[15] appeared unrelated to the reading problems in 100 cases. Monroe and Backus suggested that economic insecurity rather than economic rating might be a cause of reading failure.

Bennett studied the occupational groups and concluded that "there was then no clear evidence that the occupational adjustment of the family was a significant factor in producing the poor readers."[16]

On the other hand, Louttit suggested that

there has apparently been no demonstration that the socio-economic condition of the home has any relation to reading except as it may have a relationship to general ability. However, in the case of homes of the lower socio-economic groups one might expect a lack of stimulation toward reading or even an antagonism toward it.[17]

It thus appears that studies to date have not given objective evidence of the relationship of socioeconomic status to reading disability or reading progress.

BOOKS IN THE HOME

Some writers were of the opinion that children who have few books at home and have little experience with books exhibit less desire to learn to read. For example, Parr[18] made a study of college students who were poor readers and found a lack of reading material in the home, lack of interest in reading in childhood, and little or no recreational reading in childhood.

Bennett[19] tabulated the size of the library in the homes of his cases of reading disability and concluded that the number of books in the home was not significant as a cause of failure to learn to read.

ORDINAL POSITION IN FAMILY

Bennett[20] studied ordinal position in the family and found that fewer only children and eldest children were reading problems than children who were intermediate or youngest. Anderson and Kelley[21] found that one-half of the control and one-third of the reading-disability cases were oldest or only children. They offered as an explanation the theory that parents probably assist oldest or only children more than children of a larger sibship.

SUMMARY

There seems to be little relationship between reading failure and education or ability of parents, socioeconomic status, foreign language in the home, or recordable attitudes. It appears from the few studies presented that the ordinal position of the child in the family may be related to reading failure, but results might be due to chance. Further studies should be made to verify this finding and a more intensive effort made to explain why such a factor would be operative. The relation of environmental factors to reading was summarized by Gray and others, who stated: "It is probable that the more subtle environmental aspects such as proper motivation, economic stability, and cultural pressures are most closely related to reading proficiency than those which, like socio-economic status, can be objectively measured."[22]

SEX

Most clinics and reports of studies agree that the majority of reading failures seem to be boys. Monroe[23] found that 84 per cent of her failures were boys, Preston[24] reported 72 per cent, and others reported varying percentages; but there seemed to be general agreement that failure to learn to read is greater among boys than among girls.

Monroe[25] believed that certain unfavorable constitutional factors were more prevalent among boys than among girls or, as with other biological variations, that boys might be more susceptible than girls. Witty and Kopel thought that the larger percentage of boys "appears to reflect in part the slower physical maturation of schoolboys, which causes larger numbers of boys than of girls at the same chronological age not to be ready for initial reading instruction."[26] This last opinion seems to be shared by Olson, who felt that "reading tends to be an aspect of the growth of the child as a whole."[27]

Perhaps more research in child growth and development will throw light on this explanation.

FACTORS IN THE SCHOOL RELATED TO READING FAILURE

Since the school is the place where reading is ordinarily learned, it would seem logical to assume that the most important cause of reading failure would appear in this area. Thus the policy of the school as a whole concerning methods of teaching, promotion, materials for instruction, and freedom in adapting this material to individual children undoubtedly influences progress in individual cases. However, it may be argued that the majority of children learn to read under these circumstances; consequently, there must be additional factors impeding the seriously retarded reader.

Gates,[28] Durrell,[29] Monroe,[30] and Betts[31] all summarized the ways in which faulty teaching methods impede progress in reading, even actually develop and promote the growth of undesirable habits in reading. It seems probable from their reports that some children in each classroom, because of physical differences, respond to methods which are not so well suited to the entire group. Notwithstanding this fact, they found considerable variation in the teacher's familiarity with different methods and in her ability to apply them. Concerning these possible causes, Betts stated:

Aversion to reading on the part of the children is built up by forcing them into situations for which they are too immature, by questionable teacher and parent attitudes, by failure on the part of teachers to analyze learning gaps and make necessary provisions, and by a general lack of understanding of problems encountered by a child with language disability.[32]

The teacher's personality was considered important as a possible cause of failure to progress in reading, especially by Witty and Kopel.[33] Preston[34] reported that 78 per cent of the teachers studied could not refrain from expressing their annoyance at slow, stumbling failures. However, there was no means of measuring or estimating the effect of these factors. Many children were moved from one teacher to another, yet they continued to fail in reading.

Even though it was not possible to measure the effect of the school and the teacher on reading failure, such factors should be considered in determining the causes of failure in individual cases.

SUMMARY

There are many factors and conditions in the school which may be conducive to reading failure. Teachers' personalities, their relationship to children, methods of teaching reading, school policy in promotions, materials available, size of classes, and many other factors should be considered as possible causes of severely retarded readers.

CONCLUSIONS BASED ON SUMMARY OF THE LITERATURE

Many hypotheses and theories have been set forth to explain children's failure to learn to read adequately. No single cause has ever been isolated; and, as many investigators have concluded, an attempt to isolate single causes would probably be an oversimplification of a complex situation.

Visual anomalies have been related to reading failure by some research investigators, and denied by others. However, most investigators agree that the visual anomaly should be considered in individual cases. Visual acuity, per se, was not believed to be related to reading success in the studies reviewed. Hyperopia, hyperopic astigmatism, binocular inco-ordination, inadequate visual fields, and aniseikonia seemed to be most closely related to reading failure. However, it appeared that many of these visual anomalies were measured by rough screening tests and were not interpreted in terms of other findings. It is possible, then, that many of the anomalies studied are symptoms rather than abnormalities themselves.

A neurological basis for reading failure has been assumed by many. Various explanations to account for this inefficiency in reading have been advanced by one or more writers, only to be criticized by others. Many eminent neurologists have felt that, although the specific area involved could not be completely localized, there might be a physical inadequacy in the brain which accounted for some retarded readers. This condition has been referred to as word-blindness, alexia, congenital alexia, developmental alexia, or diplexia. Direct methods of examining the brains of children who have failed to learn to read have not been possible in many cases. Therefore, indirect methods have been used, and none have proved very satisfactory. In general, alexia has been the diagnosis in many cases in which no other cause seemed apparent. Thus for many years the term "alexia" has been used in referring to many cases of failure to learn to read. Newer methods of indirect investigation and controlled studies of children whose difficulties have been diagnosed as alexia should aid in clarifying the exact function of cerebral defects in preventing reading growth.

Conflicting views prevail concerning the role of dominance in reading. After much theoretical discussion and research on the part of specialists in the field of reading, there is still little agreement. The dominance tests most commonly used have been questioned as to validity, and the most desirable combination of preferences to expedite reading has not been established. It appears, however, that dominance should not be entirely neglected as a cause for reading failure until further research has been done.

Inadequate auditory acuity has been considered a cause of poor reading by a few investigators. The results of studies of auditory acuity of good and poor readers, while few, indicated that the latter had slightly poorer auditory acuity than the former, although both appeared to be within the normal range. Adequate auditory acuity did not appear to guarantee adequate hearing, since poor auditory discrimination and insufficient auditory memory span were found to be possible causes of reading failure. Howes's findings, indicating that a small percentage of undetected hearing loss was serious in its effect on school achievement, showed the need for further research in this area.

Articulatory defects have been considered as a cause of poor reading or as a possible concomitant of it. Little critical research, however, was found in this field and standards of judging articulatory defects were not given. On the basis of the evidence available, articulatory defects may be conceded to be important in oral reading but of little significance in silent reading.

General physical conditions were included among most lists of causes of reading disabilities. Malnutrition, infections, and endocrine disturbances were the three most commonly recognized, although no conclusive evidence of their relationship to reading failure has been established.

Intelligence was conceded to have a positive relationship to reading success. However, since many children who are not mentally retarded fail to learn to read, lack of sufficient intelligence is only one of the many causes of severely retarded readers. At the time of writing, the Binet intelligence test was considered the best single measure of expectancy, although some preferred to supplement it with performance tests. Thus it is probable that, when the primary abilities are isolated and a profile is made of intelligence instead of a single composite measure, reading expectancy can be more accurately estimated.

Emotional and personality maladjustments in children who failed to learn to read properly seemed to be very common. Emotional maladjustments appeared to be either a cause or a result of reading failure, or each might interact on the other, intensifying both. The data secured indicated that emotionally immature children might fail to learn to read when starting school. It was likewise stressed that neurotic children should be carefully studied before reading training is provided. Children who failed to read either accepted their failure and lost confidence, or explained away, or refused to accept failure. The latter groups tended to become aggressive, to withdraw, or to lose emotional affectivity. The evaluation of children's emotional responses is such a complex problem that few studies have been made in this field, although most investigators recognize the problem.

Several investigators believe that delinquency is associated with reading failure, since a number of delinquents studied appeared to be retarded in reading. However, this relationship could not be evaluated without more controlled studies.

A number of other social factors have been investigated, among which are parents' education, their reading ability, physical health, and emotional reactions, as well as their economic status, the language spoken in the home, neighborhood conditions, and ordinal position of the child in the family. Two studies showed that the ordinal position in the family appeared to be the only factor which is related to reading failure. An effort should therefore be made to explain why such a factor should be operative. Many other subtle environmental problems may not have been considered, or it may not have been possible to determine their relationship to reading disability.

The school itself might be a very important cause of reading failure. Administrative policies, materials, size of classes, training and personality of teachers, must all be taken into consideration and, if possible, evaluated as causes of severe retardation in reading.

The following statement by Monroe and Backus should be cited in conclusion:

Reading disabilities are usually the result of several contributing factors rather than one isolated cause. Studies of the causes of reading disabilities reveal no clear-cut factors which occur only in poor readers but never in good readers. Some children who possess the impeding factors appear to be able to read in spite of them. . . . . A few good readers are found who have poor vision, poor hearing, emotional instability, who come from environment detrimental to reading and who have had inferior teaching. . . . . We may conclude that in most cases one factor alone is not sufficient to inhibit the act of reading, if compensating abilities are present, and if the child's reaction to the difficulty is a favorable one.[35]

NOTES

1. Gertrude Whipple, "Causes of Retardation in Reading and Methods of Eliminating Them," *Peabody Journal of Education*, XVI (November, 1923), 196.

2. Edward H. Stulken, "Retardation in Reading and the Problem Boy in School," *Elementary English Review*, XIV, No. 5 (May, 1937), 180.

3. Marion Monroe and Bertie Backus, *Remedial Reading: A Monograph in Character Education* (Boston, Mass.: Houghton Mifflin Co., 1937).

4. Chester C. Bennett, *An Inquiry into the Genesis of Poor Reading* ("Teachers College Contributions to Education," No. 755 [New York: Bureau of Publications, Teachers College, Columbia University, 1938]), p. 68.

5. Mary I. Preston, "The Reaction of Parents to Reading Failures," *Child Development*, X, No. 3 (September, 1939), 173.

6. Margaret Rhoads Ladd, *The Relation of Social, Economic, and Personal Characteristics to Reading Ability* ("Teachers College Contributions to Education," No. 582 [Bureau of Publications, Teachers College, Columbia University, 1933]).

7. Marion Monroe, *Children Who Cannot Read* (Chicago: University of Chicago Press, 1932).

8. *Op. cit.*, p. 63.

9. Grace E. Bird, Personality Factors in Learning," *Personnel Journal*, VI (June, 1927), 56–59.

10. "The Reaction of Parents to Reading Failure," *op. cit.*

11. *Ibid.* p. 173.

12. *Op. cit.*

13. *Op. cit.*

14. Margaret Anderson and Mae Kelley, "An Inquiry into Traits Associated with Reading Disability," *Smith College Studies in Social Work*, II (September, 1931), 46–63.

15. "The Reaction of Parents to Reading Failure," *op. cit.*

16. *Op. cit.*, p. 65.

17. C. M. Louttit, *Clinical Psychology: A Handbook of Children's Behavior Problems* (New York: Harper & Bros., 1936), p. 210.

18. F. W. Parr, "Factors Associated with Poor Reading Ability of Adults," *School and Society*, XXXV (May 7, 1932), 626.

19. *Op. cit.*

20. *Ibid.*

21. "An Inquiry into Traits Associated with Reading Disability," *Op. cit.*

22. William S. Gray (ed.), *Reading in General Education* (Washington, D.C.: American Council on Education, 1940), p. 317.

23. *Op. cit.*

24. "The Reaction of Parents to Reading Failure," *op. cit.*

25. *Op. cit.*

26. Paul Witty and David Kopel, *Reading and the Educative Process* (Boston: Ginn & Co., 1939), p. 220.

27. Willard C. Olson, Reading as a Function of the Total Growth of the Child," in William S. Gray (comp. and ed.), *Reading and Pupil Development* ("Supplementary Educational Monographs," No. 51 [Chicago: University of Chicago, 1940]), p. 233.

28. Arthur I. Gates, *The Improvement of Reading* (New York: Macmillan Co., 1929).

29. Donald Dewitt Durrell, *Improvement of Basic Reading Abilities* (Yonkers-on-Hudson, N.Y.: World Book Co., 1941).

30. *Op. cit.*

31. Emmett A. Betts, *The Prevention and Correction of Reading Difficulties* (Evanston, Ill.: Row, Peterson & Co., 1936).

32. *Ibid.*, p. 233.

33. *Op. cit.*, p. 233.

34. Mary I. Preston, Reading Failure and the Child's Security," *American Journal of Orthopsychiatry*, X (April, 1940), 239–52.

35. *Op. cit.*, p. 12.

PART II
THE EXPERIMENTAL STUDY

CHAPTER IX

DESCRIPTION OF THE INTENSIVE STUDY
OF THIRTY CASES

A PLAN for considering every angle of the child's developmental life was recognized as essential in attempting to isolate the causes of severe reading retardation. As indicated in chapter i, most previous studies had considered one cause or a limited number of possible causes. In line with the newer philosophy of education, it seemed desirable to explore as many areas as possible in each case studied. To do this thoroughly involved (1) securing specialists in each area to collect valid data and render expert opinion; (2) analyzing the constellations of concomitant factors so as to identify true causes of reading difficulty, if possible; and (3) attempting to institute appropriate therapy as an aid in ascertaining whether the assumed causes were the correct ones.

INITIAL ORGANIZATION

In the autumn of 1936 a group of specialists who had previously expressed interest in reading problems met to discuss the wisdom of the proposed study, to indicate their willingness to co-operate, and to help plan its general scope and procedures.

The initial group included the director of Billings Hospital, University of Chicago, and the acting chairman of the Department of Education; a reading specialist, a psychiatrist, and a pediatrician from the Department of Education; two social workers from the School of Social Service Administration; three ophthalmologists, a neurologist, one otolaryngologist, an endocrinologist, and a speech specialist from the staff of Billings Hospital; and the investigator, who acted as psychologist and reading technician.

During the conference, each of these specialists agreed to co-operate and discuss the steps necessary to secure adequate data relating to reading-disability cases. It was decided that each case should have a similar type of examination, in order to insure comparable data, which could be interpreted in terms of the findings for all cases. It was recognized at once that an adequate developmental history was needed by all who examined the subjects. Furthermore, each examiner agreed to make out a form into which he could insert findings of his examinations on each case and on which he might record all pertinent data. Following the conference, each participant provided such a form and also indicated what information he would want from a history. This desired historical information was sorted, classified, and organized by the investigator.

After the examination routine was established, the forms were developed. The services of the following specialists were involved:

A social worker, who interviewed the parents while the child was being examined and obtained a history of the case in harmony with the suggestions of the group of specialists. In some instances the worker also interpreted the results to the parents after the examinations had been completed.

A psychiatrist, who usually saw the child when he made his first visit to the institution for examination and often saw him frequently thereafter. He sought early to establish rapport with the child in order to identify the nature of his emotional responses and to evaluate them and particularly to study his responses to reading situations in which he had failed.

A pediatrician, who made a general physical examination of each child and who was especially interested in determining the child's level of nutrition, evidence of infections, and his physical status in the various respects emphasized by the literature in this field.

A neurologist, who examined each child to determine the integrity of the nervous system and to identify cases of alexia.

Three ophthalmologists, who co-operated in making the visual examinations. Two were concerned largely with refractions, and the third, who was interested in orthoptics, gave functional visual tests and orthoptic training to those needing it.

A speech-correction specialist, who studied the speech of the subject and also investigated the status of auditory memory span for sounds and his auditory discrimination of paired words.

An otolaryngologist, who examined ears, nose, and throat for evidence of infections or abnormalities and also tested hearing.

An endocrinologist, who examined most of the children and had basal metabolic rate and fasting blood-cholesterol tests made.

The investigator gave all reading tests, except the Standardized Oral Reading Paragraphs. She also gave the psychometric tests and did much of the remedial work.

The reading specialist examined all the test data and administered the Standardized Oral Reading Paragraphs. He acted as chairman at the conferences and as consultant on remedial treatment.

The investigator was responsible for selecting cases; making the initial psychological and reading examinations; securing the social history from the social worker and taking it with the child to visit each specialist, who would, in turn, add his findings to the total report. When all the tests and examinations had been completed, the medical data were taken to the pediatrician, who summarized them and interpreted the technical findings. The whole case was then summarized and presented for discussion at a conference of the co-operating group. Following the conference, the experimenter reported findings to the parents and was responsible for seeing that the recommendations were carried out. Each case was carefully followed by the investigator as far as possible, and reports of progress were obtained. If necessary, a second or third conference was held concerning a given child, and the relationship of possible causes restudied or revisions made in the plan for treatment.

DESCRIPTION OF CASES

Thirty children were studied according to the plan described above, and the findings on each case were summarized. The various cases were referred to the investigator for study by the following: members of the committee, 8; parents, 8; social agencies, 1; physicians, 2; schools, 8; and private reading tutors, 3.

Pupils were accepted as subjects in the study, provided the following requirements were met:

1. The child had to have an I.Q. on the New Stanford-Binet of at least 85, thus eliminating the most serious cases of mental retardation and insuring intellectual readiness for reading.

2. The parents had to agree to bring the child for several appointments at scheduled times and to comply with special requests, such as no food on the morning of a basal metabolic rate reading.

3. After being informed concerning the examination routine, the

parent had to indicate willingness to co-operate in a remedial plan for the child.

Many poor readers referred to the investigator did not meet the foregoing standards, and findings on such cases are not included in this report. However, some of these cases were examined and given remedial treatment by the Orthogenic School of the University of Chicago or were referred to some other agency for appropriate help.

The children were studied in the order of their referral. Five of the thirty cases thus secured were girls and twenty-five were boys. All had attended public or private schools or both and had failed to learn to read.

The thirty cases studied ranged in chronological ages from 6 years 9 months to 15 years 3 months. The median chronological age was 10 years 3.5 months.

The amount of retardation in reading varied from 9 months to 75 months, in terms of chronological age. Monroe[1] has indicated that children with reading indices[2] below .80 are sufficiently retarded to need correctional reading work. All the cases in this study fell below .80, with a median at .48. Thus each child was seriously retarded in reading, although his intelligence score was within the normal range or superior.

PSYCHOMETRIC AND EDUCATIONAL EXAMINATION

All cases referred for examination were given an application blank, a part of which was to be filled in by the parent, another part by the parent and the school, and a third part by the subject's reading or home-room teacher. Through a study of the information on the blank, an attempt was made to determine whether a referral met the requirements of the present study. Some cases had been studied elsewhere, and fairly complete information was available. If it appeared that a further study might aid in diagnosis and in prescribing treatment, a case was accepted for preliminary examination.

PRELIMINARY EXAMINATION

In a child's first visit he was greeted by the investigator, who spent some time getting acquainted with him and gaining his confidence. In most cases this could be done in a short time. However, one girl could not be studied intensively for about two months after she entered the Orthogenic School because she was very much afraid of tests and felt insecure with any examiner. After the investigator had gained the child's confidence and established rapport, she described the tests that were to be given. She also attempted to show the child the need for seeing so many specialists and explained the function of each. This resulted in better co-operation between the children and the examiners.

The child was then given the New Stanford-Binet Intelligence Test, Form L, according to the directions given by Terman and Merrill.[3] The mental age and intelligence quotient were computed according to directions, even though it appeared to the examiner in certain cases that the child was being penalized by inability to read.

If the child could read, he was given the New Stanford Achievement Test[4] or the Metropolitan Achievement Test,[5] according to the directions accompanying the respective tests. The Stanford Achievement Test was given to each child who could read above Grade II; however, the Metropolitan seemed better suited to any whose reading level was Grade II or below and was used with such cases. An attempt was also made to estimate informally the ability of a subject by permitting him to select one of a number of small books at various levels of difficulty and to read from it both orally and silently.

If the average reading grade, as revealed by the test given, was found to be at least 0.9 year below the mental age and the chronological age in the case of a child below nine years of age, he was accepted for further study. If the average reading grade was two years below both the mental and the chronological ages in the case of a child nine years or older, he was accepted for further study. This procedure was based on opinions of previous investigators concerning a sound estimate of reading retardation.

PSYCHOMETRIC EXAMINATION

As pointed out previously, a New Stanford-Binet rating was obtained on each child. There is general agreement that, when possible, the Stanford-Binet should be supplemented by other tests requiring less verbal ability. The performance tests were investigated, and the Arthur Point Scale of Performance[6] was chosen because it includes nine different performance tests and because satisfactory results had already been reported with defective readers through its use.[7] This series of performance tests was given according to the manual of directions prepared by Dr. Arthur. A mental age rating was secured on each test within the group and on the group of tests as a whole.

The Chicago Non-verbal Examination[8] was used to supplement the two tests mentioned above. It was selected because it requires a minimum of verbal responses and tests types of reasoning different from those sampled by the other two tests. It contains two tests composed of forms which are different from the forms of our letters, and it seemed interesting to investigate the behavior of poor readers in this area. The test was given according to the mimeographed verbal directions included with the test blanks that accompany the test. The raw scores were obtained and converted into mental ages according to the table dated May, 1939.[9]

The mental ages obtained on the three tests were all considered in an attempt to determine the mental ability of each child. As indicated in chapter ii, Binet scores correlate higher than nonverbal tests with reading success; hence the mental age obtained on the Binet was used in predicting reading expectancy.

After a number of the cases had been examined, the Durrell-Sullivan Test of Reading Capacity[10] for Intermediate Grades became available and was used as an additional measure of reading expectancy with children whose ability appeared to be between Grades II and VII. This test was administered and scored according to the directions accompanying the test. The results of these tests were recorded on the form prepared for this purpose.

ACHIEVEMENT TESTS AND READING TESTS

As mentioned previously, either the Stanford Achievement tests or the Metropolitan Achievement tests were given to each child. The purpose of using such tests was to secure a cross-section of a pupil's achievement in all school subjects. The scores secured made possible a comparison of achievement in reading, spelling, and arithmetic, as well as in other subjects at the upper-grade levels. If the scores on arithmetic computation were as low as those in reading and spelling, the child was considered a general learning problem, because a pupil with only reading disability can do well in nonreading subjects.

Some of the cases examined were nonreaders, so it was not possible to measure achievement through the use of reading or other school tests. Instead, an attempt was made to determine the level of preparedness for beginning to read, through the use of one of the reading-readiness tests. The Monroe Reading Aptitude Test[11] was usually given; but in a few instances it was supplemented by the Metropolitan Readiness Test,[12] especially if the former had been given previously to the subject.

The Monroe Diagnostic Reading Examination[13] was given to all children who rated Grade I or higher in reading. The purpose of this test was to aid in determining specific characteristics of a child's performance in reading, in order that treatment could be directed to the areas of greatest need. As an example, the errors made on two subtests of the Monroe test and on the Gray Standardized Oral Reading Paragraphs[14] were analyzed into the following types of errors: faulty vowels, faulty consonants, reversals, addition of sounds, omission of sounds, substitution of words, repetition of words, addition of words, omission of words, words refused, and words aided.

The test was given according to Monroe's *Manual of Directions*[15] and the directions in her book,[16] except that, to avoid duplication, tests 11 and 12 were omitted because handedness was measured in another battery and spelling was measured by a different test. The Monroe Reading Index, which is designed to indicate percentage of reading achievement as compared with chronological age, mental age, and achievement in arithmetic, was calculated according to her directions.[17] The profile of errors reveals the proportional number of errors in each area measured above and was prepared according to the directions in Monroe's *Children Who Cannot Read*.[18] This profile has obvious limitations, as indicated by the fact that certain errors may be classified in any one of several different ways.

In certain instances the Monroe Diagnostic Test was sufficient to show up the types of difficulties encountered by the child. In other instances, further testing seemed desirable. Accordingly, parts of the Gates Reading Diagnosis Tests[19] or the Durrell Analysis of Reading Difficulty[20] were used. Only selected parts were used, since the administration of all of either of the tests required a great deal of time and added to the large battery already being employed.

The Standardized Oral Reading Paragraphs were administered to each child by the reading specialist, and many characteristics of the child's reading were noted at this time. The test was scored according to Gray's directions,[21] and the specific errors made were analyzed according to Monroe's directions, as well as according to Gray's suggestions.

A motion-picture photograph of the behavior of the eyes during reading[22] was made for each child who could read. In most cases, two or three records were secured, and the examiner took the average rather than depending on only one. From these records the examiner could identify certain reading habits and characteristics of the subject and study the maturity of the reading process. This record was also scrutinized by the ophthalmologists for additional evidence of changes in relative position of the two eyes while working at close range. The analysis of the film was made according to the manual[23] accompanying the instrument, and the norms prepared were used in determining the level of achievement.

The Keystone Visual Survey tests administered through the Telebinocular were given to each child. These tests were originally a part of the Betts Ready To Read tests.[24] Some cards have been changed, and different norms and directions have been provided by the makers of the instrument.[25]

The Gray Oral Reading Check tests,[26] adapted to the Telebinocular, were also administered to all children who could read them, in order to check reading efficiency with each eye separately and with both eyes reading together. The results of these tests were recorded on forms developed for this purpose.

PREFERENCE TESTS

Since some investigators have emphasized hand and eye preference, it seemed essential to secure evidence of the preferred hand and eye. Questions on preference were asked the parents, and the eye clinic determined the preferred eye by its own methods. It seemed to the writer that the preferred foot would be less subject to change than the preferred hand, because social pressure is used to train a child to be right-handed. Hence the determination of foot preference was included in the study. It also appeared that some children had preferences as to ears, accordingly tests for ear preference were used.

Few laterality and preference tests are standardized, and their reliability and validity are still questioned. The use of a question-naire, such as Witty and Kopel suggest, was also questioned for these children after a few were observed to give one set of answers but to behave otherwise.

The series of tests finally selected provided six opportunities to observe hand preference, five to observe foot preference, five for ear preference, and five for eye preference. They were selected from unpublished tests used in a previous study by Dr. Louise F. Davis and Dr. William S. Gray. The chief characteristics of these tests are that (1) each hand, foot, ear, or eye has an equal chance, as one is not favored or used for any other purpose at the same time; (2) the child is asked to perform the tasks without being told or shown by the examiner which hand, foot, ear, or eye to use; and (3) the child performs the work without knowing that he is being observed for that purpose. However, a few children became aware of what was being measured after the tests were partly finished.

No formal interest inventory was filled out. During the testing the examiner noted the subject of the conversation which the child enjoyed, the things he chose to do during rest periods, the type of children he selected as playmates during the lunch hour, his skill in the games they played, and the extent of his participation. These facts were recorded as an aid in understanding the child. Children often related stories of things they had done at home or in other schools. The parents and teachers were also asked about the child's interests, and the psychiatrist often obtained further information concerning the things he most enjoyed.

SOCIAL HISTORY

The social history was taken, according to the outline previously described, by a trained social worker. The workers changed during the period of study, but the outline served as a guide, and those participating were members of the Department of Social Service of the University of Chicago.

The trained worker usually took the original history from the mother when she brought the child for psychometric or reading tests. In most instances the mother was seen several times, so that she would be more at ease and more willing to give full information. In some instances, fathers, tutors, and doctors were interviewed;

and, whenever possible, reports from schools or other clinics were obtained.

The social worker attempted to study the family interrelationships as they affected the child's reading, and, in many cases, this step revealed possible causes of difficulty. Unfortunately, social factors are not subject to measurement. Consequently, expert opinion is considered preferable to that of an untrained worker. The outline made by the worker and the investigator was used as a guide to collect uniform data.

PSYCHIATRIC STUDY

The psychiatrist saw each child from one to five times before the final diagnostic report was made. Usually the child was seen two or three times. The interview method was used to identify and evaluate the various emotional responses.

An outline was used as a guide to the study. In certain very severe or baffling cases, more objective measures of emotionality, such as the photopolygram or the electroencephalogram, were made. However, such records were secured on only about eight of the cases.

PEDIATRIC EXAMINATION

Each of the cases was taken to the office of the pediatrician, where a general physical examination was made. The record form included details concerning all the physical factors considered in this examination. It was not the opinion of the pediatrician that all these factors might be related to reading; but the fact was recognized that anything less than a complete examination might omit some of the important symptoms. Therefore, a form used for previous examinations was made the basis for collecting this information.

The pediatrician examining these cases was the school physician for the University Elementary and High Schools and assistant professor of pediatrics at Billings Hospital. The same pediatrician examined all thirty cases.

NEUROLOGICAL EXAMINATION

A neurologist at Bobs Roberts Hospital examined each of the children, and if one visit was not sufficient, a second was made. The chief purpose of this examination was to identify possible cases of alexia and other types of neurologic interference which might make the teaching of reading very difficult. All thirty cases were seen by the same neurologist. One skull X-ray was required, and one encephalogram was made.

VISUAL EXAMINATION

Each child was taken to the University of Chicago Eye Clinic, where he was seen by an ophthalmologist. The external examination was made and signs of pathology were recorded. Unaided vision was measured by the use of the Snellen chart. The child was then given atropine, to be put into his eyes at home, and returned for a second examination with his pupils dilated. A third visit was made one month later, when he had recovered from the effects of the atropine. Vision was then tested again and a study made of the phorias and ductions.

Furthermore, the blind spot was charted and the visual field plotted to determine whether they were normal. Whenever there were questions concerning the functioning of the eyes in reading, the child was seen by another ophthalmologist, who did specialized work in orthoptics. During the time the data were being collected, five different ophthalmologists co-operated in examining the children.

EXAMINATION OF HEARING

Each child was examined by an otolaryngologist, who made an audiometer record in a soundproof room. The Western Electric Audiometer was used. An examination was also made of the ears, nose, and throat to identify any local conditions which might contribute to hearing loss or especially bad tonsils, adenoids, or sinuses which might lower the child's energy. Two different doctors made the examinations, although the original specialist continued to co-operate in the interpretation of all data.

SPEECH EXAMINATION

The speech pathologist examined each child to determine the presence or absence of a speech defect and also attempted to be more specific in classifying speech defects than many other investigators had been.

Among the first cases was one child who appeared to have a short auditory memory span for sounds. The speech pathologist decided to check the auditory memory span for sounds of each child, using a technique similar to that reported by V. A. Anderson.[27] However, the vowel and consonant sounds were intermingled rather than given in isolation. Unfortunately, no adequate norms have been established for the test, but variations within this group may be noted.

Since many of the so-called "auditory discrimination tests" were not well organized phonetically, a test was devised by the speech pathologist to measure auditory discrimination. It was organized to test vowel discrimination and consonant discrimination separately. After a preliminary trial, the test was revised and is now being standardized. All the thirty cases were examined by the same speech pathologist.

ENDOCRINE EXAMINATION

Since a number of references indicated the possibility of relationship between poor reading and thyroid deficiency, pituitary deficiency, or delayed sexual development, an endocrinologist who could determine the presence of these conditions in severely retarded readers seemed very pertinent.

A basal metabolic rate was charted on each child at the clinic in Billings Hospital. The Benedict-Roth procedure was used, and the findings were compared with standards.[28] However, some studies[29] have indicated that these norms are somewhat high. This fact was taken into consideration by the endocrinologist in making his final diagnosis. The report was made on a regular form designed for this purpose. A note accompanied the report stating the endocrinologist's diagnosis.

A fasting blood cholesterol in whole blood, Lieberman-Burchard calorimetric determination in Bloor's alcohol-ether extract, was also made for each child. The results are reported in milligrams per cent per 100 cc. of blood. The normal range is about 130–250 mg. per cent. In cases of hypothyroidism this fasting blood-cholesterol rating is elevated.

Most of the cases had a radiogram made of the wrist to determine the stage of ossification of the carpal bones. These radiograms were compared with Carter's standards.[30] This, too, was considered by the endocrinologist in making his final diagnosis.

The same endocrinologist co-operated throughout the study and saw the majority of the cases. Basal metabolic rates and fasting blood cholesterols are available for the thirty cases.

GROUP CONFERENCE

When the specialists had completed their examinations, the medical findings, except for those of the psychiatrist, were summarized and interpreted by the pediatrician. The investigator assembled all reports and called a conference. The findings on the case were reported, so that each specialist would be acquainted with the findings of others. The factors which might be causes were discussed, and an attempt was made to evaluate each factor to determine whether it was a cause of reading failure or merely a concomitant. In some instances, factors could be associated with each other.

The conference served as a means of planning remedial treatment for the poor reader. If the group decided on one factor as being the most important cause, it was treated first to determine the effect on reading. An example to clarify this procedure is the case of K. C. The diagnosis showed that he could not concentrate for more than 5 minutes without falling asleep. The endocrinologist pointed out that his metabolic rate was very low and that the rate of learning might be improved through administration of thyroid. The ophthalmologist reported that the two eyes were not functioning as a team and that the condition was such as to produce discomfort and fatigue. The psychiatrist thought he was sufficiently disturbed emotionally to be unable to concentrate on learning.

On the basis of the evidence presented, the committee decided to have orthoptic exercises given to the boy. After twelve weeks of treatment he ceased falling asleep and learned to read. Furthermore, the psychiatric problem which he had exhibited disappeared without treatment. After he had about reached expectancy in ability to read, thyroid was administered to improve his health, but it was of no value in reading. Any one of these factors found in isolation might have been considered as a cause of the reading failure. When every angle had been investigated, three were identified, and the treatment of one proved satisfactory.

Remedial plans were always tentative and subject to revision at any time that they seemed inadequate. The investigator was responsible for calling additional conferences on a case when progress was not satisfactory. She also made follow-up appointments and was responsible for retesting and reporting progress back to the group.

The conference provided an excellent medium for interchange of ideas and explanations of diverse points of view. Every member of the group found it a valuable opportunity to become acquainted with various interpretations of the evidence secured and with factors affecting reading. They agreed that no one of the group was capable of making a complete analysis of causes of severe reading retardation and believed that progress in solving this problem must be based on co-operative research.

LIMITATIONS OF THE TECHNIQUES USED

Such an extensive and intensive study is subject to limitations just as are the less detailed studies. The limitations of this study are recognized. Some of the major ones follow:

1. The number of cases examined was necessarily small, because of the number and extent of examinations made and because an attempt was made to treat each case so as to further evaluate causes of reading retardation.
2. Cases had to be selected largely from the Chicago area because of the length of time required for testing and remediation.
3. Even though an intensive effort was made to anticipate the pertinent data needed, there were times during the study when many of the specialists felt that some other minor aspect should have been included.
4. Tests were not available for the purpose of evaluating all phases of progress. Some were constructed during the time the data were being collected; hence results were not available for all cases.
5. Although parents were carefully informed in advance of the details of the examination and treatment planned, some were unable to carry out the remedial measures as well as were others. In some cases particularly, the group felt that part of the treatment should be directed toward the parents. Such cases presented special difficulty, because maladjusted parents could seldom recognize the vital relationship between their own attitudes and problems and those of their children.

6. The least satisfactory results were obtained on the children selected from the public school. The school co-operated fully, but many of the parents did not keep appointments for treatment and were not so co-operative, on the whole, as were those who voluntarily brought their children to the clinic.

7. Much of the data obtained were not quantitative or objective and therefore did not lend themselves to statistical treatment.

NOTES

1. Marion Monroe, *Children Who Cannot Read* (Chicago: University of Chicago Press, 1932), p. 17.

2. *Ibid.*, p. 14.

3. Lewis N. Terman and Maud A. Merrill, *Measuring Intelligence—a Guide to the Administration of the New Revised Stanford-Binet Tests of Intelligence* (Boston: Houghton Mifflin Co., 1937).

4. Published by World Book Co., 1930.

5. Published by World Book Co., 1933.

6. Grace Arthur, *A Point Scale of Performance* (New York: Commonwealth Fund Division of Publications, 1930).

7. Grace Arthur, "An Attempt To Sort Children with Specific Reading Disability from Other Non-readers," *Journal of Applied Psychology*, XI (August, 1927).

8. *Chicago Non-verbal Examination.* Prepared by Andrew W. Brown, Institute for Juvenile Research, with the assistance of Seymour P. Stein, and Perry L. Rohrer, Chicago, Ill.

9. Mimeographed table from Institute for Juvenile Research.

10. *Durrell-Sullivan Reading Capacity and Achievement Tests, Intermediate Test, Form A, for Grades 3–6* (Yonkers-on-Hudson, N.Y.: World Book Co., 1937).

11. Marion Monroe, *Reading Aptitude Tests* (Boston: Houghton Mifflin Co., Riverside Press, 1935).

12. Gertrude H. Hildreth, and Nellie L. Griffiths, *Metropolitan Readiness Tests* (Yonkers-on-Hudson, N.Y.: World Book Co., 1933).

13. Marion Monroe, *Diagnostic Reading Examination, for Diagnosis of Special Difficulty in Reading* (Chicago: Institute for Juvenile Research, C. H. Stoelting Co., 1932).

14. William S. Gray, *Standardized Oral Reading Paragraphs* (Bloomington, Ill.: Public School Pub. Co., 1916).

15. Marion Monroe, *Diagnostic Reading Examination: Manual of Directions* (Chicago: C. H. Stoelting Co., 1930).

16. *Children Who Cannot Read*, Appendix.

17. *Ibid.*, p. 191.

18. Pp. 37–57.

19. Arthur I. Gates, *Gates Reading Diagnosis Tests* (New York: Bureau of Publications, Teachers College, Columbia University, 1933).

20. Donald D. Durrell, *Durrell Analysis of Reading Difficulty* (Yonkers-on-Hudson, N.Y.: World Book Co., 1937).

21. *Standardized Oral Reading Paragraphs.*

22. This was made on the Ophthalm-O-Graph, made by American Optical Co., Southbridge, Mass.

23. *The Ophthalm-O-Graph, the Metron-O-Scope—Manual for Controlled Reading*, ed. Bureau of Visual Science, American Optical Co. (Southbridge, Mass.: American Optical Co., 1937–38).

24. Emmett A. Betts, *The Prevention and Correction of Reading Difficulties* (Evanston, Ill.: Row, Peterson & Co., 1936), Appen. B.

25. Keystone View Co., Meadville, Pa.

26. William S. Gray, *Keystone Tests of Binocular Skill: An Adaptation of the Gray Oral Reading Check Test for Use in the Keystone Telebinocular* (Meadville, Pa.: Keystone View Co., 1938).

27. "Auditory Memory Span as Tested by Speech Sounds," *American Journal of Psychology*, LIII, No. 1 (January, 1939), 95–99.

28. Walter M. Boothby, Joseph Berkson, and Halbert L. Dunn, "Studies of the Energy of Metabolism of Normal Individuals: A Standard for Basal Metabolism, with a Nomogram for Clinical Application," *American Journal of Physiology*, CXVI (July, 1936), 468–94.

29. Nathan W. Shock and Mayo H. Soley, "Average Values for Basal Respiratory Functions in Adolescents and Adults," *Journal of Nutrition*, XVIII (August, 1939), 143–53.

30. Thomas Milton Carter, "A Study of Radiographs of the Bones of the Wrist as a Means of Determining Anatomical Age," (Doctor's thesis, Department of Education, University of Chicago, 1923), pp. 62–87.

CHAPTER X

FINDINGS OF THE STUDY OF THIRTY CHILDREN INTERPRETED ACCORDING TO PREVIOUS STANDARDS

THE purpose of this chapter is to present the detailed data collected by each examiner on the thirty children examined. They include the objective findings and the individual opinions of each examiner as to the presence or absence of an abnormality in his particular field. In this respect the data in the tables are comparable to those summarized in chapter ii. In addition, there is a composite of all findings on each child. The analysis and evaluation of the findings appear in chapter xi.

The original plan was to obtain the same type of data on all the children studied, so that the findings could be treated quantitatively. Unfortunately, this was not possible because some children did not complete their appointments. For example, one girl was afraid to wear glasses for fear others would tease her, so she did not return to the ophthalmologist for her last examination. One boy came from some distance, and when the initial visual study showed no abnormality, his parents would not bring him again for a complete refraction. In addition, some children were totally unable to read, hence could not score on the reading tests included in the battery. These factors account for incomplete data in some of the tables of this chapter.

GENERAL INFORMATION

The distribution of the chronological ages of the pupils is shown in the second column of Table 1. The third column shows the distributions of mental ages as determined by the New Stanford-Binet, and the last column shows the distribution of mental ages as determined by the Arthur Point Scale.

The range in chronological age from 6 years 9 months to 15 years 3 months indicates a fairly wide sampling of ages.

The mental ages, obtained by giving the Terman-Merrill revision of the Stanford-Binet, show that all this group of children rated above 7-0 years, a level considered adequate for learning to read, as pointed out previously.[1] Thus it is evident that all the children included in this study were old enough and had the requisite general intelligence to have learned to read. However, each child studied had been referred for examination because of reading difficulty. Since each child had adequate general intelligence, it was necessary to search for other causes of reading failure.

TABLE 1

DISTRIBUTION OF CHRONOLOGICAL AND MENTAL AGES OF THIRTY SUBJECTS

Age Ranges	Chronological Age	New Binet Mental Age	Arthur Point Scale Mental Age*	Age Ranges	Chronological Age	New Binet Mental Age	Arthur Point Scale Mental Age*
6-0 to 6-11...	1	0	0	14-0 to 14-11...	4	1	1
7-0 to 7-11...	1	2	1	15-0 to 15-11...	1	1	12
8-0 to 8-11...	3	1	2				
9-0 to 9-11...	3	5	3	Total no. of cases......	30	30	30
10-0 to 10-11...	6	5	4				
11-0 to 11-11...	3	4	6				
12-0 to 12-11...	5	5	0	Median.......	11-3.5	11-5.5	11-8.3
13-0 to 13-11...	3	6	1				

* The highest norm on this test is 15-6.

EXTENT OF READING RETARDATION

Table 2 shows the amount of reading retardation of the children examined. The ordinary conception of retardation in any school subject bases expectancy on chronological age, so age appears in the second column of the table. The range of retardation is from 0.9 grade to 6.4 grades, and the median is 3.9 grades. This was obtained by subtracting the average achievement in reading from the expected grade when the chronological age alone was considered. In general, the younger children were least retarded and the older ones most retarded, as will be shown in detail later in this chapter.

In the case of very bright children, mental age must also be considered as a basis for determining expectancy in reading. Accordingly, the difference between mental age expectancy and average reading achievement is presented in the third column of Table 2. The range is from 0.9 grade to 7.5 grades, with a median of 3.7 grades.

The entries in this table show that these children are all seriously retarded in reading.

Another objective measure of the amount of reading retardation is Monroe's reading index.[2] It is the ratio of the average reading grade to the average of chronological age expectancy, mental age

TABLE 2

DISCREPANCIES IN MONTHS BETWEEN READING GRADE
AND CHRONOLOGICAL AND MENTAL AGES

Grade Ranges	Discrepancy between Chronological Age and Reading Age	Discrepancy between Binet Mental Age and Reading Age	Grade Ranges	Discrepancy between Chronological Age and Reading Age	Discrepancy between Binet Mental Age and Reading Age
7.0–7.5........	0	1	2.5–2.9......	3	4
6.5–6.9........	0	2	2.0–2.4......	1	2
6.0–6.4........	4	1	1.5–1.9......	2	1
5.5–5.9........	1	1	1.0–1.4......	1	1
5.0–5.4........	2	1	0.9......	1	1
4.5–4.9........	5	4			
4.0–4.4........	3	2	Total.....	30	30
3.5–3.9........	1	6			
3.0–3.4........	6	3	Median.......	3.95	3.7

TABLE 3

DISTRIBUTION OF READING INDICES

Range	No. of Cases	Range	No. of Cases
0.15–0.19...................	1	0.45–0.49..................	6
.20– .24...................	0	.50– .54..................	6
.25– .29...................	0	.55– .59.................	3
.30– .34...................	3	.60– .64..................	3
.35– .39...................	1	0.65–0.69..................	2
0.40–0.44...................	5	Median reading index......... .487	

expectancy, and the arithmetic grade. The grade expectancy is obtained by subtracting five years from the chronological age or the mental age. This reading index was calculated for each child, and the distribution appears in Table 3.

According to Monroe's standards, all the children included in this study were severely retarded. She considered any child with a reading index of 0.80 or lower to be in need of diagnosis and remedial help. She found that less than one child per thousand has a reading index below 0.45, so nearly half the thirty cases represent the lowest percentile of reading efficiency reported by Monroe.

VISUAL FINDINGS

The findings of the ophthalmologists appear in Table 4. The data in the table were taken from the detailed record of each child, and the methods of determining each of these findings is described below. The last six columns represent decisions made by the co-operating ophthalmologists and subjective reports of parents, children, or teachers concerning the value of the treatment in improving reading achievement.

VISUAL ACUITY

Visual acuity was measured on the Snellen chart at 20 feet under 20-foot candles of light. The findings were recorded in decimal notation with 1.0 being equal to the commonly recorded 20/20 on the Snellen chart, or 100 per cent visual efficiency. Less than 1.0 indicates less than 20/20 vision, and more than 1.0 indicates better than 20/20 vision.

The second, third, and fourth columns of Table 4 show the visual acuity of the right eye, the left eye, and both eyes as determined by the ophthalmologist on the Snellen chart the first time that the child visited the eye clinic.

MYOPIA, HYPEROPIA, AND ASTIGMATISM

The refraction, or study of the needed correction by lenses, was made only after one drop of 1 per cent atropine sulphate solution in each eye had been administered four times daily for four days. Visual acuity was tested before the administration of atropine, and the ductions and phorias recorded one month after the atropine cycloplegic refraction. Only one child (Case 30) failed to have the atropine refraction, but this boy came from some distance and could take only one week for the entire examination.

The atropine correction gave evidence of some hyperopia and astigmatism in a number of cases. The findings under the column marked "Sphere" are either + or −. The + correction indicates hyperopia and the − correction, myopia.

TABLE 1

FINDINGS OF OPHTHALMOLOGIST

Case Number	Visual Acuity Right Eye (Snellen Chart)	Visual Acuity Left Eye (Snellen Chart)	Visual Acuity Both Eyes (Snellen Chart)	Atropine Correction: Sphere	Atropine Correction: Cylinder	Atropine Correction: Axis	Correction Ordered	Considered as a Possible Cause of Reading Failure	Subjective Reports of Child, Parent, or Teacher Indicate Improvement with Glasses	Ductions Base-in/Base-out Far (20 Feet)	Ductions Base-in/Base-out Near (13 Inches)	Phorias (Exo.-Eso.) at 20 Feet	Phorias at 13 Inches	Considered Significant for Reading	Orthoptics Recommended	Subjective Reports Indicate Orthoptics Was Helpful in Reading	Near-Point of Convergence	Type of Fusion	Accommodation	Rotations	Interpupillary Distance (20 Feet)	Near	Visual Difficulty of Significance
1	1.2+2	1.2+2	1.2+2	+.25* / +.50			No	No		6/16	12/16	2 Eso.	3 Eso.	No	No		8 cm.	III		Smooth	52 mm.	51 mm.	No
2	0.6	1.0+1	1.0-3	+1.12	+1.00*	180	Yes	?	Yes	4/16	4/10	4 Eso.	10 Eso.	No	No		2 in.	III		Smooth	46	43	?
3	1.5-1	1.5-2	1.2	+1.00	+0.50	75	Yes	No	Yes	14/14	22/4	0	2 Exo.	?	Yes	Yes	3 cm.	III		Smooth	62	55	Yes
4	1.2-2	1.2-3	1.5-3	+1.00	+0.75	90	Yes	?	Yes	2/29	15/3	8 Exo.	1 Eso.	No	No		2 in.	III		Smooth	57	57	?
5	2.0-2	2.0-2	2.0	+1.00 / +1.25	+0.50	90	No	No		2/10		6 Eso.	4 Eso.	No	No		2 in.	III		Smooth	59	52	No
6	1.5-4	1.5-3	1.5-3	+1.00	+0.25	90	Yes	No	Yes	2/10	6/10	2 Eso.	14 Exo.	?	Yes	Yes	2½ in.	III		Smooth	58	55	?
7	0.5+1	0.4+1	0.5	-2.50	+0.25	90	Yes	Yes	Yes	4/10	12/12	12 Eso.	10 Eso.	Yes	No	?	1½ in.	II		Jerky	57	50	Yes
8	0.4+1	0.5-1	0.8+1	-2.75	+2.75	100	Yes	?		10/26	8/30	18 Eso.	4 Eso.	Yes	Yes		6 in.	III		Smooth	62	53	Yes
9	1.5	1.5	1.5	-0.50 / -0.25	+1.75 / +1.75	75 / 95	No	Yes	No	8/16	4/14	0	4 Exo.	Yes	Yes	No	1½ in.	I		Jerky	55	50	No
10	0.8+3	0.8+1	0.5	+2.00	+0.50 / +0.25	135 / 45	Yes†	?	?	6/16	6/24	Alternates		No	No		1½ in.	III	14, 14, 18	?	52	52	?
11	1.5-3	1.2+2	1.2-2†	+1.25 / +1.75	+2.75 / +1.75	75 / 75	No	?	?	4/18	3/12	8 Eso.	4 Eso.	No	No		2 in.	III		?	56	56	?
12	0.4+2	0.3	0.5-1	+3.00 / +2.75	+3.00 / +2.75	105 / 85	No	?	?	4/16	10/16	4 Eso.	3 Eso.	No	No		1 in.	III	10, 10	Smooth	59	58	No
13	1.5	1.5	1.5	+1.25 / +1.75	+2.25 / +2.75	85 / 75	No	No		10/10	8/8	3 Eso.	4 Eso.	No	No		2 in.	III	11	Smooth	60	60	No
14	1.5	1.5-1	1.5	+0.75 / +1.00	+0.75 / +0.75	100 / 80	No	No	Yes	†	†	4 Eso.	3 Eso.	No	Yes*	Yes	2½ in.	III	11	Smooth	64	55	?
15	1.0	1.0	1.0	+0.50 / +0.75	+1.75 / +2.00	90 / 90	Yes	Yes		10/10	8/8	4 Exo.	4 Exo.	No	No		3 in.	III	11	Smooth	59	55	Yes

* Top number, right eye; bottom number, left eye.

† Findings unsatisfactory.

TABLE 4—Continued

Case No.	Visual Acuity (Snellen Chart) Right Eye	Visual Acuity (Snellen Chart) Left Eye	Visual Acuity (Snellen Chart) Both Eyes	Atropine Sphere	Atropine Cylinder	Atropine Axis	Correction Ordered	Considered as a Possible Cause of Reading Failure	Subjective Reports of Child, Parent, or Teacher Indicate Improvement with Glasses	Ductions Far (20 Feet) Base-in/Base-out	Ductions Near (13 Inches) Base-in/Base-out	Phorias (Exo.-Eso.) at 20 Feet	Phorias at 13 Inches	Considered Significant for Reading	Orthoptics Recommended	Subjective Reports Indicate Orthoptics Was Helpful in Reading	Near-Point of Convergence	Type of Fusion	Accommodation	Rotations	Interpupillary Distance (20 Feet)	Near	Visual Difficulty of Significance
16.	1.2-3	1.2-3		-1.50 / -1.50	+0.25 / +0.25	90 / 90	Yes†	No		16/20	16/20	3 Eso.	3 Eso.	?	Yes*	No	2 in.	III	12 / 12	Smooth	59 mm.	57 mm.	?
17.	1.5	1.5	1.5	+1.50 / +1.50	+0.25 / +0.25	90 / 90	Yes	?	No	6/14	16/12	2 Eso.	8 Exo.	?	Yes	No	2½ in.	III	17	Smooth		
18.	2.0-3	1.5-4	2.0-3	+1.50 / +1.50	+0.25 / +0.25	90 / 90	No	No		10/8	23/17*	0	10 Exo.	?	No		7 in.	III		Smooth	64	59	?
19.	1.2	2.0-4		+1.00 / +1.25	+0.25 / +0.25	90 / 90	No	No		10/12	16/12		0	No	No		to nose	II / III	9.5 / 9.5	Smooth	59	55	No
20.	1.5	1.5		+1.25 / +1.25	+0.75 / +0.50	100 / 75 / 90 / 20	Yes	No	Yes	4/2	16/20	1 Eso.	2 Eso.	No	Yes	Yes	115 mm.	III	10	Smooth	61	56	Yes
21.	1.5+4	1.5-2	1.2+1	+1.50 / +1.50	+0.50 / +0.25	105 / 75 / 90	No	?		6/4	34/16	0	4 Exo.	?	Yes	?	75 mm.	III	12.5 / 12.5	Smooth	58	54	?
22.	1.5-2	1.5+2	1.2+2	+0.75 / +0.75	+0.25 / +0.25	90 / 90	No	No		4/12	12/4	0	10 Exo.	No	No		60 mm.	III	14	Jerky	61½	58½	No
23.	1.5-2	1.2-3		+0.75 / +0.75	+0.75 / +0.75	90 / 90	No	No	?	6/4	24/0	4 Exo.	24 Exo.	Yes	Yes	?	75 mm.	III		Jerky	63	60	Yes
24.	0.4	0.3	0.4	+1.25 / +1.25; +3.00 / +3.00	+4.50 / +3.90	90 / 90 / 120	Yes	Yes		4/12	12/4	2 Eso.	4 Exo.	Yes	Yes		65 mm.	III / 60%		Smooth	56	52	Yes
25.	1.5	1.5-2	1.2-3	+1.00 / +1.00	+0.50 / +0.25	90 / 90	No	?	No	6/4	24/0	0	20 Exo.	Yes	Yes		125 mm.	III		Jerky	56	52	Yes
26†	1.5-3	1.2-1		+2.50	+0.75 / +0.75	90	Yes	?		6/12	16/12	Not taken	8 Exo.	No	No			III			66	62	?
27.	1.5-1	1.5-1	1.5	+0.75 / +2.00	+0.75 / +0.75	90 / 90	No	No		4/4	20/12	0	16 Exo.	?	Yes		80 mm.	III		Jerky	66	62	?
28.	1.5	1.5-2	1.5-2	+2.25	+0.25 / +0.25	90 / 90	No	No		4/22	8/24	6 Eso.	8 Eso.	?	Yes		85 mm.	III		Smooth	58	55	?
29.	1.5	1.5	1.5	+0.75 / +0.75	+0.25 / +0.25	90 / 90	No	No		4/24		0		No	No		8 in.	III		Smooth	57	55	No
30†	1.5-1	1.5-2		Not done			No	No				Not taken	Not taken	No	No								No

† Findings unsatisfactory.

One of the controversial issues at present is the amount of + lens a child seems to need before any correction is given him and how much the child himself can compensate for this without lenses. This difference of opinion may readily account for the differences in findings concerning the relationship of hyperopia to reading disability. There was some difference of opinion among the ophthalmologists making this study. One felt that, in general, a child who has more than +1.50 diopters of hyperopia should have a correction to be used when reading. Another believed that the minimum could not be set, as it depended upon other findings, such as phorias, etc., as well as the total makeup of the child.

The lack of consistency may best be illustrated by examining the sphere correction of Case 2, where the correction was +1.12 and +1.00 in the two eyes and for which glasses were prescribed. Contrast that with Case 5, where the sphere correction was +2.00 in each eye and no correction was ordered.

According to any standard set of norms, corrections would be ordered routinely without considering other factors. Case 30 had no atropine refraction, and 3 cases evidenced some myopia. Twelve out of 29 cases, or 41 per cent, were fitted with glasses for hyperopia or astigmatism.

In order to portray better the discrepancy between the amount of measured hyperopia and the corrections made, Table 5 was constructed.

Eames[3] states that he considers more than +0.50 significant and would correct for it. Therefore, he would have found 25 of the 29 cases to have a significant amount of hyperopia, whereas the ophthalmologists co-operating in this study considered only 12 out of 29 to be sufficiently abnormal to prescribe glasses.

The amount of cylinder gives an indication of the amount of astigmatism that the child evidences. In general, according to the co-operating ophthalmologists, anything over 1.00 is considered sufficiently serious to indicate the need for lenses for the child. Thus the findings show that 6 cases out of 29, or 20 per cent, had a significant amount of astigmatism. However, 3 of the 6 cases evidenced myopia, and only 3 of the 12 children with hyperopia were also complicated by astigmatism. One of these 3 cases (Case 2) had low degrees of both hyperopia and astigmatism, but the other 2 cases (Cases 12 and 24) had high degrees of both. Therefore, glasses would probably have been prescribed for those 2 on the basis of the hyperopia, if the astigmatism had not existed. Thus, 11 out of 29 cases, or 38 per cent of the children studied, might be said to have sufficient hyperopia to require correction, according to the standards of the co-operating ophthalmologists.

Fifteen of the 30 cases, or 50 per cent in all, were given glasses to correct either myopia, hyperopia, or astigmatism or combinations of these. According to the ophthalmologists, not nearly so high a per-

TABLE 5

AMOUNT OF HYPEROPIA AMONG TWENTY-NINE
SEVERELY RETARDED READERS

Sphere	Number of Cases Evidencing Stated Amounts of Hyperopia or More in Both Eyes	Number of Cases Evidencing Stated Amounts of Hyperopia or More in Either Eye	Number of Last Group of Cases Having Glasses Prescribed	Sphere	Number of Cases Evidencing Stated Amounts of Hyperopia or More in Both Eyes	Number of Cases Evidencing Stated Amounts of Hyperopia or More in Either Eye	Number of Last Group of Cases Having Glasses Prescribed
0.00...	26	26	12	+1.75...	5	6	5
+0.50...	24	25	12	+2.00...	4	6	5
+0.75...	23	24	12	+2.25...	1	4	4
+1.00...	17	19	11	+2.50...	1	3	3
+1.25...	11	16	9	+3.00...	1	2	2
+1.50...	7	9	6				

centage of children who come for examination would be given glasses. Since a small percentage of school children go to the clinics for examination, it is probable that the proportion of severely retarded readers requiring glasses is greater than it is in the general population.

Thus lenses were prescribed for 15 children when a thorough and careful ophthalmological examination was made; yet only 6 of these cases showed less than normal visual acuity on the Snellen chart. Therefore, the Snellen chart alone identified only about 40 per cent of children needing correction with lenses.

There were some children for whom lenses were prescribed when it was felt by the ophthalmologist that there was no relationship between the needed correction and reading disability. Table 5 shows that the visual difficulty requiring lenses was considered sufficient to be a cause for reading failure in 4 of the 30 cases, or 13 per cent. In another 10 cases it was not possible to determine any direct causal relationship, but the ophthalmologists thought there might be a relationship. In 16 cases the need for lenses was definitely not considered to be a cause of reading failure. Thus, in 47 per cent of the cases a visual difficulty, which could be corrected by lenses, may have been a cause for failure to learn to read adequately.

Some of the children liked their glasses and reported improved vision at the reading distance. Some teachers noted more accuracy in reading with the glasses; in other instances, parents reported improvement. These were recorded, and, as Table 5 indicates, 9 of the 15 cases seem to have obtained help from their glasses. No reports were received on 2 of the cases, and 1 pupil (Case 26) refused to get her glasses. There is a question concerning the value of the lenses in 1 case (No. 14). Another child had not worn his glasses long enough to determine their effectiveness, and in still another case there was evidence that the glasses were of no value in improving reading.

DUCTIONS

The ductions were taken with rotary prisms, with a target at 20 feet and another at 13 inches. The findings were complete on only 24 of the 30 cases. One case (No. 30) was not completed because of insufficient time for the examination. Another case (No. 26) refused to return after she was told that she needed glasses. No ductions could be taken on one child (Case 10), because he did not have simultaneous binocular vision. One child (Case 15) was not sufficiently co-operative to give adequate responses. The ductions were not recorded in 2 instances (Cases 19 and 20).

Of the 24 cases on which ductions at 20 feet have been recorded, only 4 approximated even closely the ratio of $1/4$, which is considered by some authorities to be adequate. Not one case approximated the $10/40$ ratio set up as a standard by Taylor.[4] Only 2 cases achieved base-in of 5^Δ or more and base-out of 20^Δ or more at the same time, which was the standard suggested by one of the ophthalmologists. Seven of the 24 cases, or about 30 per cent, had ratios of $1/1$, or the base-in was greater than the base-out at 20 feet. Thus the ductions were considered inadequate in at least 30 per cent of the cases and questionable in another 54 per cent of the cases.

The near-point ductions, taken with targets at 13 inches, were completed on only 23 cases. Of this number, 12 cases had larger base-in ratings than base-out, or the two were equal. Thus the near-point ductions were inadequate in at least 52 per cent of the cases.

PHORIAS

Phoria findings were not available on 3 cases. In one instance (Case 10) the child had alternating central fixation, using first one eye, then the other, but never both at once. Two children (Cases 26 and 30) were not completed, as explained previously.

The phorias taken at distance, or 20 feet, showed that 9 cases, or about 33 per cent, had orthophoria. Twelve other cases, or about 44 per cent, had from 1 to 4 prism diopters of esophoria or exophoria. Thus 27 per cent of the cases showed phoria findings at 20 feet, between 4 prism diopters of esophoria and 4 prism diopters of exophoria. Three cases exhibited 5–9 prism diopters of exophoria. One case evidenced 10–14 prism diopters of esotropia, and 1 case showed between 15 and 20 prism diopters of esotropia. Thus, about 22 per cent of the cases exhibited more than 4 prism diopters of esophoria or exophoria at 20 feet. One co-operating ophthalmologist considered 0–6 prism diopters of esophoria at 20 feet to be normal, and 0–3 prism diopters of exophoria. Using these standards, 6 out of 27 cases, or 22 per cent, fell outside the normal range, considering phorias taken at 20 feet.

At reading distance, or 13 inches, 8 cases, or about 30 per cent, had 5 or more prism diopters of exophoria, while 6, or 22 per cent, had more than 10 prism diopters of exotropia at this distance. Three cases exhibited 5 or more prism diopters of esophoria. One co-operating ophthalmologist suggested that at 13 inches there should be no more than 6 prism diopters of esophoria and no exophoria. Using these standards, 17 out of the 27 cases, or 63 per cent, were outside the normal range for phorias at near-point, or 13 inches.

In 6 of the 29 cases, or 20 per cent, the duction and phoria findings were considered significant as causing reading failure. There was a question as to the significance in 8 other cases. In 15 of the 29 cases, or 52 per cent, the phoria and duction findings were considered insignificant as a cause of reading disability. Orthoptic training was recommended for 14 of the 29 cases, or 48 per cent. In 1 case (No. 10) this training was combined with an operation to straighten the crossed eyes, while, in another instance (Case 7), wearing lenses removed double vision at the reading distance so that no orthoptic training was needed. In 2 instances (Cases 14 and 20), orthoptics were recommended after a restudy of the case had been made, but this was not considered significant at the time of the initial study.

Six, or 20 per cent of the cases for whom orthoptics was recommended, did not need correction by lenses. Thus 50 per cent of the 30 cases were fitted with glasses, and another 20 per cent had orthoptic training, so that 21, or 70 per cent of the 30 cases, were either fitted with glasses or had orthoptic treatment. In 7 of these 21 cases, the deficiency calling for the correction recommended was considered significant as a cause of reading disability, and in 13 others there was a question as to whether or not the visual difficulty was a cause. In 10 cases, or 33 per cent of the cases, it was definitely not considered a cause.

NEAR-POINT OF CONVERGENCE

Near-point of convergence was the nearest point at which the two eyes could continue to fixate on the same object. It is recorded in Pcb., which is the near-point measured in millimeters plus 25 mm. The normal range for adults, according to the co-operating ophthalmologists, was 75–100 mm. Seven cases, or 24 per cent, were not able to attain convergence at 100 Pcb.

ACCOMMODATION

Accommodation was measured on only 6 cases but in all instances was considered normal. It ranged from 9.5 to 18 diopters, with 10 diopters being considered normal.

ROTATIONS

In 20 of the 30 cases the rotations were smooth and adequate. In 4 cases the results were not recorded. In 6 cases rotations were jerky. One of these cases was fitted with glasses, and the rotations became smooth after he had become accustomed to them. In 4 of the 6 cases of jerky rotations, orthoptics was recommended, and in 1 case it was not. There was no attempt made to evaluate the jerky rotations as a cause of failure to learn to read.

There is no standard for interpupillary distance. The data are presented because the literature indicated that one writer believed this to be one of the visual factors in reading failure.

These tests were given to all 30 cases. They were given by the investigator in an attempt to determine the value of this test in selecting reading-disability cases who should be referred to a refractionist for a detailed study of the eyes.

Columns 1–11 of Table 6 show the results of the tests. Column 12 shows the score obtained according to the suggestions of the representative of the Keystone View Company.[5] Whenever this score is below 85, the child should be referred to the refractionist. On this basis, 25 of the 30 cases would be selected for a careful visual examination. It is especially significant to note that the 5 cases whose scores were above 85 were all either fitted with glasses or given orthoptic exercises.

Among the cases who were not fitted with glasses or for whom orthoptic exercises were not recommended, was one with a score of 35. He was the youngest case studied, and the reliability of his responses was questioned. However, 2 cases scored 60, 1 scored 70, 3 scored 75, and 2 scored 80.

Thus, for these severely retarded readers, the Keystone Visual Safety tests did not appear to be sufficiently discriminating, when the *suggested* method of scoring was used. Perhaps the final judgment of an experienced examiner might be better than the suggested scores.

Visual acuity was taken on the Snellen chart by the ophthalmologists, and the scores were transmuted into percentage of visual acuity. The visual-acuity scores on the Keystone Visual Safety tests are usually recorded in percentages, and the two scores have been placed consecutively in Table 7. It is evident that the two scores are identical on more than half of the cases and very similar on the

TABLE 6

Scores on the Keystone Visual Safety Tests

Case Number	Visual Acuity Both Eyes*	Visual Acuity Left Eye*	Visual Acuity Right Eye*	Stereopsis Level	Vertical Imbalance	Far-Point Fusion	Near-Point Fusion	Lateral Imbalance—Far-Point	Lateral Imbalance—Near-Point	Ametropia—Near-Point	Ametropia—Far-Point	Score According to Keystone Rating	To Be Referred to Eye Clinic by Test	Ophthalmologists Made Recommendations on Case
	(1)	(2)	(3)	(4)	(5)	(6)	(7)	(8)	(9)	(10)	(11)	(12)	(13)	(14)
1...	100%	70%	50%	80%	P	P	P	P	P	P	F	60	Yes	No
2...	90	90	80	100	P	?	F	F	F	F	F	25	Yes	Yes
3...	110	100	105	100	P	P	P	P	P	P	P	100	No	Yes
4...	105	100	100	100	P	P	P	F	P	P	P	90	No	Yes
5...	110	110	105	In-valid	P	P	P	F	F	P	F	60	Yes	No
6...	105	105	105	100	P	P	P	F	P	P	P	90	No	Yes
7...	60	70	60	100	P	P	?	F	?	F	F	30	Yes	Yes
8...	90	80	90	90	P	P	P	?	P	F	F	50	Yes	Yes
9†..	80	70	40	0	?	?	P	?	P	P	F	35	Yes	No
10...	90	100	90	0	F	F	F	F	F	P	P	30	Yes	Yes
11...	105	110	105	100	P	F	F	F	F	P	P	60	Yes	Yes
12...	90	80	70	90	P	P	F	?	P	P	F	45	Yes	Yes
13...	105	100	105	100	P	F	F	P	P	P	P	80	Yes	No
14...	105	105	105	100	P	P	F	P	P	P	P	90	No	Yes
15†..	90	90	90	60	P	P	P	F	P	P	P	65	Yes	Yes
16...	70	30	40	60	P	P	F	P	P	P	F	30	Yes	Yes
17...	100	100	100	100	P	P	P	P	P	P	P	100	No	Yes
18...	105	100	105	70	P	?	F	P	P	P	P	75	Yes	No
19...	105	90	90	100	P	?	F	P	P	P	P	75	Yes	No
20...	110	105	110	70	P	F	F	P	P	P	P	75	Yes	Yes
21...	100	90	90	100	P	F	?	F	P	P	F	55	Yes	Yes
22...	105	100	105	90	P	?	F	P	P	P	P	80	Yes	No
23...	105	110	105	100	P	?	F	P	P	P	P	85	Yes	Yes
24...	90	80	90	90	P	?	F	P	P	F	F	40	Yes	Yes
25...	105	110	100	100	P	F	?	P	P	P	P	85	Yes	Yes
26...	105	105	105	100	P	?	?	P	P	P	P	90	No	Yes
27...	110	110	110	100	P	F	F	P	P	P	P	80	Yes	Yes
28...	110	105	110	100	P	?	P	P	P	P	P	90	No	Yes
29...	105	70	105	100	P	F	P	P	P	P	F	In-valid	No	No
30...	105	105	100	90	Not‡	P	F	P	P	P	F	75	Yes	No

* Less than 85 per cent is failure.
† This child was very young, and results are questioned.
‡ Line goes away.

others. Case 16 is the only one in which there is considerable difference in the findings.

Table 8 shows the ametropia at near-point and at 20 feet, as compared with the cylinder requirements found by the ophthalmologists. If a cylinder of more than 1.00 was found, it was considered significant. There was agreement in 21 of the 29 cases recorded, or 72 per cent. In only one case was there complete disagreement.

Thus it appears that the various parts of the Keystone Visual Safety tests agree with the findings of the ophthalmologists better than with the final score.

TABLE 7

PERCENTAGE OF VISUAL EFFICIENCY AS SHOWN BY KEYSTONE
VISUAL SAFETY TESTS AND SNELLEN CHART

CASE NUMBER	BOTH EYES		LEFT EYE		RIGHT EYE	
	Keystone Visual Safety	Snellen Chart	Keystone Visual Safety	Snellen Chart	Keystone Visual Safety	Snellen Chart
1	100	100	70	100	50	100
2	90	100	90	100	80	91.4
3	110	100	100	100	105	100
4	105	100	100	100	100	100
5	110	100	110	100	105	100
6	105	100	105	100	105	100
7	60	83.6	70	76.5	60	83.6
8	90	95.6	80	83.6	90	76.6
9	80	100	70	100	40	100
10	90	100	100	95.6	90	95.6
11	105	100	110	100	105	100
12	90	83.6	80	66.8	70	76.5
13	105	100	100	100	105	100
14	105	100	105	100	105	100
15	90	100	90	100	90	100
16	70	....	30	100	40	100
17	100	100	100	100	100	100
18	105	100	100	100	105	100
19	105	....	90	100	90	100
20	110	....	105	100	110	100
21	100	100	90	100	90	100
22	105	100	110	100	105	100
23	105	....	110	100	105	100
24	90	76.5	80	66.8	90	76.5
25	105	100	110	100	100	100
26	105	....	105	100	105	100
27	110	100	110	100	110	100
28	110	100	105	100	110	100
29	105	100	70	100	105	100
30	105	....	105	100	100	100

TABLE 8

RESULTS OF KEYSTONE VISUAL SAFETY AMETROPIA TESTS
COMPARED WITH THE OPHTHALMOLOGISTS' FINDINGS

Case Number	Near Ametropia	Far Ametropia	Cylinder Required	Agreement
1............	Pass	Fail	None* None	?
2............	Fail	Fail	1.00 0.50	Yes
3............	Pass	Pass	0.75 0.50	Yes
4............	Pass	Pass	0.50 0.75	Yes
5............	Pass	Fail	0.25 0.25	?
6............	Pass	Pass	0.25 0.25	Yes
7............	Fail	Fail	2.75 2.75	Yes
8............	Fail	Fail	1.75 0.75	Yes
9............	Pass	Fail	0.50 0.25	?
10............	Pass	Pass	0.50 0.50	Yes
11............	Pass	Pass	0.50 0.75	Yes
12............	Pass	Fail	3.00 2.75	?
13............	Pass	Pass	0.25 0.25	Yes
14............	Pass	Pass	0.75 0.75	Yes
15............	Pass	Pass	1.75 2.00	No
16............	Pass	Fail	0.25 0.25	?
17............	Pass	Pass	None None	Yes
18............	Pass	Pass	0.25 0.25	Yes
19............	Pass	Pass	0.25 0.25	Yes
20............	Pass	Pass	0.75 0.50	Yes
21............	Pass	Fail	0.25 0.25	?
22............	Pass	Pass	None None	Yes
23............	Pass	Pass	0.75 0.75	Yes
24............	Fail	Fail	4.50 3.50	Yes
25............	Pass	Pass	0.50 0.50	Yes

* More than −1.00 considered significant.

TABLE 8—*Continued*

Case Number	Near Ametropia	Far Ametropia	Cylinder Required	Agreement
26.............	Pass	Pass	0.25 None	Yes
27............	Pass	Pass	0.75 0.75	Yes
28............	Pass	Pass	None None	Yes
29............	Pass	Fail	0.25 0.25	?
30............	Pass	Fail	....	....

SUMMARY OF VISUAL FINDINGS

Hyperopia was found more frequently than any other of the refractive errors. Several cases evidenced astigmatism, and all but one of these likewise exhibited hyperopia or myopia.

Glasses were prescribed for half the cases examined, whereas the Snellen chart identified only 6 of the 15. The visual difficulty for which this correction was made may have been a factor in failure to learn to read, according to the co-operating ophthalmologists.

Ductions at both near-point and distance were inadequate in at least a third of the cases and questionable in another 50 per cent of them. Thus, in over two-thirds of the cases, the norms of the co-operating ophthalmologists were higher than the duction findings.

About one-fourth of the cases exhibited phorias at distance, outside the normal range. Over half of these children exhibited phorias outside the normal range at near-point.

Considering all the visual findings, 21 of the 30, or 70 per cent, showed some type of difficulty requiring either lenses or orthoptic training or both. In only one-third of these cases did the ophthalmologist feel that the visual difficulty would cause the reading deficiency.

Finally, the ophthalmologists pointed out that individual visual findings are not significant except when interpreted in the light of all the findings. Thus, many individual findings were outside the norms but were not judged significant when considered as a part of the total visual findings.

NEUROLOGICAL AND DOMINANCE FINDINGS

Of the 30 cases examined by the neurologist, 6, or 20 per cent, were considered to have some difficulty in this area, which might interfere with learning to read. Of this group, 5 were diagnosed as alexia, and in 4 of the 5 cases there seemed to be a history of difficulty in learning to read on the part of one of the parents.

The other case with neurological findings was a boy who had suffered a skull fracture before entering school. This had affected his speech, and the neurologist believed that it might also have affected his ability to learn to read. An encephalogram showed some cortical

TABLE 9

NEUROLOGICAL FINDINGS

CASE NUMBER*	C.A.	BINET M.A.	I.Q.	INITIAL READING LEVEL	RETARDATION		READING GAIN	TIME REQUIRED	PROBABLE FINAL DIAGNOSIS
					M.A.	C.A.			
3....	14- 0	13-10	101	3.2	5.7	6.6	1.1 grade	6 mo.	Alexia
5....	8-10	9- 0	102	1.2	2.8	2.6	.5 grade	6 wk.	Left tutoring before finished
7....	10- 8	9- 4	88	1.0	3.3	4.7	....	......	Alexia
12....	10- 1	11- 4	112	1.4	4.9	3.7	Not known	......	?
21....	11- 8	12-11	110	3.2	4.7	3.5	1.7	8 wk.	Reading disability
22....	14- 4	13- 2	95	3.2	5.0	6.1	Reported satisfactory	......	?

* Findings were negative in all cases omitted.

atrophy in the left occipitoparietal region. He exhibited right-sided pyramidal signs.

From the gains made in reading, as shown in Table 9, Case 21 did not appear to respond as slowly as would be expected of a true case of alexia. There was no tendency to slower progress, and he rated nearly Grade V in reading.

Cases 12 and 22 were not treated by the investigator, and progress was not measured. Cases 3 and 7 responded very slowly. Case 3 made rapid gains at the very outset but progressed more slowly as the work became more difficult. When she reached the middle of Grade IV her progress curve leveled off, and she appeared to be unable to make additional progress. Case 7 also made very slow progress, but reading training should have been continued to make sure that he was a true case of alexia.

SUMMARY

Among 30 cases of severe reading disability, 6, or 20 per cent, were believed by the neurologist to have a defect which would seriously hamper reading progress. Treatment of these cases led the investigator to conclude that 1 case was not hampered by any neurological difficulty, as he responded very quickly to remedial-reading training. Two of the cases responded very slowly, and 2 were not treated.

DOMINANCE FINDINGS

The preferred hand, foot, ear, and eye were tested as described in chapter ix. The parents were also asked about the child's hand

TABLE 10

RESULTS OF THE PREFERENCE TESTS

	HAND PREFERENCE		FOOT PREFERENCE		EAR PREFERENCE		EYE PREFERENCE		CLINIC REPORT		PARENTS' REPORT	
	Right	Left	Right	Left	Right	Left	Right	Left	Right	Left	Right	Left
Number of cases.	26	4	28	2	14	16	18	12	16	10	14	3*
Percentage......	87	13	93	7	47	53	60	40	61	39	47	10

* Remainder not reported.

preference, and the ophthalmologist tested eye preference. Table 10 gives all the findings on the 30 cases tested.

At least five measures of preference were used for each of the types. If the child preferred the right in three or more of the five trials, the preference was recorded as right, or vice versa.

According to Table 10, about 87 per cent of the cases studied preferred the right hand, and 93 per cent preferred the right foot. Since the cerebral centers for right hand and foot are known to lie on the left side of the brain, then at least 87 per cent of the cases had left-dominant cerebral hemispheres. Since this is conventionally preferred, then the dominant side seems to be favorable for these cases.

Looking further into these preferences, a few discrepancies may be noted. For example, the right ear is preferred in only 47 per cent of the cases. Since little is known about centers for hearing and the percentage of persons with right-ear preference in the general population, it is not possible to say what this finding may signify.

Among the 30 cases, 18, or 60 per cent, preferred the right eye. Thus, if right-eye preference is a desirable condition for learning to read effectively, then 40 per cent of these cases were handicapped by left-dominant eyes.

Some authorities consider the agreement of preferred hand, foot, ear, and eye to be more important than preference itself. Table 11 is presented to show the percentage of agreement among the various types of preference.

TABLE 11

AGREEMENT OF PREFERENCE TESTS

Preference	Percentage of Agreement	Preference	Percentage of Agreement
Hand and foot...........	93	Foot and ear............	53
Hand and ear............	60	Foot and eye............	67
Hand and eye............	73	Ear and eye.............	60

Hand and foot preferences agree most frequently, as would be expected, since the brain centers controlling the right hand and right foot are believed to be on the same side of the brain. Hand and eye preferences agree in 73 per cent of the cases, and foot and eye preferences are next, as they agree in 67 per cent of the cases.

Since hand and eye preferences seem most important in poor readers, agreement in 73 per cent of the cases is probably most significant.

The ophthalmologist also tested 26 of the 30 cases for eye preference, and the findings of the preference tests administered by the investigator agreed with those of the ophthalmologist in 24 of 26 cases, or 92 per cent of the cases, which showed very high agreement. In analyzing the 2 cases in which there was disagreement, the investigator's findings in both cases were borderline, with only 1 choice of the 5 being toward the opposite side. In 4 of the cases the preferred eye was not recorded by the ophthalmologist.

SUMMARY

Among the 30 cases studied, 26, or 87 per cent, preferred the right hand, and 93 per cent preferred the right foot. The right ear was preferred by 47 per cent of the cases, and the right eye by 60 per cent of the cases according to the investigator's tests, and by 61 per cent according to the ophthalmologist's tests.

Hand and foot preferences were the same in 93 per cent of the cases, and hand and eye preferences were the same in 73 per cent of the cases. Other agreements among preferences were lower.

The tests given by the investigator and the ophthalmologists showed very high agreement, there being only a slight difference in two of the cases.

OTOLARYNGOLOGICAL FINDINGS

Each child was examined in the clinic for abnormalities of hearing and to identify their causes. An audiometer record, made by the specialist in a soundproof room, showed some loss of hearing in certain cases. Table 12 indicates the amount of hearing loss in each ear if it was more than 10 sensation units. If less than 10 sensation units, no numbers appear.

In only 2 of the cases was there sufficient hearing loss for it to be considered a possible cause of failure to learn to read. Case 19 learned to read before the adenoids were removed and the hearing improved. In Case 17 the hearing was normal in one ear and the loss not so great in the other as to be an absolute cause of reading failure.

It is impossible to interpret this hearing loss at present, since specialists in this field are not agreed as to how much loss a child may have and yet function adequately. However, it seems probable that low auditory acuity is not a cause of failure to learn to read in many cases.

In 5 of the 30 cases, or 17 per cent, infectious tonsils or adenoids or both were found. Two cases were post-mastoid, and 3 cases were allergic.

SUMMARY

Considerable loss in auditory acuity was found in 2 cases; in one of these the loss was in only one ear, and the other case learned to read without correction; so it appears that loss of auditory acuity was not a cause of serious reading retardation in any of the 30 cases studied. This evidence is not conclusive, since the exact effect of smaller losses of auditory acuity is not known and since the norms of performance for children are not yet well established.

TABLE 12

SENSATION UNITS OF HEARING LOSS

CASE NUM-BER	FREQUENCIES								CON-SIDERED SIG-NIFI-CANT	NOSE AND THROAT PATHOLOGY	CON-SIDERED CAUSE OF READ-ING FAIL-URE
	64	128	256	512	1,024	2,048	4,096	8,192			
1....	X*	X	X	X	X	13	20	22†	No	No	No
	X	X	X	X	X	11	11	20‡			
2....	22	15	13	13	X	.....	12	14	No	No	No
	28	21	21	21	12	.....	15	16			
3....	X	X	X	X	X	X	X	12	No	T-A infection-al	No
	X	X	X	X	X	X	X	12			
4....	12	X	X	X	X	X	12	23	No	No	No
	X	X	X	X	X	X	11	23			
5....	11	X	X	X	X	X	X	28	No	No	No
	X	X	X	X	X	X	X	22			
6....	X	X	X	X	X	X	X	23	No	No	No
	X	X	X	X	X	X	X	23			
7....	13	X	X	15	19	11	20	15	No	No	No
	18	12	13	24	21	13	X	X			
8....	15	X	X	14	19	18	20	24	No	No	No
	15	12	X	13	18	16	19	23			
9....	X	X	X	X	X	X	20	12	No	No	No
	X	X	X	X	X	X	X	12			
10....	X	X	X	X	X	X	X	X	No	No	No
11....	X	X	X	X	X	X	X	X	No	No	No
12....	X	X	X	X	X	X	15	X	No	No	No
13....	X	X	17	20	15	X	X	20	No	Chr. pharano-gitis adenoid remnant	
	20	15	26	20	20	12	18	21			
14....	X	X	X	X	X	X	X	X	No	Deflected sep-tum	No
15....	X	X	X	X	X	X	X	X	No	No	No
16....	X	X	X	X	X	X	12	12	No	No	No
	X	X	X	X	X	X	X	X			
17....	X	X	X	X	X	X	X	15	Yes	No (post-mas-toid)	?
	35	34	38	35	43	50	58	58			
18....	X	X	X	X	X	X	X	X	No	No	.....
19....	25	25	32	32	41	29	40	42	Yes	Adenoid rem-nant inject-ed—otitis media	?
	15	X	X	X	X	X	X	32			
20....	15	X	14	X	X	X	X	18	No	No (post-mastoid)	No
	X	X	X	X	X	X	X	X			
21....	X	X	X	X	X	X	X	X	No	No	.....
22....	18	12	X	X	22	30	33	33	No	Mild conduc-tion deaf-ness	No
	12	16	X	X	12	X	20	22			

* X means 10 or less.
† Top number, left ear.   ‡ Bottom number, right ear.

TABLE 12—*Continued*

CASE NUMBER	FREQUENCIES								CONSIDERED SIGNIFICANT	NOSE AND THROAT PATHOLOGY	CONSIDERED CAUSE OF READING FAILURE
	64	128	256	512	1,024	2,048	4,096	8,192			
23....	X	X	X	X	X	12	40	X	?	Hypertrophied tonsils—infected	No
	X	X	X	X	X	X	40	X			
24....	....	....	....	....	....	....	....	....	....	....	......
25....	X	X	X	X	X	X	X	15	No	No	No
	X	X	X	X	X	X	X	X			
26....	X	X	X	X	X	X	X	X	No	Hypertrophied tonsils—infections	No
27....	X	20	18	X	X	X	X	X	No	Hay fever	No
	X	20	18	X	X	X	X	X			
28....	X	X	X	X	X	X	X	X	No	No	No
	X	15	12	X	X	X	X	X			
29....	19	12	X	X	X	X	18	21	No	No	No
	15	X	X	X	X	X	16	33			
30....	X	X	X	X	X	X	X	X	No	Allergic rhinitis	No
	16	15	16	16	X	X	X	X			

Infectious tonsils and adenoids were found in 17 per cent of the cases but were not believed by the specialist to be associated with failure to learn to read.

Two post-mastoid cases were found, and 3 cases of allergy. In one of the post-mastoid cases there was some hearing loss, but, other than that, the abnormalities of the ears, nose, and throat appeared to be unrelated to reading failure.

SPEECH FINDINGS

The reports from the speech specialist were tabulated and appear in Table 13. Only 1 of the cases stuttered consistently. In another case there was a slight stutter noted, but it appeared only when the child became excited. In neither instance was it considered a factor in reading failure. The case in which stuttering was most pronounced was also considered to be unstable emotionally, so that stuttering may have been a symptom of this emotional instability.

Dyslalia, which includes misformation of letters, was found in 6,

TABLE 13

Findings of Speech Specialist

Case Number	Stutters	Other Defect	(Average No. of Isolated Sounds Reproduced) Auditory Memory Span for Sounds	Evaluation of Auditory Memory Span	Auditory Discrimination (Per Cent Correct) Vowels	Auditory Discrimination (Per Cent Correct) Consonants	More than 15 Units of Hearing Loss	Frequencies of Loss	Considered Significant as a Cause of Reading Failure
1	No	Dyslalia Rhinolalia Aperta	......	......	.....	.....	Yes	Upper	?
2	Yes	No	......	......	.....	.....	Yes	Lower	No
3	No	No	......	......	.....	.....	No	....	No
4	No	No	......	......	.....	.....	Yes	Upper	No
5	No	Dyslalia	......	......	.....	.....	Yes	Upper	No
6	No	No	......	......	.....	.....	Yes	Upper	No
7	No	No	3	?	100	90	Yes	Upper and lower	?
8	No	Dyslalia Dysphonia	3½	?	.....	.....	Yes	All	Yes
9	No	Dyslalia	3½	?	100	100	Yes	Upper	?
10	No	Dyslalia	2½	Poor	100	47	No	....	Yes
11	No	No	4½	Normal	100	100	No	....	No
12	No	Dyslalia	4½	Normal	100	93	No	....	?
13	No	No	4½	Normal	80	90	Yes	All	?
14	No	No	4 con. 5 vow.	Normal	90	83	No	....	?
15	No	No	3	Normal	70	80	No	....	No
16	No	No	5	Normal	100	93	No	....	No
17	No	No	5	Normal	100	90	Yes	All	No
18	No	No	4	Normal	93	93	No	....	No
19	No	No	3	?	70	97	Yes	All	?
20	Slight	No	4½	Normal	100	90	Yes	Upper	No
21	No	Dyslalia	3	?	100	90	No	....	?
22	No	No	5	Normal	100	97	Yes	Upper and lower	No
23	No	No	4	Normal	100	97	Yes	Upper	No
24	No	No	4	Normal	100	100	....	....	No
25	No	No	4½	Normal	93	100	No	....	No
26	No	No	4½	Normal	100	100	No	....	No
27	No	No	3	?	100	90	Yes	Lower	?
28	No	No	5	Normal	100	83	No	....	?
29	No	No	3½	Normal	81	90	Yes	Upper and lower	?
30	No	No	5	Normal	87	93	Yes	Upper and lower	?

or 20 per cent, of the cases examined. This finding may be significant, since dyslalia is believed to be present in only about 2 per cent of the general school population. Its effect as a cause of failure to learn to read could not be determined in many of the cases. In Case 8, which was a very young child, training was instituted to correct the dyslalia and the child learned to read readily. In the other cases no direct relationship could be established, nor could such relationship be denied.

Auditory memory span for sounds was tested on the last 24 cases. Norms have not yet been established, but it appears that there is some increase with age. Thus the adequacy of the auditory memory span for sounds, as recorded in Table 13, is the opinion of the speech specialist. Only 1 case evidenced extreme deficiency in auditory memory span for sounds, although it appeared to be questionable in 6, or 25 per cent, of the cases. The speech specialist believed that this deficiency in auditory memory span for sounds might be a cause of failure to learn to read in the cases of pupils who were taught by phonetic methods.

Auditory discrimination tests were not administered to the first 6 cases, since the test was just being formulated at that time. Twenty-three cases were given the test, and the percentage of success on vowels and consonants was recorded. A percentage of success of 90 or above was considered normal by the speech specialist. On the basis of this tentative norm, 5 cases, or 22 per cent of the children examined, had insufficient auditory discrimination of vowels. Four cases, or 17 per cent, had insufficient auditory discrimination of consonants. As was noted earlier, only 1 of the cases was found deficient in both consonants and vowels. This child was very inattentive during examination, which might account for her low score. Even if this case is eliminated, 7 of the 22 remaining cases, or 32 per cent, are still below expectancy in their ability to discriminate either consonants or vowels. The lowest score of 47 per cent was made by Case 10, who also had dyslalia and insufficient auditory memory span for sounds.

There appears to be no relation between dyslalia, auditory memory span for sound, or auditory discrimination and hearing loss, or the frequency at which the loss occurs.

SUMMARY

Stuttering appears to be insignificant as a cause for reading retardation among the cases studied.

Dyslalia was present in 20 per cent of the cases. This is much more prevalent than in the general school population, where it is believed that its presence does not exceed 2 per cent. In one of these cases, dyslalia was the only possible cause of reading failure, and treatment for the dyslalia led to reading improvement. The relationship was considered questionable in the other 5 cases.

There is a possibility that deficient auditory memory span for sounds may be one of the causes of failure to learn to read in 25 per cent of the 24 cases tested. This possibility should be explored further when adequate norms are established.

Auditory discrimination tests were constructed and are in the process of being standardized. On the basis of tentative findings, 7 out of 22 cases for whom the results seemed reliable were below expectancy in their ability to discriminate either vowels or consonants. When this test is standardized, auditory discrimination should be studied further as a cause for serious reading retardation.

In 17 cases, or 57 per cent, the speech specialist did not believe that speech difficulties, inadequate auditory memory span for sounds, and unsatisfactory auditory discrimination were causes of severe reading retardation in this study. In 37 per cent of the cases there was a possibility that one or all of these factors were causes of reading difficulty. In 2 cases dyslalia and questionable auditory memory span were considered causes. Inadequate auditory discrimination was also present in one of the two cases just mentioned.

GENERAL PHYSICAL DIFFICULTIES

Each child was examined by the pediatrician, and all the medical data were collected and interpreted by him. Table 14 presents the data which might be significant in their relation to reading disability.

The percentage of underweight or overweight was calculated by the Baldwin-Wood averages, which take into account both height and weight in relation to age. The range of normality is from 10 per cent underweight to 15 per cent overweight. According to this norm,

8 of the cases, or 27 per cent, fell outside the normal range. Two of these cases were overweight, and 6 were underweight. In some studies weight alone has been used as an index to malnutrition.

The rating of abdominal protrusion is a subjective estimate by the pediatrician. The rating of o means normal and 3 means extreme protrusion. Four of the cases exhibited considerable abdominal pro-

TABLE 14

FINDINGS ON GENERAL PHYSICAL CONDITION

Case Number	Per Cent Overweight or Underweight	Abdominal Protrusion	Hemoglobin	Malnutrition	Posture	Pulse Rate, Sitting	Pulse Increase after Exercise	Increase or Decrease in Pulse Rate, Sitting, Two Minutes after Exercise	Number of Carious Teeth	Genitalia	General Physical Factors May Be Causes
1....	0	0	100	No	C	78	18	0	0	Normal	No
2....	− 7	0-1	95	No	B	102	18	0	0	Normal	No
3....	0	0	95	No	B	84	18	0	1	Normal	No
4....	−19	0	100	Yes	B	84	24	−12	0	Normal	Yes
5....	−14	0	85	?	C	102	12	− 8	2	Normal	?
6....	20	3	95	No	D	72	30	0	4	Normal	No
7....	− 6	2	90	No	D	72	12	− 6	1	Normal	No
8....	− 7	2	95	?	D	108	12	−12	0	Undescended testes	?
9....	0	2	95	No	D	84	24	−12	0	Normal	No
10....	0	0	100	No	C	78	24	− 6	0	Undescended testes	?
11....	− 6	0	100	No	B	66	66	0	0	Normal	No
12....	−17	0	100	?	C	90	42	0	1	Normal	?
13....	0	0	100	No	B	114	12	− 6*	0	Normal	Yes
14....	32	0-1	95	.....	C	90	60	6	1	Normal	No
15....	0	0	.....	No	B	90	24	0	0	Normal	No
16....	− 9	0	100	No	C	96	42	4	0	Normal	No
17....	− 4	0	95	No	C	90	42	− 2	0	Normal	No
18....	− 7	0	100	No	B	102	42	0	0	Normal	No
19....	−10	0	100	No	C	84	54	− 6	2	Normal	No
20....	0	0-1	90	No	C	74	40	10	0	Normal	No
21....	0	0	100	No	C	96	12	− 6	1	Normal	No
22....	0	0	100	No	B	76	52	2	2	Normal	No
23....	0	0	95	No	.....	72	36	0	0	Normal	No
24....	−15	0	95	No	C	72	60	18	4	Normal	?
25....	−14	0	85	Yes	C	60	54	0	0	Normal	Yes
26....	− 6	0	100	No	B	102	18	−18	2	Normal	No
27....	0	0	100	No	C	78	42	− 6	0	Normal	No
28....	0	0	100	No	C	90	18	−14	0	Normal	No
29....	−14	0	95	Yes	C	90	24	0	0	Normal	Yes
30....	9	0-1	100	No	B	102	12	0	0	Penis small	No

* This boy had a serious heart condition.

trusion, which is not abnormal in itself but is a further symptom of malnutrition.

The hemoglobin was estimated by the Tallqvist standard, which was the only means available at the time of examination.

According to these considerations, 3 of the cases, or 10 per cent, were believed to be cases of malnutrition, and there was a definite question concerning the nutritional status of 3 others. Thus, 80 per cent of the cases gave no conclusive evidence of malnutrition.

The systolic blood pressure ranged from 82 to 126, but the child who rated 126 was one whom the pediatrician considered especially tense and apprehensive. The diastolic blood pressure ranged from 44 to 70. Since these findings were within the normal range, they were not included in the table for each case.

The pulse rate taken when the child was sitting varied from 66 to 114, which was considered to be within the normal range. Each child was asked to hop twenty times on one foot, and the increase in pulse rate after this exercise was recorded in the eighth column of Table 14. The ninth column of this table shows the change in pulse rate taken while the child was sitting and 2 minutes after the exercise had ceased, as compared with the first pulse rate taken while sitting. In some instances the pulse rate dropped below that taken before exercise. This was not considered significant by the pediatrician. One case maintained a pulse rate 18 points higher after exercise than before, which would indicate fatigue. This, together with the previous findings, suggested that this boy was suffering from lowered resistance, which might operate to reduce his efficiency of learning.

Case 13 was known to have a serious heart condition, which caused him to tire easily and which had kept him in bed two years, thus retarding him in school.

The number of carious teeth appears to be insignificant, except in the case mentioned above, where there were four carious teeth in the six-year molars. These may have been present for a long period and, combined with the other findings, added to the possibility of a general physical condition causing learning failure, which might affect all learning as well as reading.

Thus, in 4 of the 30 cases, or 13 per cent, some general physical condition was present which the pediatrician believed might cause failure to learn to read. In five other cases the pediatrician believed that there was a question as to whether the physical condition could be responsible. Thus it is apparent that in 9 cases, or 30 per cent of the children examined, some physical difficulty may be operating as a cause for reading failure.

SUMMARY

Ten per cent of the 30 severely retarded readers examined by the pediatrician were cases of malnutrition, and 10 per cent were questionable. Thus, 20 per cent of the cases were possible malnutrition cases.

One of these cases exhibited further unfavorable symptoms, as the pulse did not return to the pre-exercise level. This same case had four carious teeth and was believed to be a case of quick fatigue. In one case a heart condition had existed for several years.

Four of the 30 children examined, or 13 per cent, had definite physical difficulties which could be a cause of failure to learn adequately. There was a possibility that a physical condition was hampering the learning in 5 other cases. Thus, in 9 cases, or 30 per cent, physical factors were found by the pediatrician, which might cause failure in learning in general, and in reading in particular.

ENDOCRINE DISTURBANCES

The endocrinologist decided whether or not there was an endocrine disturbance. Some of his objective measures are recorded in Table 15, as well as his opinion and the treatment instituted.

Only 29 of the 30 cases were examined, as Case 26 would not co-operate for a basal metabolism. If a normal basal metabolic range is -15 to $+15$, then 7 of the 29 cases, or 24 per cent, had basal metabolic rates outside the normal range, and all were too low. The median basal rate was -11, which also tends toward the lower limit of the normal range.

A second measure of endocrine function is the fasting blood cholesterol. This test was made on 26 of the 30 cases. The range was from 115 to 233, which is within the normal range. The highest rating was on a case that had a borderline basal metabolism but was 32 per cent overweight and presented a picture of hypothyroidism.

In a few instances there were other findings which the endocrinologist considered very important in making a final diagnosis.

For example, a radiogram was made of the wrist to determine the level of ossification of the wrist-bones. In some cases the symptoms presented by the child led to decisions concerning endocrine disturbances.

Three of the 28 cases showed definite symptoms of hypothyroidism and were treated by thyroid therapy. There was a question as to whether 4 other cases were hypothyroid. Thus 7 cases, or 26 per cent of the 28 cases, exhibited some symptoms of glandular disturbance.

TABLE 15

ENDOCRINE FINDINGS

Case Number	Basal Metabolic Rate	Fasting Blood Cholesterol (Mg. %)	Miscellaneous Symptoms Found by Endocrinologist	Endocrine Disturbance	Thyroid Therapy Instituted	Considered Significant as a Cause of Reading Failure
1...........	− 3	193	Yes	No	Yes	No
2...........	−16	....	No	No	No	No
3...........	−13	155.5	No	No	No	No
4...........	−20	190	No	No	No	No
5...........	−18	115	No	No	No	No
6...........	−17	165	No	?	Yes	No
7...........	−15	192	Yes	?	No	?
8...........	−11	142	Undescended testes	?	No	No
9...........	−18	166	No	?	No	?
10...........	− 4	129	Undescended testes	?	No	?
11...........	−13	168	No	No	No	No
12...........	4	129	No	No	No	No
13...........	− 9	177	No	No	No	No
14...........	−14	233	Yes	Yes	Yes	Yes
15...........	−13	160	No	No	No	No
16...........	−21	144	No	Yes	Yes	Yes
17...........	− 9	....	No	No	No	No
18...........	− 6	167	No	No	No	No
19...........	4	140	No	No	No	No
20...........	− 9	202	No	No	No	No
21...........	− 6	166	No	No	No	No
22...........	0	....	No	No	No	No
23...........	−11	167	No	No	No	No
24...........	......	....	....	....	....	....
25...........	−13	161	No	No	No	No
26...........	......	....	Would not co-operate	....	....	....
27...........	− 6	160	No	No	No	No
28...........	− 2	157	No	No	No	No
29...........	− 3	148	No	No	No	No
30...........	−22	198	?	Yes	Yes	?
Median.......	−11	....	....	....	....	....

In 5 cases thyroid therapy was carried out according to the directions given by the endocrinologist. Of these 5 cases, 2 showed definite improvement in learning after the thyroid feeding was instituted, while 1 case was not observed. One case learned to read first, and thyroid therapy was instituted later. Another case showed no improvement.

The endocrinologist found no evidence of pituitary disturbance; but he did find 2 cases of undescended testes. If undescended testes is considered a glandular disturbance, then 8 of the 28 cases, or 29 per cent of the cases examined, showed evidence of need for treatment by the endocrinologist.

SUMMARY

Seven of the 28 cases examined had basal metabolic rates below −15, which is usually considered the lower limit of the normal range. No cases rated above the upper limit. The median tended toward the lower limit.

Fasting blood cholesterol was within the normal range in all cases, but the highest one gave other evidence of hypothyroidism.

Other means of diagnosis, such as the radiogram of the wrist, were used in some cases. The presence of endocrine disturbance was determined by the endocrinologist when he considered all these data. In 8 of the 28 cases, or 29 per cent, there was evidence of some endocrine disturbance.

PSYCHOMETRIC FINDINGS

Each of the 30 children was examined with Form L of the Revised Stanford-Binet, as explained in chapter ix. The Grace Arthur Performance Test battery and the Chicago Non-verbal tests were also given to most of the children. The results of the tests are shown in Table 16.

The Binet mental ages range from 7 years 10 months in the youngest child to 15 years 7 months in the oldest child. The mental age of each child was sufficient, according to all previous standards, to justify hope that the child would learn to read. Therefore, insufficient mental age, as such, was not a cause of failure to learn to read in any of the cases considered in this study.

The Binet I.Q.'s ranged from 85 to 137, with a median of 101. Since 9 of the 30 children had Binet I.Q.'s under 100, any one of these might have been somewhat immature when he entered school and, for this reason, have failed to learn to read adequately. Since so many children with I.Q.'s equivalent to those of the group tested learn to read without difficulty, this small amount of retardation does not appear to be adequate to cause reading failure in these 9 cases.

TABLE 16

PSYCHOMETRIC FINDINGS

Case Number	Chronological Age	Binet Mental Age	Binet I.Q.*	Arthur Performance Mental Age	Arthur Performance I.Q.	Chicago Non-verbal Mental Age	Chicago Non-verbal I.Q.	Arthur M.A. minus Binet M.A. (In Months)	Arthur I.Q. minus Binet I.Q.	Chicago Non-verbal M.A. minus Binet M.A. (In Months)	Chicago Non-verbal I.Q. minus Binet I.Q.
1	10- 6	9- 2	87	10-10	104	9- 1	87	20	17	− 1	0
2	8- 6	11- 8	137	11- 1	130	9-10	115	− 7	− 7	−22	−22
3	14- 0	13-10	101	15- 6	110	17- 3	123	20	9	41	22
4	9- 6	10- 6	112	15- 6	123	10- 7	111	60	11	1	− 1
5	8-10	9- 0	102	9- 7	108	8- 8	98	7	6	− 4	− 4
6	10- 6	10- 7	101	11- 7	110	9- 8	92	12	9	−11	− 9
7	10- 8	9- 4	88	8- 7	81	8- 2	76	− 9	− 7	−14	−12
8	11- 8	9-10	85	10- 9	92	8-11	76	11	7	−11	− 9
9	6- 9	7-10	118	8- 4	125	6- 7	99	6	7	−15	−19
10	13- 1	12- 4	94	11-11	90	10- 6	79	− 5	− 4	−22	−15
11	13- 5	13- 2	98	15- 6	115	16- 7	124	28	17	41	26
12	10- 1	11- 4	112	9- 5	95	....	....	−23	−17	....	....
13	12- 1	12- 2	101	15- 5	127	15- 0	124	39	26	34	23
14	11- 1	13- 4	120	15- 6	140	14- 0	120	26	20	8	0
15	7- 7	7-11	105	7- 6	97	....	....	− 5	− 8	....	....
16	8- 7	9- 8	112	9- 3	106	8- 5	97	− 5	− 6	−15	−15
17	9- 9	10- 2	104	11- 7	120	10- 8	108	17	16	6	4
18	14- 0	13- 8	100	15- 5	110	15- 8	111	21	10	24	11
19	10- 6	10- 2	95	13- 3	118	9- 0	80	25	23	−14	−15
20	9- 8	10- 6	107	10- 5	108	10- 5	108	− 1	1	− 1	1
21	11- 8	12-11	110	15- 5	132	12- 8	113	30	22	− 3	3
22	14- 4	13- 2	95	15- 6	109	15- 9	106	28	14	31	11
23	12- 6	13- 0	104	15- 6	124	14- 4	115	30	20	16	11
24	12- 1	11- 9	98	11- 6	95	10-11	90	− 3	− 3	−10	− 8
25	12- 4	14- 6	118	14- 1	114	14- 3	116	− 5	− 4	− 3	− 2
26	14- 1	14- 4	103	15- 6	110	18- 9	133	14	7	53	30
27	13-10	12- 6	93	15- 6	114	16- 1	116	36	21	43	23
28	15- 3	15- 7	107	15- 6	102	16- 8	109	?	− 5	13	2
29	10- 2	8-10	87	10- 0	98	9- 8	95	14	11	10	12
30	12- 9	11-10	93	11- 8	91	12- 3	99	− 2	− 2	5	6
Median	11-4.5	11-8.5	101.3	11-9.5	110	10-9.5	108	14	8	0	0.5
Average	......	......	......	....	......	......	......	13.1	......	7.3	......

* Uncorrected for reading disability; determined by table in Terman and Merrill.

The Arthur Performance Test gave evidence of ability higher than the Binet in 19 of the 30 cases, or 63 per cent. The Arthur test yielded a median of 14 months higher mental age than the Binet, and an average of 13.1 months higher. Thus it can be concluded that the majority of the cases studied rated higher on the Arthur Performance Test than on the Binet.

On the Chicago Non-verbal Test, about half of the cases rated higher than on the Binet, and half rated lower; hence the median difference was 0. However, the average difference was 7.3 months, in favor of the Chicago Non-verbal Test scores.

An analysis of the findings on the Binet tests was made to determine whether or not the basal age was exceedingly low or the range

TABLE 17

ANALYSIS OF BINET TEST

Case Number	Binet Basal Age	Range in Years	Vocabulary Level	Binet M.A.	Binet M.A. *minus* Vocabulary Level (In Years)	
1........	8	3	8	9- 2		1
2........	8	7	8	11- 8		4
3........	10	7	S.A.I.	13- 0	About	2
4........	8	5	12	10- 6		−1.5
5........	7	4	8	9- 0		1
6........	8	6	8	10- 7		3
7........	8	4	8	9- 4		1
8........	8	5	12	9-10		−2
9........	6	2	8	7-10		0
10........	11	3	14	12- 4		−2
11........	10	5	14	13- 2		−1
12........	8	6	14	11- 4		−3
13........	9	5	12	12- 2		0
14........	9	7	14	13- 4		−1
15........	5	5	10	7-11		−2
16........	7	6	8	9- 8		2
17........	7	4	10	10- 2		0
18........	11	4	A.A.	13- 8	About	2
19........	8	5	10	10- 2		0
20........	8	5	8	10- 6		2.5
21........	10	5	12	12-11		1
22........	12	2	12	13- 2		1
23........	11	3	12	13- 0		1
24........	9	4	10	11- 9		2
25........	9	5	10	14- 6		4.6
26........	12	3	14	14- 4		0
27........	10	4	10	12- 6		2.6
28........	14	3	A.A.	15- 7		0
29........	8	3	8	8-10		1
30........	9	5	14	11-10		−2
Median...	8.7	5	11	11- 8	About	1 year
Average...	9.0	4.5	About 11	....	....	

in years exceedingly high. Table 17 shows that the basal ages were not exceedingly low on any of the cases, and the median range seems about what would be expected with an unselected group. In 3 cases the range was seven years, but these were very seriously retarded readers, and in 2 of these cases the basal ages were reduced because of their inability to read.

In order to determine the level of vocabulary as compared with mental age, the last column in Table 17 was constructed. In some cases the mental age was above the vocabulary level and vice versa. In the group as a whole the two are approximately equal. In no case

TABLE 18

ANALYSIS OF ARTHUR PERFORMANCE TEST FINDINGS

Case Number	Binet M.A.	Binet I.Q.	Arthur Point Scale (Mental Age)	Arthur I.Q.	Knox Cube	Seguin Form-board	Casuist Form-board	Feature Profile	Mare and Foal	Healy Picture Completion I	Porteus Maze	Koh's Block Design
1......	9- 2	87	10-10	104	8-6	10-6	9-7	11-1	10-7	9-11	11-6	10-5
2......	11- 8	137	11- 1	130	6-9	10-6	11-1	11-8	12-6	9- 8	12-6	11-0
3......	13-10	101	15- 6	110	8-6	14	15	14-9	15	15	14	15
4......	10- 6	112	15	123	12-0	14-0	15	15	15-0	15	14-0	15
5......	9- 0	102	9- 7	108	6-6	9-3	9-4	9-1	10-3	10- 6	8-9	9-7
6.......	10- 7	101	11- 7	110	6-6	11-6	11-4	10-9	13-3	11- 7	12-6	12-5
7......	9- 4	88	8- 7	81	6	8-9	9-5	9-0	7-9	9- 7	7-9	8-0
8......	9-10	85	10- 9	92	9	7-9	11-1	11-6	8-3	12- 5	14	11-0
9......	7-10	118	8- 4	125	5-3	9-0	7-6	9-6	12-6	7- 9	6-9	8-3
10......	12- 4	94	11-11	90	9	14	15	8-0	13-8	7- 8	14-0	9-5
11......	13- 2	98	15- 6	115	12	14	15-0	15	15	12- 3	14	15
12......	11- 4	112	9- 5	94	6	10-5	11-3	11-0	8-5	7- 6	......	11-6
13......	12- 2	101	15- 5	127	11	14	15	13-3	15	12- 6	14	14-1
14......	13- 4	120	15- 6	140	12	14	15	8-0	15	15	14	14-6
15......	7- 2	105	7- 6	97	......	8-0	8-8	5-5	6-8	8- 8	8-0	6-2
16......	9- 8	112	9- 3	106	8-0	8-0	7-6	5-6	8-9	11- 9	10-0	9-4
17......	10- 2	104	11- 7	120	5	12	14-0	9-0	12-0	12- 0	10-0	13-0
18......	13- 8	100	15- 5	110	12-0	14-0	14-0	10-7	15	15	14-0	11-6
19......	10 -2	95	13- 3	118	12	14	11-0	14-8	7-2	15	14-2	12-4
20......	10- 6	107	10- 5	108	7	12	10-0	15	11-5	7- 5	10-0	10-5
21......	12-11	110	15- 5	132	12	10	15	15	15-0	15-	14-0	14-0
22......	13- 2	95	15- 6	109	12	14	8-6	9-8	15	15	14	11-4
23......	13- 0	104	15- 6	124	7	14	15	15	15	15	14-0	15
24......	11- 9	98	11- 6	95	12	10	15	9-0	12-6	9- 9	12-6	9-4
25......	12- 6	119	14- 1	114	12	14	14-0	15	13-7	7- 8	14-0	15
26......	14- 4	103	15- 6	110	12-0	14-0	15	15	15	15	14-0	15
27......	12- 6	93	15- 6	114	7-0	14	15	15	14-0	15	14	15
28......	15- 7	107	15- 6	102	8-0	14-0	15	11-7	15	15	14	15
29......	8-10	87	10- 0	98	9-0	9-5	7-5	13-2	11-5	12- 0	9-0	8-0
30......	11-10	93	11- 8	91	8-0	10	10-0	15	15	8- 5	14-0	11-5
Median..	......	......	......	......	8-6	12-0	11-3.5	11-6.5	13-5	12- 0	14-0	11-6

was inadequate speaking vocabulary considered to be a cause of reading failure.

An analysis of the scores on various tests in the Arthur Performance series shows that the lowest scores were made consistently on the Knox Cube test. In 18 of the 30 cases, or 60 per cent, the Knox Cube mental age equivalent was the lowest of the series of tests. The cases were not counted when the highest possible score on the Knox Cube test was reached. In 6 other cases the mental ages on the Knox Cube were higher than on only one of the other tests. Thus in 24 of the 30 cases, or 80 per cent, the score on the Knox Cube test was one of the two lowest. The exact meaning of this low rating on the Knox Cube test is not clear at present. Further testing of good and poor readers with this series may show that this test is associated with reading failure and thus may give some clue as to the cause for failure in these cases.

SUMMARY

The Binet mental ages ranged from 7 years 10 months to 15 years 7 months, and the I.Q.'s from 85 to 137. The mental ages were high enough in every case that the child should have learned to read. In a few of the cases with I.Q.'s below 100, the maturity of the child when he first entered school might be questioned.

The Arthur Point Scale of Performance yielded mental ages with a median 14 months higher than the Binet. There was little difference between the Binet mental ages and those obtained on the Chicago Non-verbal examination.

An analysis of the Binet scores showed no special vocabulary difficulty and no unusually large ranges of testing, that is, difference between the age levels at which all tests are passed and at which all tests are failed.

The Knox Cube test yielded the lowest mental age equivalent of the Arthur series in 60 per cent of this group of severely retarded readers and was one of the two lowest in 80 per cent of the group studied. This may have some significance in pointing to causes.

PSYCHIATRIC FINDINGS

The psychiatrist attempted to evaluate the emotional responses of 28 of the 30 cases examined. Although the reports are largely descriptive, Table 19 summarizes the findings. Cases 26 and 28 were seen only once by the psychiatrist, and, as a result, no satisfactory evaluation could be made.

Only 4 of the 28 cases examined, or 14 per cent, accepted failure to learn to read. Ten of the cases, or 36 per cent, had no clearly defined attitudes toward success and failure. One case emphasized success in other areas; 1 exhibited a feeling toward success and failure, although it was not verbalized; 1 felt it necessary to quit school, thus exhibiting no necessity for choice; and 1 thought a tutor was better than a teacher with whom he had associated failure. In 5 cases, or 18 per cent, the psychiatrist found that the children felt "intense," "anxious," or "rebelled against failure." One case feared failure, 1 was confused, and only 1 appeared to recognize it and expected to improve.

The methods of explaining deficiency in reading varied. Seven of the 28 cases, or 25 per cent, had no method of explaining the reading failure. Poor eyes were credited by 8 of the 28 cases, or 29 per cent, as a cause of failure to learn to read properly. In 2 cases, "dumbness" was believed by the children to be the cause of reading failure. Other causes mentioned by no more than one child were: school absence, teachers, physical defects, accidents, and fear of reciting in class. One child accepted the responsibility, 1 denied its importance, and 1 was not aware of the deficiency.

Some of the children studied felt that they had lost status, while others did not. No reaction to loss of status was reported by 11 of 28 cases, or 39 per cent. Compensation by various methods were reported by 6 of the 28, or 21 per cent. It was not possible to evaluate the reaction to loss of status in 1 case, 1 was anxious about the loss, 1 retreated, 1 was isolated and reported no play, 1 played with children who would accept him, while 1 made no effort to do anything about it.

A normal or average emotional response was recorded by the psychiatrist in 8 of the 28 cases, which is 29 per cent of them. Other cases described as "anxious," "tense," "unresponsive," or "timid" included 11 children, or 39 per cent of the cases. Three were described as tractable, 1 as responsive but tense, 1 as blocked, and 1 as withdrawn. One child showed no change in emotional intensity, while another vacillated. The emotional responses in 1 case were described as "immature."

Physical reactions during discussion of reading failure evidenced tension or tics in 16 out of 28, or 57 per cent of the cases. In 10 cases, which is 36 per cent, no physical reaction was noted. Two cases were hyperactive, and no physical reaction was recorded on 1 child.

Evidences of mental conflict were recorded in 14 of the 28 cases, or 50 per cent. One exhibited no conflict except when reading was discussed; 12 showed no evidence of mental conflict; and 1 was not recorded.

Perhaps none of these findings alone is of special significance.

However, when combined, they led the psychiatrist to decide that there was no psychiatric problem associated with 13 of the 28 cases examined, or 46 per cent of them. Of the remaining 54 per cent, there was a psychiatric finding which was considered important. Three of the children studied were diagnosed as neurotics. The others were diagnosed as psychiatric problems, and in 1 case there was lack of emotionality. Another case was described as evidencing no present problem, but it appeared incipient.

In 9 cases, which is 32 per cent, direct psychiatric therapy was recommended. In the other cases the psychiatrist felt that reading would progress without direct psychiatric therapy.

Improvement in psychiatric adjustment was reported in 14 children, or 50 per cent of those examined. In 7 cases there was no psychiatric improvement reported, while 7 cases were not followed long enough to determine definitely the results.

Emotional maladjustment was considered to be a possible cause of reading failure in 12 cases, or 43 per cent of the 28 children studied. The emotional maladjustment was considered to be a result of reading failure in the same number of cases. Nine of these 12 cases are the same, since the emotional problem was considered both a cause and a result of the reading failure. Three cases of emotional maladjustment were considered to be coincidental with the reading failure.

SUMMARY

Of the 28 severely retarded readers studied, 14 per cent accepted failure; 36 per cent had no clearly defined attitudes toward success and failure; 18 per cent felt intense, anxious, or rebelled against failure; the other 32 per cent had individual types of reactions to success and failure.

Twenty-five per cent of the cases had no method of explaining deficiency. Poor eyes were blamed by 29 per cent as the cause for failure. Forty-six per cent of the children used other methods of explaining failure or did not attempt to do so.

In 39 per cent of the cases there was no loss of status or no reaction to loss of status. Compensations were reported by 21 per cent of the cases, and isolated responses were reported by 40 per cent.

Normal emotional responses were found in 29 per cent of the cases, while 39 per cent were described as "anxious," "intense," "unresponsive," or "timid." In 33 per cent there were individualized responses.

There were evidences of physical tension, or tics, in 57 per cent of these severely retarded readers, while in 36 per cent no physical reaction was noted. Others were hyperactive, or no response was noted. There was some evidence of mental conflict in 54 per cent of these children, and no evidence of mental conflict in 43 per cent. Findings for others were not recorded.

There was a psychiatric problem of some kind in 54 per cent of the cases and none in 46 per cent. Only 32 per cent of the cases were thought by the psychiatrist to be in need of direct psychiatric treatment.

Improvement in emotional adjustments were reported in half the cases, some of whom submitted to psychiatric therapy, while others were treated for reading disability only.

Emotional maladjustment was considered as a possible cause of reading failure in 43 per cent of the cases and as a result in an equal number, 9 of whom overlapped in the two groups.

READING LEVEL

On the Standardized Oral Reading Paragraphs, 12 of the 30 children studied, or 40 per cent, were unable to read well enough to score. These cases are often described as "nonreaders." However, this was not true in all 12 cases, because some of them could read silently and thus obtained a score on comprehension tests. Excessive time and too many errors prevented scoring on the oral reading tests. No child rated above grade 4.4 in oral reading.

Even though the child did not score on the Standardized Reading Paragraphs, the Stanford Achievement Test, primary or advanced, was given to some children and the Metropolitan Achievement Test was given to others. Some of the poorest readers could score on the Metropolitan test for Grade I, where they could not score on the Stanford Achievement Test.

One of the three reading scores just discussed was obtained on all children to secure an objective measure of reading achievement.

The scores on the Monroe Diagnostic Reading Examination were not especially helpful in determining whether there was a methodological cause of failure to learn to read. The scores substantiated the findings in the other tests and showed that these children were retarded in reading. The reading indices supplied objective evidence of this retardation, considering life-age, mental age, and arithmetic scores as reference frames.

The Gates Primary Reading Test or the Gates Reading Diagnosis tests were given to a number of the children but not to all, as indicated in Table 20. The scores on all these tests indicate that they are not of great diagnostic value when grade scores alone are considered.

TABLE 20

GRADE EQUIVALENTS ON READING TESTS

Case Number	Gray Oral Paragraphs	Stanford or Metropolitan Word Meaning	Stanford or Metropolitan Paragraph Meaning	Average Reading	Monroe Diagnostic Iota Word Test	Monroe Diagnostic Word Discrimination Test	Monroe Reading Index	Gates Tests			
								1	2	3	4
1....	3.2	3.8	3.0	3.3	2.2	2.7	.65	3.8	3.7	....	....
2....	1.0	1.7	1.7	1.5	1.6	1.8	.35	2.3	1.6	1.8	....
3....	1.0	3.0	3.2	2.4	3.9	4.2	.42	3.1	3.4	3.5	3.3
4....	1.0	1.0	1.0	1.0	2.5	2.5	.47	2.5	2.1	1.9	....
5....	1.0	1.6	1.1	1.2	1.2	1.0	.33	....	....	....	....
6....	1.8	3.5	2.9	2.7	2.5	2.6	.55	2.9	3.1	3.1	....
7....	1.0	1.0	1.0	1.0	1.4	1.5	.30	1.7	1.4	1.5	....
8....	1.0	2.8	2.3	2.0	2.5	2.0	.41	3.0	2.4	2.2	....
9....	1.0	1.0	1.0	1.0	1.0	1.0	.53	....	....	....	....
10....	1.0	1.0	1.0	1.0	1.0	1.0	.15	....	....	....	....
11....	3.4	5.7	6.1	5.1	5.8	5.1	.63	3.6	3.7	4.5	3.8
12....	1.0	1.1	2.2	1.4	2.6	4.0	.49	3.2	2.9	4.0	....
13....	2.8	3.2	4.0	3.3	3.1	2.7	.52	....	....	....	....
14....	2.3	3.0	3.0	2.8	3.2	2.9	.45	3.0	2.8	....	....
15....	1.0	1.0	1.0	1.0	1.0	1.0	.60	....	....	....	....
16....	1.8	2.7	2.8	2.4	2.4	2.7	.68	2.4	2.6	2.2	....
17....	1.6	2.2	2.5	2.1	2.4	2.0	.45	....	....	....	....
18....	2.3	2.6	2.5	2.5	2.0	2.1	.31	....	....	....	....
19....	1.0	2.5	2.1	1.9	1.8	2.3	.48	2.6	2.1	2.4	....
20....	1.0	2.9	2.4	2.1	2.1	3.2	.56	....	....	....	....
21....	2.8	3.1	3.8	3.2	2.2	2.4	.44	3.3	....	....	....
22....	3.3	2.5	3.9	3.2	3.4	4.4	.50	3.3	3.3	3.8	3.9
23....	3.6	4.0	3.9	3.8	4.2	3.9	.50	3.1	3.0	3.2	2.9
24....	1.8	2.6	2.5	2.3	2.4	4.0	.46	2.9	2.6	2.4	....
25....	2.4	2.9	3.1	2.8	3.1	4.0	.44	3.3	3.3	3.7	....
26....	4.4	6.3	4.7	5.1	5.0	5.0	.59	3.5	3.9	4.5	4.0
27....	3.1	5.5	4.8	4.5	4.9	5.0	.64	3.1	3.1	3.5	3.0
28....	3.1	4.5	6.3	4.6	5.1	4.5	.52	4.2	6.0	5.5	3.5
29....	1.6	3.1	Below 2.0	2.2	1.8	1.9	.51	1.45	1.95	2.0	....
30....	2.4	2.5	2.7	2.5	2.2	....	.41	....	....	....	....

They do indicate a level of achievement against which later gains can be compared. The analysis of the performance on the various tests provided clues to the difficulty in individual cases.

METHODS OF TEACHING AND INTERESTS

At the time of examination it was not possible to evaluate the methods of teaching reading which had been used on each child in the years before examination. Probably this is important in evaluating causes but, with present facilities, an evaluation of methods was not feasible.

Interests in reading have been recorded on as many cases as possible. Some parents had observed no interests in their child, and some children expressed no interests. Even though attempts were made to record and evaluate interests and ambitions of the children the data secured were of little value. The social workers, who discussed the children's interests with the parents, felt, in many instances, that the parents were very guarded in their statements regarding them. Many of these children were sufficiently retarded in school or upset emotionally that defenses were noted rather than genuine interests.

Many of these children were taught to read under conditions where the writer could observe interests. The records indicate great changes as these children began to succeed in school.

SUMMARY

Interests should be evaluated more carefully than was done in the present study.

SOCIAL FACTORS

The social factors most frequently studied are indicated in Table 21. As generally accepted, most social factors do not lend themselves to quantitative treatment. Therefore, it was essential to consider the diagnosis made by the social worker, who obtained a detailed case history and attempted to establish a good relationship with the parent in a number of interviews. The different social factors which might have caused reading failure varied with each case, as noted in Table 22.

In 16 of the 30 cases, or 53 per cent, there was some abnormality in the family structure or relationship. In 4 other cases this was questionable. Six of these cases had lost either the father or the mother by death. In 2 cases the fathers had deserted, and in 1 case the mother did not live with the children. Two children were adopted,

TABLE 21

CHILDREN'S INTERESTS

Case Number	Parents' Opinion of Child's Interests	School's Opinion of Child's Interests	Child's Voiced Interests	Parents' Choice of Profession
1......	Sports	Social studies	....	None
2......	Sports, movies	....	....	....
3......	Nature study	None	Girl Scouts	....
4......	Mechanics	Collecting, handi-work	....	....
5......	Movies, parties	?	Engineer	None
6......	Movies, sports, parties	Drawing	....	....
7......	....	None	....	....
8......	Mechanics	....	....	None
9......	Movies	....	....	....
10......	None	None	None	None
11......	Mechanics	Athletics	Scouts, choir	Mechanics
12......	Mechanics	Art	Scouts, mechanics	College
13......	....	Drawing	....	....
14......	Drawing	....	....	None
15......	....	....	....	None
16......	Church, play	Science, art	....	....
17......	Mechanics	Mechanics	....	....
18......	....	....	....	....
19......	Playing	....	....	....
20......	....	None	....	....
21......	Building, drawing	....	........?......	Mechanics
22......	Sports, airplanes	Sports, science	Mechanics	Pilot or doctor
23......	Craftsman, club	Science, airplanes	....	....
24......	Sports, movies	Camera, science	....	....
25......	Movies, Scouts	History, Scouts	....	....
26......	Leaving school	None	None	....
27......	Mechanics	....	....	None
28......	None	None	Mechanics	Profession
29......	Drawing	....	....	....
30......	Sports, handicraft	Construction	....	....

and in both cases there was considerable home tension. Table 22 gives some indication of the central problem, which was elaborated in the case history. In many instances minor problems were also found.

The occupations of the fathers showed considerable variety and indicated the wide range in socioeconomic status of the children examined. Seriousness of retardation seemed in no way related to either occupation of father or socioeconomic status.

The education of the parents ranged from Grade VI to college graduation. Most of the parents' education tended toward the upper end of this range. English was spoken exclusively in all the homes.

Lack of books, magazines, or newspapers could not be considered a

TABLE 22

SOCIAL FACTORS

Case Number	Number of Rooms in House or Apartment	Number of Books in Home	Number of Children's Books	Number of Daily Papers	Number of Magazines	Education of Mother	Education of Father	Occupation of Father
1.....	5	0	0	1	2	12	12	Salesman
2.....	5	?	?	?	?	14	16	Manager passenger agency (foster)
3.....	6	Over 500	?	1	5	8	16	Attorney
4.....	10	Many	Many	1	?	?	?	Naval officer (deceased, foster)
5.....	8	0	0	0	1	13	14	Druggist (deserted)
6.....	8	300	?	1	5	12	16	Veterinarian
7.....								Businessman
8.....	6	?	?	2	7	16	16	Engineer (civil)
9.....	3		0			16	17	Teacher
10.....								Electrical contract engineer (deceased)
11.....	7		0	2	10	16	8	Implement dealer
12.....	8	25	0	2	8	12	10	Mechanic
13.....	6	0	0	1		12	12	Elevator man
14.....	6	?		2	9	13	16	Manufacturer
15.....						14	16	Chemist
16.....	8		75	2	13	16	16	Architect
17.....	8		Small	1	1	14	15	Contractor
18.....								Real estate salesman
19.....						6	8	Checker at dairy
20.....	6	?	?	1	2	14	16	Superintendent of a press
21.....			0	1		12	12	Mechanic (deceased)
22.....		30		1		6	8	Serviceman on ice machines
23.....	8	0	0	0	4	12	12	Foreman
24.....	5	0	0	1		8	8	Taxi driver
25.....	4		Small				7	Catering manager
26.....								Deceased
27.....	2	0	0	2	1	11	14	Clerk
28.....								Unknown
29.....	5	?	0			8	8	Laborer
30.....	1	0	0			8	9	Roofer

cause of reading failure in these cases. Some of these children were exposed to none, while others had the opportunity to contact many in the home.

The ordinal position of the child in the family is interesting. Five, or 17 per cent, were only children, and another 5 were first children. Thus 10, or about 33 per cent of the cases examined, were first or only children, and about 67 per cent had older brothers or sisters. Ten of the cases were youngest in the family, excluding only children.

SUMMARY

The social workers who interviewed the parents found many factors in family relationships which they believed were not conducive to academic achievement. In 53 per cent of the cases there was evidence of a social situation which was believed to disturb the child, while in 14 per cent of the cases there was a question about existing relationship.

The education of parents; occupations of fathers; and number of books, magazines, or newspapers appeared to be unrelated to reading failure.

One-third of the children were only or first children, one-third were medially placed, and one-third were the youngest in their families.

GENERAL SUMMARY

The data presented in this chapter show that each of the 30 children examined possessed sufficient intelligence, as shown by a battery of individual intelligence tests, to make average or better-than-average progress in reading. However, each child was seriously retarded in reading, as shown by the discrepancy between (a) chronological age and reading grades; (b) mental age and the reading grade achieved; and (c) by the Monroe reading index.

To summarize the complete findings of each specialist, Table 23 has been constructed. The cases are presented in descending order of severity, as indicated by the Monroe reading index. The final opinion as to the presence or absence of any anomaly in the area of specialization is recorded. In some instances the difficulty is of such a slight degree as to be called questionable.

If the 30 cases are divided into three groups, the 10 most seriously retarded readers exhibit 39 anomalies, and the 10 least seriously retarded exhibit only 26, showing that the most seriously retarded tend to exhibit the greatest number of anomalies. The entries in this table justify two general conclusions: (1) the most seriously retarded readers had the greatest number of anomalies, and the least seriously retarded cases exhibited fewer defects; (2) the pattern of anomalies

TABLE 23

ANOMALIES FOUND FOR EACH CASE

Case Number	Monroe Reading Index	Visual Difficulty (Table 4)	Neurological Difficulty (Table 9)	Auditory Difficulty (Table 12)	Speech or Discrimination Difficulty (Table 13)	General Physical Difficulty (Table 14)	Endocrine Disturbance (Table 15)	Emotional Maladjustment (Table 19)	Social Problems	Number of Possible Hampering Factors
10	15	Yes	No	No	Yes	?	?	Yes	Yes	6
7	30	Yes	Yes	No	?	No	?	Yes	?	6
18	31	?	No	No	No	No	No	Yes	Yes	3
5	33	No	Yes	No	Yes	?	No	Yes	Yes	5
2	35	?	No	No	No	No	No	No	Yes	2
8	41	Yes	No	No	Yes	?	?	Yes	Yes	6
30	41	No	No	No	No	No	No	No	Yes	1
3	42	Yes	Yes	No	No	No	No	No	Yes	3
21	44	?	Yes	No	?	No	No	No	?	4
25	44	Yes	No	No	No	Yes	No	Yes	No	3
14	45	?	No	No	?	No	Yes	No	No	3
17	45	?	No	?	No	No	No	Yes	No	3
24	46	Yes	No	No	No	?	No	Yes	No	3
4	47	?	No	No	No	Yes	No	No	Yes	3
19	48	No	No	?	?	No	No	Yes	?	4
12	49	?	Yes	No	Yes	?	No	No	No	4
22	50	No	Yes	No	No	No	No	No	No	1
23	50	Yes	No	No	No	No	No	No	Yes	2
29	51	No	No	No	?	Yes	No	No	No	2
13	52	No	No	No	?	Yes	No	No	Yes	3
28	52	?	No	No	?	No	No	No	Yes	3
9	53	No	No	No	Yes	No	?	No	Yes	3
6	55	?	No	No	No	No	?	Yes	No	3
20	56	Yes	No	No	No	No	No	Yes	?	3
26	59	?	No	No	No	No	No	No	Yes	2
15	60	Yes	No	No	No	No	No	No	Yes	2
11	63	?	No	No	No	No	No	No	No	1
27	64	?	No	No	?	No	No	No	No	2
1	65	No	No	No	?	No	No	No	Yes	2
16	68	?	No	No	No	No	Yes	Yes	Yes	4
Number of anomalies	.....	22	6	2	14	9	7	12	20	......
Per cent of Yes and ?	.....	73	20	6.7	46.7	30	23.3	40	66.7	......

found varied from case to case. This latter fact will be considered further in the study of individual cases in chapter xi.

The relative importance of each anomaly as judged by the frequency of its occurrence among the 30 cases is shown in the last row of entries in Table 23 and in graphic form in Figure 1. The percentages indicated include those cases in which a defect was found that was considered either a possible or a "questionable" cause of

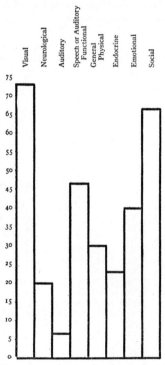

Fig. 1.—Percentage of cases showing various anomalies

reading failure. From Figure 1 it is evident that visual difficulties requiring either lenses or orthoptic treatment, or both, were found most prevalent and were present in 73 per cent of the cases. Social and emotional maladjustments were the two factors next in order of frequency. These two factors are necessarily closely related and often could not be distinguished separately.

Figure 1 shows also that a speech difficulty or a functional auditory disturbance, such as inadequate auditory discrimination or insufficient auditory memory span for sounds, was present in about 46 per cent of the cases. Auditory acuity, on the other hand, was noted in very few cases and was not considered significant as a cause of reading failure in any of this group of cases. General physical difficulties were reported in 30 per cent of the cases. Endocrine disturbances were found in 23 per cent of those studied, and neurological difficulties, including alexia, were identified in 20 per cent of the cases examined.

In many of the previous studies of seriously retarded readers, each anomaly identified was often accepted as a causal factor of reading disability in the cases examined. This study considered further steps essential before conclusions were drawn concerning the causes of reading disability in individual cases. The techniques employed are described in chapter xi. Whereas this chapter has dealt with the mass data relating to the anomalies found, chapter xi presents a detailed analysis of the findings in each case and an evaluation of each anomaly as a causal factor.

NOTES

1. Chap. vi.

2. Marion Monroe, *Children Who Cannot Read* (Chicago: University of Chicago Press, 1932), p. 16.

3. Thomas H. Eames, "The Ocular Conditions of 350 Poor Readers," *Journal of Educational Research*, XXXII (September, 1938), 10–13.

4. Earl A. Taylor, *Controlled Reading* (Chicago: University of Chicago Press, 1937).

5. Each doubtful score reduces a perfect score of 100 per cent by 5 per cent; each failure reduces the score 10 per cent.

CHAPTER XI

FINDINGS OF THE STUDY OF THIRTY CHILDREN INTERPRETED BY THE CONFERENCE OF SPECIALISTS

THE purpose of this chapter is to present the conclusions reached when all findings on each child were pooled and an attempt was made to evaluate them.

After each specialist had completed his individual examination and recorded his findings and opinions, the group met for the purpose of evaluating these factors and making appropriate recommendations for treatment. In some cases treatment was followed out and the results were recorded. In others, no follow-up was available, so it was not possible to evaluate the accuracy of the group opinions. When it was possible to follow results, it was often necessary for the group to reconsider the case and make secondary recommendations. After treatment was completed, the group attempted to identify the probable causes of the reading failure. Unfortunately, only a limited amount of the detailed case history and findings can be considered in this discussion, and only the pertinent facts in each case can be presented.

The cases will be discussed in the order in which they were studied. For the detailed findings of each specialist, reference is made to the tables in chapter x, where the cases are listed in the same order.

CASE I

This ten-and-a-half-year-old boy came to the attention of the group because he had a speech defect about which his mother had consulted the speech specialist. At that time she asked for help with his reading because he was not keeping up with his classmates.

INDIVIDUAL FINDINGS

This boy's intelligence score placed him in the lower part of the normal range; all his responses were slow. He showed no interest, ambition, or desire to progress in school. From his history and his reactions, it seemed probable that he was immature when he entered school.

The speech specialist classified his defect as dyslalia. It was characterized by slowness of articulation and oral inactivity. The mother had a slight speech defect of another type, but the boy apparently had not imitated her difficulty.

The social worker considered the mother to be very tense and to hold standards of perfection so high that the boy could never reach them. As a result he had ceased trying and had withdrawn from most activities, even with other children. She had become emotionally upset over his first failure in school, and it was believed that the boy felt very guilty about it.

GROUP EVALUATION

The discussion of the group centered around the boy's immaturity and slow reactions. After each specialist had emphasized this fact but was unable to offer suggestions for treatment, the endocrinologist expressed the opinion that, in spite of a basal metabolic rate of -3, the boy might be speeded up by means of thyroid therapy. If such treatment did speed up his reactions and activity, it was assumed that he might become more interested and active and, as a result, might improve in reading and speech. This seemed the only remedy for immaturity that might be adopted. It appeared difficult to alter the family relationships because the distance to their home precluded frequent contacts. However, the medication was given under the direction of the endocrinologist, and after one year there was still less-than-average gain in reading, with no change in his speed of reactions. Thus the endocrine disturbance was ruled out as a cause for reading failure.

A second consideration by the group centered on the family relationships and especially the mother's great tension and dissatisfaction with this boy. Therefore, the second recommendation was that the social worker endeavor to establish a more satisfactory relationship between the mother and the boy by helping her to accept him as slower than the average. The worker also tried to impress upon the mother the fact that her goals were so high that her son could never reach them and that therefore he was always fearful of attempting anything. The mother refused to accept any such explanation as relevant to her son's progress in reading and, instead, exaggerated his problem by having him tutored after school and on Saturdays. Two years later, the boy was considered more withdrawn than ever by the psychiatrist and was making less-than-average progress in reading, according to his school reports. The speech difficulty was considered a symptom of a larger reaction to family maladjustments and unimportant as a cause of reading failure.

A summary of the evaluation of the case follows:

Anomalies Found by Individual Examiners	Factors Considered Important by the Group	Probable Causes
Poor family relationships	Family relationships	Family relationships
Speech difficulty	Endocrine imbalance (?)	
Immaturity		

CASE 2

This bright, eight-year-old boy was the adopted child of wealthy parents, who had no other children. He had failed to learn to read during his two-and-a-half years at school, and the mother sought help for him because she believed he was a disgrace to her.

INDIVIDUAL FINDINGS

The ophthalmologist recommended glasses to correct 1 diopter of hyperopia in each eye and 1 diopter of astigmatism in one eye and .50 in the other. The ophthalmologists thought that the visual difficulty was so small that it could scarcely cause a serious reading retardation.

The social worker believed that the source of the trouble was in the family interrelationships and attitudes. From the boy's history she learned that he had been hyperactive as a child and had finally become almost uncontrollable. The parents had been dissatisfied with him even before he had entered school and failed to learn to read. He had not wished to go to school, and after he entered, he had spent most of his time trying to gain security with the teacher and the other children. His attention span was very short, and he never appeared to hear directions. He said he did not want to learn to read because then his mother would not read to him any more. It was evident that he failed at first because his attention was constantly elsewhere, and that he enjoyed the failure and saw it as a means of maintaining the undivided attention of his mother.

The group considered this boy's major difficulty to be one of a family relationship which was not conducive to learning. A second possible contributing factor was a slight visual difficulty. They recommended that he obtain glasses, since that step seemed to offer possibilities. In addition, the social worker was asked to help the parents to accept their adopted child. The social worker explained to the parents that the child was intelligent and capable of learning. She gave them specific methods for helping him, so that he would learn to read and, in turn, they would be better satisfied with him.

Both the parents and the school were assisted in the handling of this boy. The school agreed to keep him in the same grade and give him work appropriate to his lower reading level. The mother agreed to cease showing visible concern over his reading failure and to discontinue questioning him about his school work. She agreed to stop reading to him, to give him simple, attractive books and to listen to his reading and praise him accordingly. He obtained the glasses and liked them very much, and his parents and teachers agreed that he read better with them.

Three months of following this plan brought reports of improvment in his attitude toward school. His teacher also reported that the boy read better. At that time he transferred to another school, where he had some individual help. One year later, reports showed no academic problem, even though he was still unstable and a behavior problem.

A summary of the evaluation of the case follows:

Anomalies Found by by Individual Examiners	Factors Considered Important by the Group	Probable Causes
Family maladjustments	Family maladjustments	Family maladjustments
Slight visual difficulty	Slight visual difficulty	Visual difficulty

CASE 3

This attractive girl was just fourteen years old when she was first seen, and at that time she was unable to read more than a few words.

On the New Binet test this girl showed average general intelligence. She ranked superior on nonverbal tests. Her meaning vocabu-

lary seemed adequate as measured by the vocabulary section of the
Binet test, which rated her at the superior adult level. In oral reading
she rated at the beginning of Grade I level; in silent reading she
ranked about Grade III.

Visual examination indicated the need for a very small correction
of about 1 diopter of plus. Orthoptic exercises were also advised.

The neurologist diagnosed the girl as a case of alexia and said that
her achievement in reading would probably never go beyond Grade
IV.

The social worker felt that undue family pressure had been exerted on this girl. An example of the effect of pressure was her stated
interests in history and nature study. Material simplified and given
to her in these fields elicited no enthusiasm on her part. She finally
admitted that she hated them and only said she liked them because
her father insisted they were the interests of any "lady." They were
his interests, too, and she had been deprived of play with other children to go on long field trips alone with her father.

GROUP EVALUATION

In this group conference, attention was concentrated on the girl's
social maladjustment, visual difficulty, and alexia. The neurologist
agreed that nothing except good training in reading could help the
girl if she were a true case of alexia; and he doubted that she would
ever progress beyond the fourth-grade reading level, even under the
most favorable circumstances. With this as a challenge, the committee decided to give the girl all available help as quickly as possible.

Attention was directed to the family problem and their pressure
on her to learn to read. It was recommended that she be placed in
the Orthogenic School at the University of Chicago, where she could
be given concentrated individual help with her reading in an environment where less emotion would be exhibited concerning her
progress. It was also recommended that the social worker see the
parents and help them to understand and accept their daughter's
problems.

The group also believed that, since the visual difficulty might be a
hampering cause of reading failure, she should have glasses and
orthoptic training.

A reconsideration of the case after six months brought out the recommendation that intensive reading training be continued and that even more attention be directed to the parents.

The girl was given individual help and daily training in reading in a small group at the Orthogenic School. She was permitted to read anything in which she evidenced an interest. She was constantly encouraged and made very satisfactory initial progress. She found reading difficult and frequently forgot words, often having to relearn them ten or fifteen times. When one method appeared unsuccessful, others were tried.

After making a good beginning, her progress slowed down until, at about Grade IV, learning reached a plateau. Whether the deceleration was due to a fundamental deficiency called "alexia" or whether not enough was known to be able to teach this girl to read with her handicaps could not be decided. The family relationships had not been fundamentally changed during the period and probably continued to exert a retarding influence.

A summary of the evaluation follows:

Anomalies Found by Individual Examiners	Factors Considered Important by the Group	Probable Causes
Family relations	Family relationships	Alexia
Alexia	Visual difficulty	Family relations
Visual difficulty	Inappropriate reading training	
Inappropriate reading training		

CASE 4

This lad was nine and one-half years old and unable to read, although his intelligence score gave him a reading expectancy of Grade V.

Examinations indicated that the boy needed a small visual correction, which could be supplied by glasses. It was questionable, however, whether the visual difficulty was a primary cause of failure to learn to read.

The boy was very thin and pale and was diagnosed as a case of malnutrition by the pediatrist. The mother explained that he had always been a feeding problem; and, at the time of the examination,

she stated that he had a very small stomach, which made it necessary for him to eat six tiny meals each day instead of three ordinary
ones. He complained of indigestion following the eating of any foods
he disliked. An X-ray of the stomach, however, did not bear out the
previous diagnosis of stomach deformity, and the pediatrist recommended normal feedings.

The boy's basal metabolic rate was − 20, but the fasting blood
cholesterol was within the normal range. The endocrinologist believed that, in spite of the low basal metabolic rate, the boy had no
abnormal endocrine symptoms.

The social worker felt that the family makeup was a very important influence on this boy's adjustment. He had been adopted when
he was an infant, and the father had died at about the time that the
boy entered school. He was one of four adopted children, having a
foster-sister of the same age who had a good command of language
and who was definitely a successful reader. Any comparisons of the
boy with his sister were to her advantage, except in handwork, where
he excelled. He had a shop in his basement and gradually withdrew
from the "sister-dominated" social contacts to shop solitude. At the
time he came in for examination, he prided himself on being the
worst reader in the family, and he was almost smug when he said he
had been tutored in reading without having learned a thing. The
tutoring had been done by an untrained person who had used reading
materials at the third- or fourth-grade level when the boy lacked a
primer sight-vocabulary.

GROUP EVALUATION

The conference centered attention on the home situation and family relationships as being the most probable cause of the reading
failure. It was also decided that malnutrition was a result of the
mother's handling of this boy and was not a cause of reading failure.

The visual difficulty was considered a possible hampering cause of
inability to learn to read; hence glasses were recommended.

The group recommended that the boy be placed in the Orthogenic
School and that he be trained to eat like other children. It was further suggested that an effort be made to improve his social adjustment. By separating him from his sister, so that no comparisons
could be made, it was felt that his tension concerning reading might

be reduced. In the meantime, he was to be given concentrated help with reading, with special methods adapted to his needs.

TREATMENT

This boy was placed in the school as recommended. He spent two school years of nine months each there and improved markedly in all areas. He gained weight, and evidences of malnutrition disappeared. He became well adjusted socially and even a leader in a selected group. When he was admitted as a member of the University Elementary School gymnasium class, he adjusted himself successfully.

His reading improved so that he ranked at the upper fourth-grade level on standardized tests of reading and read social science material of upper fifth-grade difficulty. In the reading of arithmetic problems, his scores were equal to that of a middle sixth-grader. These gains were considered satisfactory.

A summary of the evaluation follows:

Anomalies Found by Individual Examiners	Factors Considered Important by the Group	Probable Causes
Family relationships	Family relationships	Family relationships
Visual difficulty	Visual difficulty	Visual difficulty
Malnutrition		

CASE 5

This boy was nine years old when he was first examined, and his mother had sought help because her son was unable to read. He had been in school almost three years and was capable in many ways.

INDIVIDUAL FINDINGS

The boy had general intelligence adequate enough to read at the level of the first part of Grade IV, but he actually made a grade score in reading of 1.2. After three years in school, his achievement in reading was equal to only two months of growth.

Further study showed that the boy had suffered a skull fracture, with considerable concussion, at the age of five years. Since the injury was on the left side, approximately in the area of the reading center, the neurologist believed it might be the cause of his failure in reading. An air-encephalogram was made and showed considerable damage and scar tissue in the area corresponding to the external damage. The neurologist predicted that this boy might never learn to read and that, if he did learn, he would require much more concentrated help than the average learner.

The speech specialist found a speech defect which he called "dyslalia." He did not believe this difficulty was a cause of reading failure, since the boy could be readily understood. He suspected that a common cause existed for the speech and reading difficulties.

The pediatrist found that this boy was 14 per cent underweight and that his hemoglobin was 85 per cent of normal. From the examination records he concluded that the boy was somewhat undernourished, although he doubted that the deficiency was sufficiently severe to interfere with the boy's school progress, especially since he had learned arithmetic.

The social worker found that the boy's parents had separated several times. The mother had been working for four years to support the children, and the father had not been heard from during that time. The boy had an older brother, who had nearly lost his sight because of cataracts and had undergone an operation on one eye. All this attention to the older brother might well have caused the younger boy to feel neglected so that he could not easily concentrate on learning. In the third place, this boy was terribly worried about the financial status of the family. His mother had discussed all such worries with him. This was the first case examined by the group in which the psychiatrist felt that there was an emotional basis for reading failure.

GROUP EVALUATION

At the conference of specialists, major attention was focused on the boy's emotional maladjustment, the family situation, and the brain injury. The speech difficulty was not considered a cause of reading failure, and the possible malnutrition was believed to be a symptom of the child's emotional reaction to family poverty.

In discussing treatment, the psychiatrist felt that, since the father was not available and the family's financial status could not be changed, direct psychiatric therapy to help the boy solve his conflicts was desirable. Concurrent with this, he recommended help in reading, since the boy had a strong drive for achievement. It was believed that even a limited amount of success might improve his attitude. The neurologist reported that nothing could be done to change the brain damage, but intensive training might help another brain center to function for the one partially destroyed.

TREATMENT

A trained tutor approached reading indirectly through games, in order to make it possible for the boy to experience some success from the beginning. In six weeks, he improved one-half year in reading and thereby gained confidence.

The psychiatrist saw the boy at regular intervals and helped him to understand and accept his family problems. He was encouraged with the boy's progress and expressed the belief that the prognosis was much better than when he first saw him.

Unfortunately, after six weeks of tutoring, the boy's mother died, and the father, learning of the situation, came for the children and took them to another community. All later attempts to contact them failed. In this case we can only assume, on the basis of six weeks of tutoring and the resultant gains, that this boy's progress would have continued.

A summary of the evaluation follows:

Anomalies Found by Individual Examiners	Factors Considered Important by the Group	Probable Causes
Brain injury	Emotional maladjustment	Family problems
Speech difficulty	Family problems	Emotional maladjustment
Malnutrition (?)	Brain injury	
Emotional maladjustment		
Family problems		

CASE 6

This ten-and-a-half-year-old boy came for examination from a neighboring state because, although he had reached Grade IV, he was still unable to read as well as he should for his age. His five older sisters had been good students, so his whole family was distressed about his reading and agreed that he should be sent to the University of Chicago Clinics for guidance.

INDIVIDUAL FINDINGS

Examinations showed the boy to have average intelligence on the Binet test and better than average on a performance test. His expected achievement on this basis was the middle of Grade V, but actually he could read only second-grade material slowly and with considerable effort. He really tried very hard to learn but became fatigued quickly when doing near-point work and often actually fell asleep.

The visual examination yielded no evidences of need for glasses, but orthoptic training was definitely recommended, since the fatigue evidenced when reading was believed to be due to inappropriate reactions of the two eyes simultaneously.

The endocrinologist felt that thyroid feeding was desirable, since the boy tired easily, was 20 per cent overweight, and was inactive, always cold, and lacked broad interests.

The psychiatrist felt that the boy was emotionally maladjusted. He had always been overprotected by his mother and sisters, so that he had never developed any initiative of his own. They had always read to him before he failed in school the first year; and when they suddenly ceased reading to him, he felt the loss very keenly. The school had told the parents that he was just lazy and had asked their assistance in helping him. They began by paying him each week for certain things he had learned. All sorts of bribery were resorted to unsuccessfully. Then they began to remove privileges as a punishment. One privilege after another was withdrawn. When his new bicycle was chained to the dining-room table until he learned to read, it is not surprising that he rebelled. He became sullen, uncooperative, and openly denounced school. All these experiences were sufficient to create an attitude of boredom toward learning to read, and he blamed reading failure for all his troubles.

GROUP EVALUATION

At the conference, the ophthalmologist, the endocrinologist, and the psychiatrist each presented evidence of possible causes of the boy's failure to learn to read. The group decided that double vision at reading distance would interfere with reading and recommended that training to overcome this defect be given first. At the same time, intensive help with reading was recommended. If there was no improvement in the length of time he could work at the near-point and no improvement in reading after three months, the group agreed that the endocrinologist should prescribe medication. As a last resort, direct psychiatric therapy was recommended.

TREATMENT

During the month while examinations were being completed, the boy continued to be unable to work for more than a few minutes at anything presented at reading distance. As the orthoptic treatment proceeded, his ability to concentrate at the reading distance improved, with a resultant gain in reading. By the time the orthoptic training was completed, reading progress was sufficiently satisfactory that no change in procedure was recommended. Progress continued until, by the end of one year of training, he was ready to enter Grade VI in the public school.

Coincident with improvement in reading came a better social adjustment to other children. Furthermore, emotional problems decreased in number as well as in intensity. The psychiatrist found him confident, relaxed, pleasant, and perfectly co-operative at the end of the year of training. He believed that no direct psychiatric therapy was indicated and that the emotional problem had been a result of reading failure. No endocrine therapy was introduced until after the remedial-reading training was completed. It was recommended at that time, because the endocrinologist believed it would be helpful to the boy's health and general reactions. The effect of this treatment on subsequent reading progress was not ascertained.

A summary of the evaluation follows:

Anomalies Found by Individual Examiners	Factors Considered Important by the Group	Probable Causes
Visual difficulty	Visual difficulty	Visual difficulty
Mild hypothyroidism	Mild hypothyroidism	
Emotional maladjustment	Emotional maladjustment	

CASE 7

This ten-and-a-half-year-old boy was one of the most seriously retarded readers examined during the study, and, at the same time, he had the greatest number of defects which might inhibit his learning to read.

He was referred for a reading examination by a psychiatrist, who stated that the boy probably would never read in his home because of the great anxiety which the family exhibited toward his failure to learn. The psychiatrist also felt that the boy had little chance in his home school, where he had been branded as mentally deficient. The principal of the school had devoted some time to helping him daily and had said that the boy would "learn a word this morning and forget it by afternoon."

Examinations showed that he had a mental age adequate to read at beginning fourth-grade level but was a nonreader or was unable to score at all on most reading tests. His Binet I.Q. classified him at the lower end of the normal range and indicated that when he had first entered school he had been somewhat immature mentally.

Further study showed that he needed glasses to correct myopia and a high degree of astigmatism. His two eyes did not function together, but the co-operating ophthalmologists felt that they might recondition themselves when he began to wear glasses to make objects appear clearer. Consequently, he was fitted with glasses and examined periodically and found to improve nicely until there was no need for orthoptic training.

This boy was diagnosed by the neurologist as a case of alexia, and the prediction was made that reading gains would be achieved very slowly and laboriously and that he would never read normally.

The speech specialist found no speech difficulty; but, on a test of auditory memory span for sounds, the boy could recall and reproduce only three sounds. This was considered inadequate for his age, and poor memory span was thought to be a possible cause of reading failure.

The basal metabolic rate was −15, and the boy's slow movements and low energy caused the endocrinologist to consider the possibility of an endocrine disturbance.

The psychiatrist agreed with the referring psychiatrist that the boy was emotionally disturbed. He was very shy and withdrawn and would permit other children to bully him. He made no effort to defend himself and would often be found crying quietly when his feelings were hurt or when he was unhappy. He was tense, as evidenced by tics and nail-biting. At times, even though he appeared to be somewhat relaxed, his entire body would stiffen if he were handed a book. His social responses were definitely immature.

The social worker was convinced that tension in the home had left its mark on this boy. The parents were very ambitious for their children, and his younger sister met their fondest expectations. Soon after the boy entered school, it became known throughout the town that he could not learn in school. The parents began to help him evenings, but this step only resulted in parent and child discord, with no progress. His teacher kept him in at recess and noontime and often after school to give him extra help. Unfortunately, the boy thought of this as punishment and was miserable when the teacher tried to give him individual instruction. It was then that the principal decided that he should help, so he tried daily to teach the boy, all to no avail.

GROUP EVALUATION

All possible factors in this case were discussed, and appropriate treatment for each was noted. Many of these difficulties could not be treated or, if they could, would require a long treatment period. The group felt that the boy could not be expected to read when he could not see well, so it was recommended that he be fitted with glasses and be examined at regular intervals by the ophthalmologist to determine if the two eyes were working together. As soon as he appeared to be able to use his eyes satisfactorily for near-point activities, the group felt that intensive reading training should be instituted. Because of his short auditory memory span for sounds, as well as his inability to profit by phonics previously, a visual method of teaching reading was recommended. At the same time, a recommendation was made that he remain at the Orthogenic School at the University of Chicago, where pressure from the family could be relieved.

TREATMENT

Three months of intensive training resulted in very little gain in reading, although there was a great deal of change in the boy's personality. He became more confident, was more inclined to defend himself if the opponent were no larger than himself, and was willing to speak above a whisper. The case was reviewed by the group again, at which time the neurologist reminded those present of his diagnosis of alexia. The group decided that another three months of more concentrated effort should be tried. At the end of that time, the group found it necessary to admit that the boy probably was a case of alexia, complicated by many other factors, and that no means of helping him learn to read seemed adequate. The emotional and social maladjustments had been cleared up. Because no progress had been made in reading, it was concluded that they had little causal relationship to reading failure.

A summary of the evaluation follows:

Anomalies Found by Individual Examiners	Factors Considered Important by the Group	Probable Cause
Visual difficulty	Visual difficulty	Alexia
Neurological difficulty (alexia)	Alexia	Visual difficulty
Inadequate auditory span for sounds	Poor auditory memory span	Poor auditory memory span
Endocrine abnormality	Emotional maladjustment	Immaturity
Emotional maladjustment	Social maladjustment	
Social maladjustment	Immaturity	
Immaturity		

CASE 8

This boy was eleven and one-half years old when he was referred for examination by his tutor, who had worked diligently with him for a couple of years with very little evidence of progress. He was infantile in his interests, reactions, play, and level of adjustment. He was thin and slightly bent forward.

INDIVIDUAL FINDINGS

Examinations showed that the boy was slightly retarded mentally. He had the capacity to do advanced fourth-grade work in reading but he read a first-grade book slowly, laboriously, and with many errors. His motor co-ordination was poor, and he was not able to co-ordinate hand and eye. Writing and drawing were crude and unsteady. He did very poorly on any test requiring speed, since his tempo of adjustment was slow.

The visual examination substantiated a previous finding of the need for lenses to correct an astigmatic error. In addition, the ophthalmologist found the near-point convergence of the two eyes to be inadequate and felt that near-point work would be very hard for this boy without orthoptic training.

The speech specialist described this boy as having dyslalia and dysphonia. His auditory memory span for sounds averaged only $3\frac{1}{2}$, and this weakness was considered a possible cause for his speech defect and his failure to learn to read, especially by a phonetic approach. There was some hearing loss at almost all frequencies, which, however, was not deemed sufficient by the otolaryngologist to cause speech or reading inadequacies.

A general physical examination by the pediatrist showed the boy to be 7 per cent underweight, with 95 per cent hemoglobin and very poor posture. Malnutrition was questioned. The examiner noted a heart murmur after exercise.

Both the pediatrist and the endocrinologist found undescended testes. The basal metabolic rate was −11, which was considered within the normal range. The endocrinologist recommended treatment to cause the testes to descend and suggested surgery if the treatment was not effective.

The psychiatrist found the boy emotionally immature. He was extremely withdrawn and had retreated from attempts to teach him. He was certain that he was "very dumb" and accepted his failure. The psychiatrist felt that the boy had had little opportunity to develop in many ways, as he had been supervised in play constantly and had never been permitted even to go to school alone. He had been ill a great deal and consequently had been overprotected.

The social worker reported that the home was not conducive to this boy's best growth and development. The father, who was very intelligent, was deaf and for this reason had served as a poor speech model. The father had educated himself and was very ambitious for his children, constantly pushing the boy to the point where he had developed feelings of extreme inferiority. The mother had been very ill following the birth of the child, so he had spent his early years with relatives. Following the death of the mother, a housekeeper cared for the children. The housekeeper definitely preferred the attractive, capable sister who was older. By virtue of the abnormal pattern of the family, the boy felt insecure and reacted in an infantile fashion.

GROUP EVALUATION

The group of examiners decided to correct several difficulties at once, if possible, since the boy was so old that progress should not be retarded too long by experimentation. Therefore, they suggested that his glasses be changed; that he have orthoptic training; that he have training to correct the speech difficulty; that the pediatrist learn whether something more could be done for his health; that the social worker attempt to improve family attitudes; and that the boy be placed in a special school, where concentrated attention could be given to his reading, as well as guidance in all school subjects and social adjustments. The relative importance of these factors could not be determined in this case.

TREATMENT

All the foregoing recommendations were carried out. The visual corrections appeared to make it easier for him to work at close range without fatigue. The speech specialist saw him regularly; but, although the boy gave maximum co-operation, there was only minimal improvement in speech and none in auditory memory span for sounds.

The family pediatrist had been aware of the physical difficulties and had tried to correct them without success. He felt that part of the boy's apparent malnutrition was a family characteristic, since both parents had been very tall and thin. He agreed that treatment should be instituted for the undescended testes but felt that it would have no bearing on the boy's personality or learning.

The social worker saw the father regularly, had several interviews with the housekeeper, and saw the older sister a number of times. She was able to bring about an improved attitude toward the boy and his problems, so that he was permitted freedom in making decisions and in going to school, store, etc., alone. He was even given family responsibilities in accordance with his age.

Pressure for achievement was reduced, and the family began to accept him as he was rather than as they had hoped he would be.

The Orthogenic School's program under the direction of an understanding but enthusiastic teacher helped this boy gradually to overcome shyness and withdrawal, so that he gained some confidence in learning to read. By the end of the first year he had begun to play with other boys, would talk to those he knew, and had finished first- and second-grade reading assignments. He spent the summer in a play group, returning to the school in the autumn, where gains continued the second year. By the end of that year, he rated at the beginning of fifth grade on reading tests.

Unfortunately, a serious heart disorder developed, and the boy was forced to spend one year in bed. During this period, it seemed desirable to omit all teaching, so he lost a great deal. After he had returned to the school for eight months, during which a careful guard was kept on his physical well-being, he showed evidence of good progress in reading. He continued to be slow, in harmony with his entire tempo of adjustment; hence there was no reason why he should make an exception and read rapidly. By this time he read voluntarily at home and was well informed on current events. He was enthusiastic about school and especially happy at home since the sister was away at college.

A summary of the evaluation follows:

Anomalies Found by Individual Examiners	Factors Considered Important by the Group	Probable Causes
Visual difficulty	Visual difficulty	Visual difficulty
Speech and auditory memory defects	Speech defects	Family relationships
General physical condition	General physical condition	Immaturity at school entrance
Possible endocrine imbalance	Endocrine imbalance	
Emotional maladjustment	Family relationships	
Family relationships	Immaturity	
Immaturity		

CASE 9

This six-year-old boy had finished one year of school without learning to read. His older sister was an excellent student, but, although he expended great effort, he learned little. In fact, at the end of his first school year, he recognized only three words. His father, who was a student at the University of Chicago, sought expert advice on the kind of attitude the family should take toward the boy's failure. He also wished to know the reasons for failure and if anything could be done to remedy the situation.

INDIVIDUAL FINDINGS

The results of intelligence tests indicated that this boy's reading capacity should be high second grade. His interest in reading was very keen, and he was a careful observer for his age.

He had dyslalia combined with a southern accent, which had been acquired when the family had lived in the South. His auditory memory span for sounds was poor. Unfortunately, he had been taught reading by the phonic method. The speech specialist believed the boy's speech defects could be corrected.

His basal metabolic rate was −18, but he was not diagnosed as a typical hypothyroid case. He was considered a borderline case, and no treatment was recommended unless further symptoms were identified.

The social worker found that the two children were living with the father, who cared for them while he attended the university. His wife taught school several hundred miles away and spent only vacations with the children. Both of these children were quite independent and capable of taking responsibility beyond their years. They were well adjusted to children, were popular, and exerted leadership.

GROUP EVALUATION

Only two factors in this case received major attention. The speech difficulty at the boy's age was unusual, and treatment was advised. The group also felt that training in reading suitable to his capacities should be tried, with special emphasis on the visual approach. The family relationships could not be changed at the time of examination; but the group felt that, if there were no improvement in reading in two or three months, the social worker should attempt to help the family work out a better solution of their problem.

TREATMENT

The speech specialist saw the boy twice each week for treatment and was able to clear up that difficulty in about six weeks. A trained tutor then combined a visual approach to reading with training in auditory discrimination. Progress was evident from the first day; and after two months the boy entered Grade II, where he was very successful. Reports since have been excellent.

A summary of the evaluation follows:

Anomalies Found by Individual Examiners	Factors Considered Important by the Group	Probable Causes
Speech and memory-span defects	Speech defect	School methods
Possible endocrine disturbance	School methods	
Social problems		
School methods		

CASE 10

This thirteen-year-old boy was a nonreader and was the most serious case examined in this study, as judged by the extent of retardation in proportion to capacity. He was referred for examination because attempts by other agencies to teach him had met with failure. The adjustment teacher in his public school had worked with him individually, and he had been taught by private tutors.

The examination indicated that he was penalized by poor motor co-ordination and had such a severe speech defect that the examiner was not always sure of his responses. He had a mental age at the lower end of the normal range. Although his capacity to read, as determined by the mental test, was beginning seventh grade, he could recognize only ten words; sometimes he said he was not sure of them. From the case history it appeared that at one time he had been able to score as high as second grade on reading tests. However, when intensive coaching was stopped, he lost the ability to recognize words he had once known.

The ophthalmologist found him to be a case of alternating internal strabismus. In addition, he needed correction for hyperopia and astigmatism. When attempting to read, the boy would look first with one eye, then with the other. During this process he would lose his place, skip lines, and even re-read. The specialist felt that visual problems alone were sufficient to have caused a serious reading impairment.

The speech specialist found that the boy had a serious dyslalia, such that it was almost impossible to understand his ordinary conversation. It was peculiar that the first sounds of his words were usually accurate, but the endings of the word trailed off indistinguishably. The speech specialist also found an auditory memory span of only $2\frac{1}{2}$ sounds, which he considered the cause of the speech defect. Further, he found complete inability to discriminate consonants in words, as evidenced by the fact that he did no better than chance in identifying words that were alike, or differed by only one consonant sound. The speech specialist predicted that learning to read would be extremely difficult with these impairments.

The pediatrist and endocrinologist found undescended testes and recommended that treatment be instituted to cause them to descend.

The psychiatrist found that the boy was badly adjusted emotionally. He reported that the boy had a schizoid personality and might become psychotic. At this age the boy was still having nocturnal enuresis and occasional diurnal enuresis. He was poorly oriented as to time and space, even evidencing fantastic orientation. He had many mannerisms and some compulsive behavior. His conversations with the psychiatrist always revealed that he thought he was "dumb," that he was concerned over his father's death, that he wanted to take care of his mother and, above everything else, wanted to learn to read. He was sensitive about the crossing of his eyes and thought he would look much better if they were straight. Emotionally, this boy reacted like a child of about six years. He would cry when injured, call for an adult if younger children teased him, and pout. Direct psychiatric therapy was recommended.

The social worker found the mother to be very intelligent and co-operative but also greatly disturbed. Her husband had died recently, leaving no insurance, and she was unprepared to go to work. It was essential that she find employment, and she was disturbed about this situation. The mother reported that the boy had grieved a great deal over the death of his father and had become more disturbed recently.

GROUP EVALUATION

In conference, the group attempted to evaluate the factors causing reading failure but decided that they were so interrelated that all resources should be pooled in an effort to relieve this boy's personality problems and help him to learn to read. They recommended that he secure glasses in an attempt to straighten his eyes; speech training was also suggested for the improvement of his talking, together with an attempt to increase his auditory memory span for sounds. Intensive psychiatric therapy was advised to help him become better adjusted emotionally. The social worker was instructed to give as much help to the mother as possible, so that she could become more secure financially and better adjusted to her new type of life. Since the boy would not fit into any ordinary school situation, the group suggested that he be placed in the Orthogenic School and be given other activities than reading until he was physiologically ready to begin the task of learning to read.

TREATMENT

These recommendations were carried out for a period of two months. The ophthalmologist found no visual improvement; hence he recommended surgery to straighten the eyes. This was done, and the cosmetic effect was excellent; but subsequent orthoptic training did not bring about fusion of the visual images of the two eyes.

Speech training yielded no improvement in speaking, although there was a definite improvement in auditory discrimination. Psychiatric help during this early period was of no apparent value. The social worker helped the mother to become stabilized, so that she obtained a job out of town. The boy was then placed in a foster-home and continued to attend the Orthogenic School as a day pupil. After all preliminary steps had been taken, the boy was considered to be as ready for training in reading as the group could make him.

Reading training was instituted with great care because the prognosis was poor. During the year and a half of concentrated reading help, a gain of only about two grades in reading achievement was made. During this period, remedial methods were changed so that visual, auditory, and kinaesthetic approaches were used in turn. Finally, combinations of these methods were tried.

At the end of two years of training, this boy showed a marked gain in emotional and social adjustment. He felt much more confident because of his straightened eyes but was still discouraged because he was not understood. He continued to wear glasses but still had monocular vision. Reading improvement had been so slow that the group decided to discontinue concentrated reading help. The boy was excused from school and placed on a farm, where he made a good adjustment.

A summary of the evaluation follows:

Anomalies Found by Individual Examiners	Factors Considered Important by the Group	Probable Causes
Visual difficulty	Visual difficulty	Visual difficulty
Speech and discrimination defects	Speech defect	Speech defect
Endocrine disturbance (?)	Emotional maladjustment	Emotional maladjustment
Emotional maladjustment		
Social maladjustment		

CASE II

This boy was thirteen and a half years old when he reported for examination. His Binet mental age was 13 years and 2 months. He could not be measured on the performance tests because he did better than the 15-6 norm on the Arthur Point Scale of Performance. On the Chicago Non-verbal Test his mental age was 16-7. These findings gave him a reading expectancy of at least Grade VIII. In oral reading, his grade score was 3.4, and his silent reading was scored at the end of Grade V.

INDIVIDUAL FINDINGS

Examinations revealed no findings of importance. Each specialist felt that he could find no possible cause for reading failure.

GROUP EVALUATION

The group reviewed the case briefly and decided that the problem was largely an educational one, unhampered by physical defects. The teachers in the small school which he attended knew only one method of teaching reading, and this method apparently did not meet his needs. The report of .50 diopter of hyperopia and very slight astigmatism by the ophthalmologist led the group to recommend glasses.

TREATMENT

It was necessary for the boy to return to the small school in the town where his parents lived. Explicit directions for remedial reading were sent to the teacher. At the end of the school year the teacher reported that the reading had improved about a grade that year. The boy was still retarded, however. He did not return to the clinic for examination and could not be followed further. He disliked the glasses and did not wear them.

A summary of the evaluation follows:

Anomalies Found by Individual Examiners	Factors Considered Important by the Group	Probable Causes
Slight visual difficulty	Slight visual difficulty	Inadequacy in teaching
Inadequacy in teaching	Inadequacy in teaching	

CASE 12

This ten-year-old lad was referred to the clinic because he had not learned to read and his school felt that there must be some physical cause for his inability. His parents brought him from some distance in an effort to determine the causes of his failure to learn and to get advice as to remedial procedures.

INDIVIDUAL FINDINGS

He had a Binet mental age of 11-4, although he did less well on a performance test. However, he should have been able to read as well as an average child in Grade V. Actually, he read at about the level of the middle of Grade I, rating lower in oral-reading and a little higher on silent-reading tests, where he could guess at some of the answers.

The visual examination showed hyperopia of +3.00 diopters in one eye and +2.00 in the other, each complicated by astigmatism. The glasses he was wearing when he came for examination were not considered adequate for near-point work; hence it was recommended that they be changed. The ophthalmologist did not think the change would increase his reading proficiency.

The neurologist diagnosed the case as alexia and was of the opinion that it was inherited, since the father had also exhibited much difficulty in learning to read.

No hearing loss was found, but he had difficulty in pronouncing some letters. The speech specialist described this condition as dyslalia. However, it was not sufficient to impede his learning to read.

The pediatrist found that the boy was 17 per cent underweight and found evidence of malnutrition. No other difficulties were found.

GROUP EVALUATION

The group conference concentrated on alexia in this case, since it appeared to be the only factor found by the group which might cause such serious reading retardation. The malnutrition could scarcely cause reading failure without causing difficulty in arithmetic, too, and the slight change in glasses did not appear to be significant. The dyslalia might have interfered with his oral reading but could not have hindered his learning to read silently.

TREATMENT

The boy's glasses were changed, and, at the suggestion of the pediatrician, his diet was improved. Definite suggestions were given concerning methods of teaching the boy, but he was not treated by a remedial-reading expert. According to reports, he made very little progress in reading. He did not return for a second checkup.

A summary of the evaluation of this case follows:

Anomalies Found by Individual Examiners	Factors Considered Important by the Group	Probable Causes
Visual difficulty	Alexia	Alexia
Dyslalia	Inappropriate teaching methods	Inappropriate teaching methods
Alexia		
Inappropriate teaching methods		

CASE 13

This twelve-year-old boy was referred for examination because he was retarded in his school subjects and was having difficulty in learning to read. The family explained that he had been absent from school a great deal because of illness.

INDIVIDUAL FINDINGS

The boy had average intelligence according to the Binet test and a mental age of 15-5 according to the Arthur Point Scale. His reading expectancy was beginning seventh grade, and he read at the beginning third-grade level. He also exhibited excessive errors in reading, which characterized him as a seriously retarded reader. The boy had no visual problem. He came from a maladjusted family, in which the father had a mediocre job while the mother had a very good one. The older brother was a great joy to the mother because of his good health and excellent scholarship. She identified this older boy with herself and made it evident that she thought the younger son would probably always be "dumb" like his father.

The otolaryngologist found a chronic pharangitis, adenoid remnant, and deflected septum, which might account for a slight hearing loss at most frequencies. It was considered unimportant as a cause of reading failure. The speech specialist found an 80 per cent score on auditory discrimination of vowels.

The pediatrist found an organic heart lesion, and the family physician reported that this was due to rheumatic fever. This heart condition had kept the boy from attending school for two and one-half years and had been one of the factors in retarding his reading progress.

GROUP EVALUATION

In conference the specialists agreed that the most important factor contributing to this boy's failure to progress in reading was the heart lesion, which had been the cause of long periods of absence from school. Attention was directed also to the mother's maladjustment and rejection of the boy. The group believed that this might contribute to his failure to learn to read and suggested that the social worker attempt some interpretation to the mother of the boy's poor school work. The Orthogenic School was suggested for an intensive program to improve his reading and arithmetic.

TREATMENT

This boy attended the Orthogenic School as a day pupil for three months. During this period he was given intensive training in reading. At the same time the social worker saw the mother frequently but obtained little co-operation in changing her basic attitude of rejection toward the boy. She described the mother as verbally responsive but "stand-offish."

During the three months a marked change was noted in the boy's attitude toward failure and work habits. He ceased daydreaming, began to learn words when they were first exposed, became confident that he could learn, and made noticeable progress. According to the Standardized Oral Reading Paragraphs, he gained from grade 2.8 to grade 4.2. According to the Stanford Achievement Tests, he gained in reading from grade 3.2 to grade 5.1. He was placed in Grade VA in the public school and with some special help made a satisfactory academic adjustment.

A summary of the evaluation of this case follows:

Anomalies Found by Individual Examiners	Factors Considered Important by the Group	Probable Causes
School absence due to physical condition	School absence due to physical condition	School absence due to physical condition
Maladjusted home environment	Maladjusted home environment	Maladjusted home environment
Questionable auditory discrimination		

CASE 14

This attractive boy was about eleven years old when he was first examined. He was brought to the clinic because he was failing in a special division of Grade V at school. With a mental age of 13-4 on the Binet test, his reading expectancy was Grade VIII. On the Arthur Performance test he had a mental age of 15-6. He had attended a good school and had been tutored, but gains were slight. In fact, his reading scores varied between second and third grade.

INDIVIDUAL FINDINGS

The boy was considered well adjusted socially and emotionally. No auditory or neurological problems were found, and his general physical condition was good. The ophthalmologist found 0.75 and 1.00 diopters of hyperopia in the right and left eyes, respectively, and glasses were prescribed for reading only. The ophthalmologist doubted that this slight correction would be of value to his reading. Since there was some complaint of discomfort when reading with the glasses and because the ductions were not very large, orthoptic exercises were prescribed.

The endocrinologist found a basal metabolism of −14 and fasting blood cholesterol of 233. These and other facts led him to advise thyroid therapy. He felt that the resulting extra energy might be a help to the boy in learning to read.

No speech defect was found, although there was a history of speech difficulty. The score on the auditory discrimination test was questionable; however, the speech specialist felt that some difficulty in sound discrimination might have contributed to his failure to learn to read.

GROUP EVALUATION

The attention of the group centered on plans for intensive help with reading for the boy, taking into account his slight difficulty in auditory discrimination. They agreed that thyroid therapy should be instituted under the direction of the endocrinologist. They advised that glasses be used for reading and that orthoptic exercises be carried out.

TREATMENT

The boy attended the Orthogenic School for nine months, where he was given intensive drill in word recognition, with emphasis on configuration of words. He was also given training in auditory discrimination, so that he could make use of auditory clues in attacking new words.

Concurrently, the boy began to take thyroid. He became more active physically and appeared to fatigue less easily. Glasses were obtained and used for reading, and orthoptic exercises were given regularly. The teacher noticed a gain in the length of time he could continue doing near-point work as the orthoptic training was given.

At the end of nine months the boy made a grade score of 8.0 on the paragraph section of the Stanford Achievement Test and a grade score above 7.0 on the social science section of the test, which required reading. On the Standardized Oral Reading Paragraphs, he made a grade score of 6.9. He was placed in Grade VII in his own school, where he continued to make good academic progress and social adjustment.

A summary of the evaluation follows:

Anomalies Found by Individual Examiners	Factors Considered Important by the Group	Probable Causes
Endocrine deficiency	Endocrine deficiency	Endocrine deficiency
Inadequate auditory discrimination	Inadequate auditory discrimination	Visual difficulty
Visual difficulty	Visual difficulty	Inadequate auditory discrimination

CASE 15

This girl was almost eight years old when she was first examined. According to intelligence-test records, her grade score should have been 2.5, but actually she had difficulty reading a pre-primer and was able to recognize only about twenty words. The statement should be added that she had spent two years in school and had been tutored during one year and a summer vacation.

INDIVIDUAL FINDINGS

The visual examination revealed a relatively high amount of astigmatic error, and glasses were recommended for constant wear.

The social worker felt that the home situation was difficult. The father was a chemist and had been ill since shortly after the girl was born, and as a result was very nervous and irritable. He created a scene with her at the table every evening. In order to avoid this difficulty, the mother had her eat earlier. An older sister was very attractive and successful, both socially and academically. She was definitely favored by the father. The mother appeared irresponsible, as evidenced by the fact that the child was frequently late for school because the mother did not get up early enough or did not get her ready in time.

The school history in this case is particularly enlightening. During the first year of school the pediatrician advised the parents to have her go to school only during the mornings, because of excessive fatigue by noon. She missed so much of the first-grade work that she had made little progress by the end of the school year. The school advised the parents to have her tutored during the summer to let her go on to the next grade. She was tutored but made little gain. The parents tried to help her, but this resulted in emotional upsets for both the child and the parents. The father and sister annoyed her, constantly taunting her. The father, particularly, felt that she could learn but just would not apply herself.

During the year before she came for examination, she was helped three times each week by the school psychologist or by the principal of the school, but with very little progress.

There were no other findings in this case.

GROUP EVALUATION

The attention of the group was called particularly to the child's problems at home and to the influence that home conditions probably had on her tardiness and inability to apply herself when she was at school. Thus the group felt that the primary cause of failure was the family situation, the school absence being a secondary cause.

The visual problem seemed to be of considerable importance, since both astigmatism and inability to use the two eyes effectively together at reading distance were factors which would make reading unpleasant or impossible.

The group recommended that the girl be placed in the Orthogenic School for treatment and that the social worker attempt to help the family in their adjustment to her. They also recommended glasses and orthoptic treatment.

TREATMENT

The parents arranged for the orthoptic training but did not keep appointments. They obtained the glasses, which the girl disliked and did not wear, probably because her parents thought them unbecoming to her. She was sent to a private school, where she was tutored in reading but made little progress. The school recommended that the girl attend the Orthogenic School because they felt that she would never learn unless she was removed from her home environment. She had been at the school only one month when this report was prepared. At that time she was learning about five new words each day. They often had to be retaught, however, and she was very fearful of making errors.

A summary of the evaluation follows:

Anomalies Found by Individual Examiners	Factors Considered Important by the Group	Probable Causes
Family problems	Family problems	Family problems
School absence	School absence	School absence
Visual difficulties	Visual difficulties	Visual difficulties

CASE 16

This quiet, retiring, disinterested boy was eight years and seven months old when he was examined. He was referred by a remedial-reading tutor, who had been very successful in treating a number of poor readers but had achieved no success with this boy. She asked for a full examination to determine the causes of failure and for recommendations for treatment. His mother brought him in for examination after the necessary arrangements had been made by the tutor.

INDIVIDUAL FINDINGS

The social worker felt that the boy did not wish to grow up. He was the youngest of four children and had always been treated as a baby. The mother had read to him every night, and, as a result, he did not wish to learn to read himself. After the first day in Grade I at school, he had to be taken to and from school by his mother. All her attempts to send him to school alone had been unsuccessful. The first-grade teacher's comment that he was an "adorable big baby" but could do nothing for himself was indicative of the boy's immaturity and infantile reactions. Later it was learned that two of the other children had had reading difficulties. The mother had provided remedial help and had assisted them through high school. Both failed to make progress in college.

The psychiatrist found the boy withdrawn and unresponsive verbally and, at the same time, physically tense and very anxious. He was afraid of every new situation and was unable to do any work without individual attention. The psychiatrist believed that pressure at home and at school had led the boy to feel very inferior. The boy excused his failure as due to a visual difficulty, but he expressed no confidence that his reading would improve after the visual difficulty was corrected. When observed with other children, he was always withdrawn, unable to make friends, and easily bullied by another boy.

The ophthalmologist found that he needed a +1.50 correction in each eye and suggested glasses for reading. He was also found to have a convergence insufficiency at reading distance; hence orthoptic training was recommended.

The endocrinologist reported a basal metabolic rate of −21 and felt that the boy should have thyroid therapy. He also believed that some of the boy's lack of energy for play might be attributed to the endocrine deficiency, which might also have affected his learning in school.

The boy had a Binet mental age one year above his chronological age. He was, therefore, sufficiently intelligent to have made average school progress, or better.

GROUP EVALUATION

The group centered their discussion around the four factors mentioned above, namely, emotional, social, visual, and endocrine disturbances. They suggested that the visual difficulty be corrected first and that the boy continue with the same tutor to see what progress could be made. If progress was not satisfactory, the group felt that the boy should enter the Orthogenic School, where psychiatric therapy and removal from the home environment might operate concurrently to improve reading progress. Finally, thyroid therapy should be given.

TREATMENT

Glasses were obtained and worn unwillingly. Orthoptic training was carried out but not to completion because the orthoptist could not secure the desired results and felt that the endocrine disturbance was a deterrent to orthoptic progress. With permission from the group, thyroid therapy was instituted; then the orthoptic treatment was readily completed. The boy remained at home and was tutored one year with no gain in reading achievement.

He then entered the Orthogenic School as a day pupil rather than as a boarder, as suggested. Psychiatric help was given and intensive reading help was provided. In nine months, he had attained a grade score of 3.1 on a standardized silent-reading test and a grade score of 4.0 in arithmetic. After three months of vacation, some loss in reading ability was noted. A year of additional training brought him to the place where he could read at the fourth-grade level, although his reading was still slow and labored. Perhaps that was to be expected, since all his reactions were slow.

A summary of the evaluation follows:

Anomalies Found by Individual Examiners	Factors Considered Important by the Group	Probable Causes
Overprotection at home	Visual difficulty	Emotional maladjustment
Emotional maladjustment	Thyroid deficiency	Overprotection at home
Visual difficulty	Overprotection at home	Possible visual and endocrine difficulties
Thyroid deficiency	Emotional maladjustment	

CASE 17

This boy was nine years old at the time he was referred for examination. He had been taught by a very good tutor for a year, but without satisfactory results. The tutor had suggested the examination as a means of securing help in understanding the boy's difficulty.

INDIVIDUAL FINDINGS

The boy had a mental age of 10-2 on the Revised Binet, Form L, and of 11-7 on the Arthur Point Scale. In spite of this standing, he belittled every answer he gave and constantly insisted that he was too "dumb" ever to learn to read. During observation he tried to break into the examiner's office to find out his I.Q., because he still believed he was "dumb" and the examiner was "kidding" him. On the basis of the tests given, it appeared that he had the capacity to read at fifth-grade level at least. However, the reading tests showed that he was still at the first- or second-grade level in reading and that he was three to four grades retarded.

The visual examination resulted in a recommendation that glasses be worn for near work to correct 1.50 diopters of hyperopia. Orthoptic training was recommended for convergence insufficiency.

The boy showed from 34 to 58 decibels hearing loss in one ear, depending on the frequency tested. This had been caused by a mastoid operation and could not be improved by treatment.

The psychiatrist reported a very serious emotional condition. He found the boy tense and fearful and unable to face a new or difficult situation. He was very irritable and subject to violent temper tantrums when slightly frustrated. During the interview, he was verbally withdrawn. His voice was pitched high, indicating tension. He had many mannerisms and was so hyperactive that he could not sit still, even when interested in something. He often walked around awhile before he could relax. He had occasional nocturnal enuresis and habitually stayed awake at night. He was unable to get along with other children, especially younger ones, whom he mistreated when they did not do what he demanded. In the schoolroom he annoyed every child and insisted on the teacher's undivided attention. He had rebelled more violently against his failure than had any child examined by the psychiatrist.

No other abnormalities were found by the examiners.

GROUP EVALUATION

The group centered attention on his visual and auditory problems as possible causes of reading failure when he first entered school and they emphasized the serious emotional problem present at the time of examination, which would impair any remedial work. The extent of the emotional problem originally was not known. The group felt that he should get glasses and receive orthoptic training, as well as psychiatric help. These steps were to be carried forward simultaneously so that every possible handicap could be removed. The group believed that, even under the most favorable conditions, the boy would be faced with grave problems in learning because of his unfortunate attitude. They recommended placement in the Orthogenic School.

TREATMENT

Glasses were obtained and worn for reading. The recommendations were not followed otherwise, and the same tutor worked with him full days for a school year. At the end of that time he was retested and had made no gains. Again the group recommended placement in the Orthogenic School, where he could have orthoptic training and psychiatric help. This time the parents accepted the suggestion, and he was placed in the school, and treatment was begun along the two lines suggested above. He responded well to the orthoptic training and seemed to be able to concentrate longer at reading distance. The psychiatric treatment advanced very slowly; gradually, however, intensive reading training got under way. For a couple of months progress was slow; but, as he gained confidence in his teacher and in himself, he improved at a more rapid rate.

At the end of nine months' treatment, the boy rated fourth grade in reading and fifth grade in arithmetic. He had learned to co-operate and to be responsible; and his work habits were also markedly improved. He returned to the Orthogenic School as a day pupil for a second school year. During that time it was necessary to reinstate orthoptic training, but it was completed readily. At the end of the school year, he was placed in the seventh grade of a good private school near his home. Later reports indicated satisfactory academic and personal adjustment.

A summary of the evaluation follows:

Anomalies Found by Individual Examiners	Factors Considered Important by the Group	Probable Causes
Visual difficulty	Emotional maladjustment	Emotional maladjustment
Slight hearing loss	Visual difficulty	Visual difficulty
Emotional maladjustment	Slight hearing loss	

CASE 18

This fourteen-year-old girl was referred for a reading examination because she was in Grade VIA but could read only at first-grade level. An examination by the school had led to the belief that she was sufficiently intelligent to learn to read.

INDIVIDUAL FINDINGS

This girl had a Binet I.Q. of 100, and she was probably more intelligent than average, for she was penalized by her inability to read on a number of parts of the Binet test. She rated higher than average on a performance test. Since her reading expectancy was Grade IX, she was about eight grades retarded.

The ophthalmologist did not suggest glasses, although a small amount of hyperopia was found. Neither was orthoptic training advised, although the question of visual difficulty at reading distance arose several times because of the girl's blinking and the irregular pattern of her eye-movements.

The social worker felt that a very large contribution to the girl's difficulty lay in the home. The girl had congenitally dislocated hips, and at the age of three years had had two serious operations and was in a cast from nine to eleven months. A sister, sixteen months younger, was sent away while this girl convalesced. When the sister returned, the girl resented her. She had to learn to walk again and resented her sister's superiority and any attention given her by the parents.

During her illness the mother read to her, and, according to the mother, the child learned to read. The progress made was doubtless due to memorization; at least the girl relied largely on memorization in reading when she entered school. No difficulty was reported until early in Grade II, when the teacher told the parents that the girl could not do her school work. She was not required to repeat the grade, but she began to be exceedingly self-conscious and disturbed. She would cry out in her sleep and was subject to nocturnal enuresis. She later repeated a grade, and her younger sister caught up with her. The latter was bright and attractive and an excellent pupil. This girl was unhappy and began to withdraw from social situations. As she did so, she became extremely shy and was unable to meet people.

The psychiatrist felt that this girl was definitely neurotic because of failure. From the history of her case, he concluded that part of the problem had been present before school failure began. He found her to be tense, afraid to recite, self-conscious, and without rationalization. She also showed many tics. He felt that the emotional condition was a partial cause of reading failure but that this condition had been intensified by the continuous frustration of failure in learning. He also believed that the pressure exerted by the parents had created, on the part of the girl, a sense of being rejected.

No other difficulties were found.

GROUP EVALUATION

The attention of the group was focused on her emotional problem. They recommended that she be treated at the Orthogenic School, where psychiatric therapy could accompany attempts at training in reading.

At the same time, the group recommended that the social worker attempt to help the parents understand and accept this girl with her limitations. If progress in reading took place, she would be more acceptable to them.

TREATMENT

The girl entered the Orthogenic School as a day pupil. She was very happy and became relaxed and was able to co-operate nicely. Her relationship with the teacher was fairly well established, and some gains had been made when she was removed from the school. She had attended the school for about three months and had made nearly one year's progress in reading.

A summary of the evaluation follows:

Anomalies Found by Individual Examiners	Factors Considered Important by the Group	Probable Causes
Emotional maladjustment	Emotional maladjustment	Emotional maladjustment
Sibling rivalry and desire to be the baby	Sibling rivalry	Sibling rivalry
Incorrect concept of reading		
Possible visual difficulty		

CASE 19

This ten-and-a-half-year-old boy was referred for examination after he had failed to learn to read during two years of regular school and two more years in a special room. With a mental age of 10-2 on the Binet test and 13-3 on the Arthur Point Scale, he had the capacity to read at fifth-grade level. Actually, he recognized no words and could not read a pre-primer.

INDIVIDUAL FINDINGS

The ophthalmologist found that the boy was slightly hyperopic but recommended no lenses, since he believed this defect too minor to affect reading. There was no evidence of endocrine, neurological, or general physical difficulties.

The social worker found the mother somewhat distractible and physically under par. She had two older children by a previous marriage and three sons by the present union. This boy was the middle one of these three and was constantly compared unfavorably to the younger brother, who was said to have learned to talk at the same time as this child. The mother reported that this child had always resented the younger brother and had been mean to him. Besides this, the oldest son by the first marriage was quiet and successful and devoted much time to his mother. From this relationship she gained much satisfaction and was frank to admit that she gained little from this boy. He had temper tantrums, was unreliable to send on errands, and brought shame on the family by being put in a class with dull children at school. On the other hand, the mother was overprotective of the boy and would not allow him to go far alone; nor would she permit him to go to the beach during the summer, although all the other children went regularly. She said he was so easily sunburned that she was afraid to let him go alone.

The boy gave evidence of insecurity, as he was afraid of every new situation. When he was first seen by the psychiatrist, however, he exhibited no strong feeling and no emotional concomitants. The decision was reached that he was not a psychiatric problem.

The speech specialist found the boy's auditory memory span for sounds to be only 3 letters, which is questionably low; his auditory discrimination for vowels is only 70 per cent, which is also questionable. He felt that these weaknesses might be causes of failure to learn to read by the phonetic approach, which had been used previously.

There was loss of hearing in the left ear, ranging from 25 to 42 decibels, depending on the frequency. The hearing in the other ear was within the normal range, except at the lower and the upper frequencies. The nose and throat specialist believed the boy's deficient hearing was caused by a remnant of adenoid tissue, which was infected, causing an otitis media. He recommended that the adenoid tissue be removed. He also believed the hearing loss might be a factor causing lowered scores on the auditory discrimination test.

GROUP EVALUATIONS

The attention of the group focused on the boy's social problem and its possible emotional effect on him, even though he showed little of this to the psychiatrist. They advised some treatment of the mother to help her understand her son. They also agreed that an adenoidectomy should be performed and that afterward his hearing and auditory discrimination should be retested. Because of the severity of the auditory problem, they advised that the boy attend the Orthogenic School, where he would be taught to read with emphasis on methods other than phonetic.

TREATMENT

He entered the Orthogenic School, where it was noted that he was unable to adjust to other children because he was shy and felt inadequate. He was afraid of every new situation and unable to work unless the teacher stood beside him giving him constant encouragement.

The social worker saw the mother once each week and attempted to change her attitude toward the boy. As the boy progressed, the mother accepted him better. At the same time, his behavior and adjustment at home improved. After nine months at the school, with the treatment centered on family and emotional adjustment and on building confidence in the boy, he made grade scores on standardized tests in reading between 3.8 and 4.1.

About the time that school was out, the adenoidectomy was performed, and the hearing became normal in about two months. However, the boy had learned to read before the hearing had improved. This does not eliminate the possibility that difficulty in hearing may have been a factor in a larger classroom, where the teacher could spend little time individually with him.

A summary of the evaluation follows:

Anomalies Found by Individual Examiners	Factors Considered Important by the Group	Probable Causes
Family problems	Family problems	Emotional maladjustment
Hearing loss	Possible emotional maladjustment	Family problems
Inadequate auditory discrimination	Hearing and discrimination difficulty	Probable hearing loss

CASE 20

This boy was nine years and eight months old when he was first referred by a psychologist in his home town because he had not learned to read. Other problems were present, such as retreat from social relationships because other boys laughed at him and called him "dumb."

INDIVIDUAL FINDINGS

The ophthalmologist found that the boy could use about a +1 lens on each eye and suggested that glasses be used for reading only. In addition, there was convergence insufficiency, for which orthoptic training was recommended.

The psychiatrist found the boy to be emotionally rigid and unaffected by pleasant or unpleasant stimuli. He smiled constantly, whether he should be pleased or not. When permitted a choice, he refused; but, if urged to choose, he always chose the easiest thing he could acquire. He showed little or no interest in anything and would sit in school as long as required but would do nothing except look blankly into space. Any teaching efforts were wasted because they did not register with this upset lad.

The social worker learned that this boy's grandmother had been the dominant person in his life. His mother was an only child who was not strong physically, so the grandmother had taken most of the responsibility for the boy's care and training. The fact that he exhibited many allergies and asthma had caused the whole family to be overanxious about him and had kept the boy from many normal social contacts. When he had a mastoid operation, followed by a brain abscess, at the age of five years, the doctors suggested a warmer climate during the winter, so the grandmother had spent three winters with him in warmer places. All this had interrupted his school training.

At the age of six, when he first entered school, he exhibited a definite tendency toward persistent reversals in reading and writing. The teacher associated this with left-handedness and suggested that he would "outgrow" this tendency as he learned to read. The latter was not accomplished, however, and the reversal tendency still persisted. He had been tutored privately every winter but had failed to learn to read even under expert guidance. The parents and grandmother had also tried helping him with reading. This abnormal school experience and the constant direction of a dominant grandmother were considered factors in his school failure.

In spite of previous suppositions that the brain abscess might have affected his reading capacity, the neurologist found no abnormality and believed that this boy should learn to read when other hampering defects were cleared up. No other difficulties than those mentioned above were found.

GROUP EVALUATION

The group felt that the important factors were the emotional rigidity and the unusual family situation, which may have been a factor in creating the emotional reactions. They felt that he should be removed from the family environment and placed under psychiatric treatment. For these reasons the Orthogenic School was recommended.

The visual problem was also emphasized, inasmuch as the boy appeared to have difficulty in concentrating, especially at reading distance. The group agreed that he should get glasses for reading and that orthoptic training should be provided before reading treatment was started.

TREATMENT

The boy entered the Orthogenic School, but only as a day pupil, since the grandmother insisted on living near the school and having him at night. This insistence created an additional social problem; hence it was necessary for the social worker to see the grandmother frequently and help her to accept the boy's problem and to co-operate with the school in treatment.

Glasses were obtained, and the boy was given orthoptic treatment three times a week. Daily exercises were carried on at the school as directed by the ophthalmologist.

In the meantime, psychiatric treatment was given to help the boy change to a pattern of emotional response which would permit him to react in a manner appropriate to the stimulus.

Work in reading followed the initial psychiatric treatment as soon as possible. Because of the tendency to move his eyes from right to left when reading and also to reproduce forms upside down, he was given concentrated training in visual perception and memory for forms, followed by the introduction of words in the same manner.

Reading was acquired at a satisfactory rate. After nine months of training he made grade scores ranging from 4-0 to 4-4 in reading and social studies, as measured by the Metropolitan Achievement Test. He was out of school three months and then returned for another nine months. At the end of that time he made grade scores of 5-8 in reading and proportionate gains in other subjects. He then entered the public school in his own town, where he was reported later to be making satisfactory gains.

While his progress in reading was gratifying, perhaps the emotional and social changes in this boy were of greater significance. He became an accepted member of the play group and independent in relation to his grandmother. He was flexible emotionally and learned to make choices and express likes and dislikes. He developed broad interests appropriate to his age.

A summary of the evaluation follows:

Anomalies Found by Individual Examiners	Factors Considered Important by the Group	Probable Causes
Family maladjustment	Family maladjustment	Family maladjustment
Emotional maladjustment	Emotional maladjustment	Emotional maladjustment
Visual difficulty	Visual difficulty	Visual difficulty

CASE 21

This attractive boy was eleven years and eight months old when he was first referred for examination by the neurologist, who had seen him in the clinic and felt that he was a case of alexia. His mental age of 12-11 was adequate for reading at the sixth-grade level at least, yet he was reading only at high second- or third-grade level, depending on the type of test used.

INDIVIDUAL FINDINGS

The ophthalmologist found compound hyperopic astigmatism of such a slight degree that it was believed unrelated to reading failure.

Although his auditory acuity was normal, the boy had a short auditory memory span for sounds, accompanied by a mild dyslalia. The latter was considered unrelated to reading, but the former may have been a factor if phonics was used as a method of teaching reading. No report on this could be obtained.

The neurologist thought he was a case of alexia, since he had failed to learn to read in a group where others had made normal progress. The neurologist also felt that this might be hereditary, since the father had failed in school and had never been able to finish eighth grade, although he was successful mechanically.

The social worker reported that the family was living on a mother's pension, since the father had died when the boy was in Grade III. The father had been a drunkard and had frequently beaten his children, and the mother had found it necessary to protect them constantly. She seemed to understand the three children well. A sister was older and a brother younger than this boy. Both the sister and the mother had tried to help him in school work, especially in reading and spelling.

Although the boy seemed very well adjusted emotionally and socially when he was examined by the psychiatrist, there was some question as to the effect on the child's school progress of the family maladjustment noted above.

During the reading diagnosis, it was learned that the boy read about 20 per cent faster with his right eye alone than with both eyes and, at the same time, made over four times as many errors with both eyes as with the right, which was the preferred one. This, too, gave weight to the significance of his visual difficulty.

GROUP EVALUATION

Emphasis was placed on the fact that the neurologist believed the boy to be a case of alexia who, therefore, would not learn to read beyond Grade IV. For experimental purposes, the group felt that the boy should be placed in the Orthogenic School as a day pupil and that reading should be taught by the sight method to eliminate the effect of his short auditory memory span for sounds. It was suggested that the ophthalmologist see if there was any way of explaining the difficulty in reading with both eyes as compared to reading with the right eye alone.

The group also agreed with the psychiatrist's suggestion that perhaps, with prolonged contact with the boy, the real influence of the father could be discovered.

TREATMENT

The boy attended the Orthogenic School for four months. During this time he was rechecked by the ophthalmologist, who recommended no treatment. The psychiatrist found no emotional problems. He felt that the father's death might have been a shock to the boy but that this fact was unrelated to reading failure.

The boy responded nicely to visual presentations of words, and during the four months, he improved in his reading from high second grade to the end of fourth grade. On the Chicago Reading Test he made a grade score of 4.9, except in rate of reading, in which his score was 3.4. He then entered Grade VI in the public school. With the help of the adjustment teacher, he continued to improve in reading and at the end of that school year was making average progress.

The evidence secured indicated that the boy's progress was different from that of a case of alexia. Rather, it appeared that his short auditory memory span for sounds had handicapped his learning by the phonetic method. It seemed probable that adapting the method of teaching reading, as well as providing individualized help, were the factors most important to his academic gains.

A summary of the evaluation follows:

Anomalies Found by Individual Examiners	Factors Considered Important by the Group	Probable Causes
Mild visual difficulty	Alexia	Short auditory memory span for sounds
Short auditory memory span for sounds	Possible visual difficulty	Inappropriate teaching methods
Alexia	Short auditory memory span	
Family maladjustments	Family maladjustments	
Inappropriate teaching methods	Inappropriate teaching methods	

CASE 22

This boy was about fourteen years old and had a reading expectancy grade of Grade VIII. On various reading tests he made grade scores between 3.2 and 3.9 and was retarded over four grades in reading.

INDIVIDUAL FINDINGS

The neurologist diagnosed this boy's case as one of alexia. The otolaryngologist found a mild conduction deafness, with a loss in auditory acuity at the upper and lower frequencies. He did not believe that this loss was sufficient to cause the boy's reading disability, although he wondered whether it might have been worse when he was younger and, if so, might have been related originally to reading failure. There were no other physical findings which merited consideration in this case.

The social worker learned that the boy was an only child and that the parents believed he was spoiled. However, his reactions did not seem to agree with their belief, since he was co-operative and persistent in attempts to learn. The mother admitted that she had been able to go to school very little because her father had lived a transient life and she had finished only Grade IV.

A report of an examination two years earlier showed that the boy had an articulatory defect, which was not described, and indicated that his hearing was "dull," although the amount of loss was not known. At that time the boy reported to the examiner that he "heard noises in his ears." He was considered a third-grade reader then. It was recommended that he sit in the front of the room, although the teacher could not carry it out because he was too tall. Nothing further could be learned about the effect of the hearing loss.

GROUP EVALUATION

The attention of the group was focused on the diagnosis of alexia and the possible effect of the hearing loss. Since the latter was not then sufficiently important to impede learning to read, no treatment was indicated. The group recommended that he come to the Orthogenic School for intensive remedial-reading training.

TREATMENT

The parents were unwilling to send the boy to the school for treatment and said that their real purpose in having the examination was to find out the cause of the defect so that recommendations could be sent to his school.

Detailed recommendations were prepared, and he was asked to return for another checkup in three months. At that time, tests showed that he had made from three to five months' progress in various types of reading. Further recommendations were made, but he did not return for further tests, as advised. Instead, at the end of the school year his mother mailed his report card from school. It indicated that he was promoted from Grade VIIA to Grade VIIIB with special commendation for industry and that his grades had all come up to satisfactory marks. Even though this evidence was not objective, it appeared questionable that the boy suffered from alexia.

A summary of the evaluation follows:

Anomalies Found by Individual Examiners	Factors Considered Important by the Group	Probable Causes
Alexia	Alexia	Hearing loss which may have been greater
Slight loss in auditory acuity	Lowered auditory acuity	Possibly a degree of alexia

The last eight cases referred to in chapter x will not be reported here, since careful evaluation of their deficiencies was not possible. Six of them, referred by a public school, were examined in an at-

tempt to identify causes of reading failure but without the thorough
diagnosis and remedial treatment given to the cases reported in this
chapter. The last two children examined (Cases 29 and 30) were
carefully studied, but the parents desired recommendations which
could be carried out quickly and were not willing to engage in the
lengthy program of training suggested.

The chief conclusions reached by the specialists in the study of the
twenty-two cases will now be summarized, with special reference to
causes of serious retardation in reading.

EVALUATION OF CAUSES OF SERIOUS READING RETARDATION

In order to summarize briefly the facts available concerning the
causes of reading difficulty exhibited by the twenty-two children
reported in this chapter, Figure 2 was prepared. It presents profiles
of individual cases. Column 1 shows profiles for anomalies found by
each examiner in each case. The profile of Case 3, for example, shows
that the ophthalmologist found a visual difficulty, the social worker
found a social problem in the home, the neurologist found a neurological difficulty, and the reading technician secured evidence that
methods of teaching reading had not been properly adapted to this
child's needs.

Column 2 shows which of the anomalies were considered by the
group of specialists at their conference to be important as possible
causes of reading deficiency in individual cases. Pursuing Case 3
again, it should be noted that the same anomalies are stressed in
Column 2 as in Column 1, except that the neurological difficulty was
not considered important as a possible cause.

Column 3 shows the probable causes of reading failure for each
case as they were evaluated after remedial treatment. Following
Case 3 again, attention is called to the fact that the visual difficulty
and the lack of adaptation of teaching methods of reading appeared
to be less important as causes of reading failure than the group of
specialists had at first believed. The anomalies found by the social
worker and the neurologist appeared to be the causes for reading
failure in this case.

In a similar manner, all the twenty-two cases presented in this
chapter are summarized. Careful examination of these individual
profiles justify several important conclusions.

First, the cases present different constellations of anomalies which might cause reading failure. This is true of the findings of individual examiners, of the group judgments as to possible causes, and of the anomalies agreed upon as probable causes of reading failure.

Considering the anomalies reported by individual examiners, Cases 3, 7, and 8 serve as illustrations of diverse patterns. A visual difficulty was found in each of the three cases, but only two cases gave definite evidence of social maladjustments, while in the third, social maladjustment was questioned; two of the cases presented emotional problems, while the third did not; one presented a speech problem, in a second case this factor was questionable, and in a third there was no speech problem; endocrine disturbances were reported as questionable in two cases but were absent in the third; a neurological difficulty was found in two cases, but not in the third; no general physical difficulties were found in two of these cases; no auditory difficulty was found in any of them; and, finally, there was evidence of inadequate adjustment of methods of teaching reading in one case but no evidence of this in the other two.

Similar comparison of anomalies found by individual examiners for any group of cases in this study will show significant variation in the pattern of anomalies reported. Likewise, anomalies considered important by the group, and again those considered to be probable causes of reading failure, differed considerably. In three instances (Cases 4, 8, and 15) the anomalies considered as probable causes by the group were the same, namely, visual difficulties and social problems. In two instances (Cases 9 and 11) the probable causes were previous use of inappropriate teaching methods. Likewise, in Cases 5 and 18, social and emotional maladjustments were considered the probable causes of reading failure. Other cases showed different combinations of probable causes. The anomalies considered as causes in the final evaluation were somewhat more alike than the anomalies reported by individual examiners. This fact suggests that certain factors exerted a greater influence in retarding reading progress than did others.

Second, the deficiencies found by individual examiners were not all recognized as causes of failure to learn to read after remedial treatment had been given. For example, the individual examiners reported in Case 6 a slight visual difficulty, which was considered

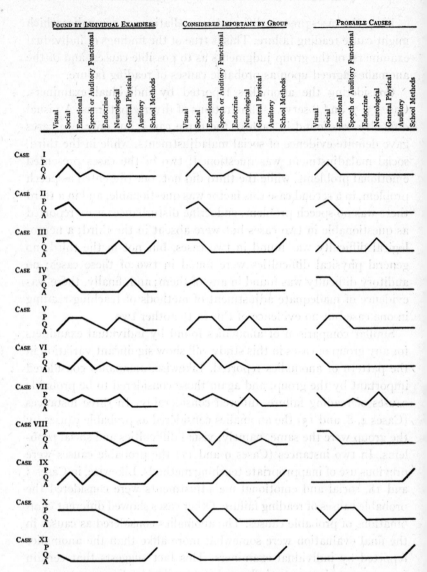

FIG. 2.—Individual case profiles. *P*, present as a cause of reading failure. *Q*, Questionable as a cause of reading failure. *A*, absent as a cause of reading failure.

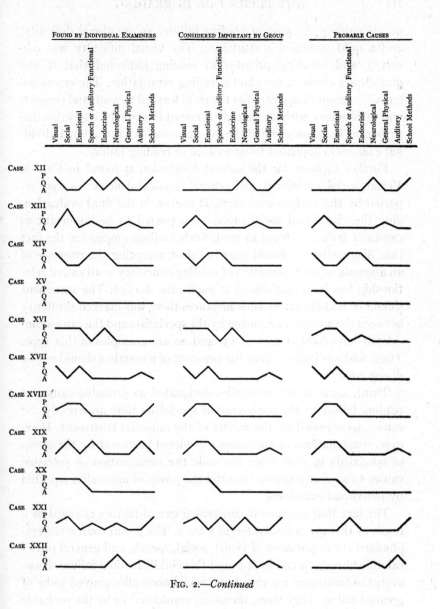

		FOUND BY INDIVIDUAL EXAMINERS									CONSIDERED IMPORTANT BY GROUP									PROBABLE CAUSES								
		Visual	Social	Emotional	Speech or Auditory Functional	Endocrine	Neurological	General Physical	Auditory	School Methods	Visual	Social	Emotional	Speech or Auditory Functional	Endocrine	Neurological	General Physical	Auditory	School Methods	Visual	Social	Emotional	Speech or Auditory Functional	Endocrine	Neurological	General Physical	Auditory	School Methods
CASE	XII																												
CASE	XIII																												
CASE	XIV																												
CASE	XV																												
CASE	XVI																												
CASE	XVII																												
CASE	XVIII																												
CASE	XIX																												
CASE	XX																												
CASE	XXI																												
CASE	XXII																												

FIG. 2.—*Continued*

213

questionable as a cause of reading failure, an emotional difficulty, and a mild endocrine disturbance. The visual difficulty was corrected, and resulting progress in reading indicated that it was doubtless a cause of the child's reading retardation. The emotional maladjustment disappeared as the child learned to read, and progress was satisfactory without therapy directed toward the endocrine disturbance. Thus, only one of the three anomalies reported by individual examiners appeared to be a cause of reading failure.

Further support for the second conclusion is found in Case 8. Visual, social, emotional, and general physical deficiencies were reported by the various examiners. However, in the final evaluation, only the visual and social problems appeared to be important as causes of failure to learn to read. Such findings emphasize the fact that diagnosticians should guard against accepting the presence of an anomaly as an explanation of reading deficiency until causal relationship has been established in each case studied. The statement should be added that in some instances there was marked similarity between the anomalies reported by the specialists and the causes considered important. Cases 2, 15, and 20 are examples of this type. These findings indicate that the presence of anomalies should not be disregarded.

Third, some of the anomalies designated as probable causes of reading failure at the conference of specialists were apparently not causes, as revealed by the results of the remedial treatment. However, constellations of anomalies considered pertinent by the group of specialists in conference resemble the combination of probable causes to a greater extent than did the group of anomalies reported by individual examiners.

The fact that judgments concerning causal factors changed as a result of therapy is illustrated in Case 8. The group conference emphasized the importance of visual, social, speech, and general physical difficulties as possible causes of this child's reading failure. However, the treatment for visual and social anomalies proved to be of greatest value. They were, therefore, considered to be the probable causes of reading failure in this case. A second example is Case 21. Visual, social, speech, or functional auditory and neurological difficulties and inappropriate use of methods of teaching reading were considered possible contributing causes of reading failure. After treatment had been given, the probable causes selected were the functional auditory inadequacy and inappropriate adaptation of teaching methods to the needs of this pupil.

In a number of instances the constellation of anomalies selected by the group of specialists was identical with, or very similar to, those which later proved to be the probable causes. For example, in Cases 2, 10, and 12 the two evaluations were identical. In a number of others, such as Cases 1 and 11, the two evaluations were very similar.

Fourth, social and visual anomalies ranked high as causes of reading retardation, as shown by their frequency in the case profiles. Emotional, speech, or auditory functional and neurological difficulties, as well as inappropriate school methods, were frequently found to be probable causes of failure in reading. Endocrine disturbances, general physical difficulties, and lack of auditory acuity were found infrequently to be causes of reading deficiency.

To summarize the anomalies considered important by the group for each of the twenty-two cases, Table 24 has been constructed. The cases are presented in descending order of severity. The number of hampering defects which the group of specialists considered important is recorded in the last column. A total of 23 such defects were identified for the seven most severely retarded and 18 for the seven least severely retarded. This difference indicates that more severely retarded readers exhibited more anomalies considered significant by the group of specialists than did the least severely retarded cases. The number of cases in which each anomaly was considered important appear at the bottom of the table, and the percentage of cases in which each anomaly was considered operative appears in the last line of Table 24.

The anomalies considered to be probable causes for each of the 22 cases are summarized in Table 25. Comparing the number of probable causes operative in the 7 most severely retarded, which was 16, with the 13 found in the 7 least severely retarded, it is evident that the number of factors that operated as causes among those most seriously retarded was, on the average, greater than for the least severely retarded cases. The difference, however, is not very large.

At the bottom of this table the frequency of occurrence of each probable cause is recorded and the percentage of cases in which each cause was considered operative.

The relative importance of certain anomalies as causal factors is represented graphically by Figure 3, which shows the percentage of

TABLE 24

ANOMALIES CONSIDERED IMPORTANT BY THE GROUP FOR EACH CASE

Case Number	Monroe Reading Index	Visual Difficulty	Neurological Difficulty	Auditory Difficulty	Speech or Discrimination Difficulty	General Physical Difficulty	Endocrine Disturbance	Emotional Maladjustment	Social Problems	School Methods	Number of Probable Hampering Factors
10	15	Yes	No	No	Yes	No	No	Yes	No	No	3
7	30	Yes	Yes	No	?	No	No	Yes	?	No	5
18	31	No	No	No	No	No	No	Yes	Yes	No	2
5	33	No	Yes	No	No	No	No	Yes	Yes	No	3
2	35	?	No	No	No	No	No	No	Yes	No	2
8	41	Yes	No	No	Yes	?	?	No	Yes	No	5
3	42	Yes	No	No	No	No	No	No	Yes	Yes	3
21	44	?	Yes	No	Yes	No	No	No	Yes	Yes	5
14	45	Yes	No	No	Yes	No	Yes	No	No	No	3
17	45	Yes	No	?	No	No	No	Yes	No	No	3
4	47	?	No	No	No	No	No	No	Yes	No	2
19	48	No	No	?	No	No	No	Yes	Yes	No	3
12	49	No	Yes	No	No	No	No	No	No	Yes	2
22	50	No	Yes	?	No	No	No	No	No	No	2
13	52	No	No	No	No	?	No	No	Yes	No	2
9	53	No	No	No	Yes	No	No	No	No	Yes	2
6	55	Yes	No	No	No	No	?	Yes	No	No	3
20	56	Yes	No	No	No	No	No	Yes	Yes	No	3
15	60	Yes	No	No	No	No	No	No	Yes	No	2
11	63	?	No	No	No	No	No	No	No	Yes	2
1	65	No	No	No	No	No	?	No	Yes	No	2
16	68	Yes	No	No	No	No	Yes	Yes	Yes	No	4
Number of anomalies	.....	14	5	3	6	2	5	9	14	5	.....
Per cent of Yes and ?	.....	63.6	22.7	13.6	27.3	9.1	22.7	40.9	63.6	22.7	.....

the 22 cases in which each anomaly was (1) recorded by individual examiners, (2) considered a possible cause by the group, and (3) considered a probable cause after remedial treatment. The percentages for the last two columns were secured from Tables 24 and 25, respectively. Examination of these three columns shows that, with one

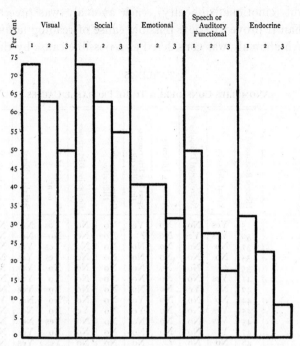

FIG. 3.—Evaluation of anomalies. *1*, percentage of 22 cases in which individual examiners found the anomaly. *2*, percentage of 22 cases in which the group considered the anomaly to be a possible cause. *3*, percentage of 22 cases in which the anomaly was recorded as a probable cause.

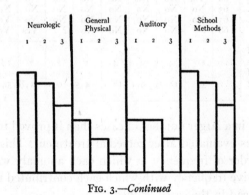

FIG. 3.—*Continued*

exception (emotional difficulty), each anomaly was present more often than it proved to be a possible cause of reading failure. Further, each anomaly was considered as a possible cause by the group

TABLE 25

ANOMALIES CONSIDERED TO BE PROBABLE CAUSES

Case Number	Monroe Reading Index	Visual Difficulty	Neurological Difficulty	Auditory Difficulty	Speech or Discrimination Difficulty	General Physical Difficulty	Endocrine Disturbance	Emotional Maladjustment	Social Problems	School Methods	Number of Probable Hampering Factors
10	15	Yes	No	No	Yes	No	No	Yes	No	No	3
7	30	Yes	Yes	No	?	No	No	No	No	No	3
18	31	No	No	No	No	No	No	Yes	Yes	No	2
5	33	No	No	No	No	No	No	Yes	Yes	No	2
2	35	?	No	No	No	No	No	No	Yes	No	2
8	41	Yes	No	No	No	No	No	No	Yes	No	2
3	42	No	Yes	No	No	No	No	No	Yes	No	2
21	44	No	No	No	Yes	No	No	No	No	Yes	2
14	45	Yes	No	No	Yes	No	Yes	No	No	No	3
17	45	Yes	No	No	No	No	No	Yes	No	No	2
4	47	Yes	No	No	No	No	No	No	Yes	No	2
19	48	No	No	?	No	No	No	Yes	Yes	No	3
12	49	No	Yes	No	No	No	No	No	No	Yes	2
22	50	No	?	Yes	No	No	No	No	No	No	2
13	52	No	No	No	No	?	No	No	Yes	No	2
9	53	No	No	No	No	No	No	No	No	Yes	1
6	55	Yes	No	No	No	No	No	No	No	No	1
20	56	Yes	No	No	No	No	No	Yes	Yes	No	3
15	60	Yes	No	No	No	No	No	No	Yes	No	2
11	63	No	No	No	No	No	No	No	No	Yes	1
1	65	No	No	No	No	No	No	No	Yes	No	1
16	68	?	No	No	No	No	?	Yes	Yes	No	4
Number of anomalies	.....	11	4	2	4	1	2	7	12	4	.....
Per cent of Yes and ?	.....	50	18.1	9.1	18.1	4.5	9.1	31.8	54.5	18.1	.....

of specialists in a larger number of cases than it proved to be a probable cause, as evaluated after remedial treatment. This figure also shows the order of frequency in which each anomaly was reported and the relative frequency with which each contributed to failure in learning to read in the cases studied.

CHAPTER XII

SUMMARY, CONCLUSIONS, AND IMPLICATIONS

THE results of this study are very suggestive to anyone interested in poor readers. They are equally valuable to school personnel who wish to prevent reading failure, because preventive measures can be planned intelligently only if causes of difficulty are understood. For the purposes of this investigation, a cause has been defined as an anomaly, which, on the basis of tangible evidence, is responsible for part or all of the reading difficulty exhibited by a pupil. The evidence required was that when the anomaly was corrected or appropriate compensations were made, improvement in reading occurred.

To achieve this aim, three steps were planned. The first was to summarize significant contributions concerning causes of reading retardation presented in the literature and, with the aid of specialists in the allied fields, to evaluate these findings.

The second step was to identify and evaluate the various causal factors in a group of severely retarded readers. To achieve this aim, the services of the following specialists were secured: a social worker, a psychiatrist, a pediatrist, a neurologist, three ophthalmologists, a speech specialist, an otolaryngologist, an endocrinologist, a reading specialist, and the investigator, who acted as psychologist and reading technician. Thirty severely retarded readers with Binet I.Q.'s between 85 and 137 were examined by each of these specialists. Anomalies were identified, and the findings were presented. Following the individual examinations, the specialists met and attempted to evaluate these anomalies and to identify possible causes of reading retardation operating in each case. Finally, an intensive remedial program for twenty-two of the thirty cases was undertaken to secure evidence of the potency of each of these possible causes.

The third step, which was to present significant general conclusions: findings with respect to causal factors, problems meriting further study, and implications of this investigation, is the function of this chapter.

219

MAJOR CONCLUSIONS

The experimental data have been studied, first, in relation to the number and percentage of cases exhibiting various anomalies and causes of reading retardation. Second, they have been treated in terms of the patterns of anomalies and causes exhibited by each individual case. Several important conclusions have been reached.

First, the pupils who were seriously retarded in reading also exhibited numerous anomalies. In fact, those most seriously retarded evidenced the greatest number of anomalies, whereas those least retarded presented fewest.

There are two possible interpretations of this finding. The first is that difficulty in reading may be a part of the general deviation from the normal pattern. For example, the child most seriously retarded (Case 10) deviated from normal expectancy in six areas besides reading, while one of the least seriously retarded (Case 1) deviated from normal in only two areas besides reading. The second possible interpretation is that the large number of anomalies act as hampering defects, thus causing more severe reading retardation. Conclusions presented later which have a direct bearing on this issue favor the first interpretation.

Second, when the group of specialists attempted to evaluate the anomalies for each child, it appeared, on the basis of all evidence available, that certain of the anomalies had no direct relationship to the reading deficiency. This conclusion was based on the data presented in chapter xi. For example, visual anomalies were found in 73 per cent of the twenty-two cases studied intensively but were considered important as possible causes of reading failure by the specialists in only about 63 per cent of them. Thus, in 10 per cent of the cases, visual difficulties were present but not considered to be a cause of reading failure.

This conclusion is important because it shows that specialists can readily identify anomalies in isolation, but, when such anomalies are considered in conjunction with all available data on each case examined, the examiners can only conclude that some anomalies are coincidental and are not causes of reading failure. Such an evaluation forms a more refined technique of identifying causes of reading failure than mere examination.

Third, a number of factors that appeared to be possible causes of reading failure, in the opinion of the specialists, did not prove experimentally to be so. Using again the example cited above, the group believed visual difficulties to be one of the causes of reading failure in about 63 per cent of the cases, while, after appropriate treatment, this cause appeared to operate in only 50 per cent of the cases. Consequently, visual difficulties appeared to be causes of reading difficulty in some cases and only coincidental in others.

This finding assumes large significance when evaluating long lists of anomalies reported for poor readers by many investigators. It shows that the mere presence of anomalies does not justify the conclusion that they are causes of reading failure. Such anomalies may be only coincidental or may represent some of the variations from the "normal" of the particular children examined. It follows that great care must be exercised before concluding that any anomaly exhibited by a seriously retarded reader operates as a cause of reading failure.

Fourth, the experimental evidence secured in this study indicated that certain types of anomalies operated as causes more frequently than others. Social, visual, and emotional difficulties appeared most frequently as causes of poor progress or failure in learning to read. Inappropriate school methods, neurological difficulties, and speech or functional auditory difficulties appeared less frequently as causes of deficient reading. Endocrine disturbances, general physical difficulties, and insufficient auditory acuity appeared to be least important, in so far as they contributed infrequently to reading failure among the particular children included in this study. This order of frequency and the probable significance of each as a cause are considerably at variance with the findings of other investigators reported in the literature. The findings relative to causal factors, therefore, merit further consideration.

FINDINGS WITH RESPECT TO CAUSAL FACTORS

The findings relative to each group of factors will now be summarized and compared with the results of previous studies. Such comparisons should aid in identifying some of the distinctive contributions of this study.

SOCIAL FACTORS

Maladjusted homes or poor interfamily relationships were found to be contributing causes in 54.5 per cent of the cases studied. This percentage is definitely higher than any reported in the literature, few other studies having considered more basic and detailed inter-family problems. Preston's[1] investigation, which points out the detrimental effects of unfortunate home relationships among poor readers, probably most nearly approximates the present intensive study of such factors. Ladd's study,[2] on the other hand, empha-sized personal, social, and economic problems, as shown by teachers' ratings and children's responses to various tests.

The relatively high percentage of cases in the present study in which family or home problems proved to be contributing causes of reading failure may be attributed to two facts. First, the inquiries concerning family problems were carried on in this study by particu-larly diligent social workers, who devoted a great deal of time to gaining the confidence of parents and to obtaining more than a superficial history of difficulties and problems. Later, these data were scrutinized carefully in relation to the child's problems. Second, the cases examined were seriously retarded in reading and were ex-amined only at the request of the parents. In this respect the cases were more highly selective than if they had included all seriously retarded readers in a particular school. However, the fact that such home and family interrelationships were associated with reading failure in some of the cases studied emphasizes the importance of greater attention to this particular area when diagnosing cases of reading deficiency.

The unusual significance is not only that organic and emotional problems of the child influence his learning to read but also that problems apparently remote from the school exert considerable influ-ence. They emphasize the importance of the home and of the social environment on the total adjustment of the child. They imply that a stable, wholesome home environment exerts a definite influence on the school progress of the child. Furthermore, such findings show that a child's failure to learn to read may be due to factors far be-yond his own control and, not infrequently, beyond the control of those charged with responsibility for his progress. Unfortunately,

many families are either unaware of the significance of the relationship just considered or are unable to control the conditions that create favorable ones.

VISUAL FINDINGS

Visual anomalies were found in 73 per cent of the twenty-two cases
which were studied fully, but were considered to be contributing
causes of reading failure in only 50 per cent of these cases. This percentage is higher than reported by some examiners but lower than
reported by others. Studies in this area are numerous. In making
comparisons, however, attention should be directed to the fact that
there is no uniformity in the methods used in examining the cases
reported in the literature. Some were tested only on the Snellen
chart, which was shown by this study to be inadequate.[3] Others
were examined by screening tests designed to be general, rather than
specific, measuring devices. Some studies considered only one phase
of the problem, such as visual fields or blind spots, and did not relate
findings to the total visual pattern. In this study each visual factor
was considered and interpreted in terms of all the findings. Furthermore, corrective procedures were administered to determine whether
or not the diagnosis was accurate. Few studies in the literature have
followed this plan of evaluation.

The types of visual difficulties exhibited are of special interest in
view of the recent pointed controversy concerning the relation of
specific visual difficulties to reading deficiency. Glasses were recommended as a corrective procedure for hyperopia in 28 per cent of the
cases in this study. Hyperopic and myopic astigmatism were each
found in 10 per cent of the children. Binocular inco-ordinations of
significance were reported in 48 per cent of the cases. This last figure
is lower than the 90 per cent reported by Selzer[4] and considerably
higher than the 29 per cent reported by Witty and Kopel.[5] Each of
these studies included 100 children; however, the method of examination used in the first was not stated, and the Keystone Visual
Safety Test was used in the second. The visual examinations reported
in the present study were made by ophthalmologists, which may
account for some of the difference in results.

Both refractive errors and binocular inco-ordination were present
in some cases, while in others only one difficulty or the other was
exhibited. Enlarged blind spots and restricted visual fields were re-

ported in no cases, although these defects had been found previously by several investigators. No tests for aniseikonia were available.

Special attention is directed to the findings concerning binocular inco-ordinations. Orthoptic training was recommended for 48 per cent of the cases examined but carried out in only 24 per cent. It was considered helpful in promoting reading growth or in prolonging attention span for activities carried on at close range in all the cases. These findings provide convincing evidence of the value of orthoptic training among reading-disability cases who exhibit binocular inco-ordinations.

It is also noteworthy that neither the Snellen chart nor the Keystone Visual Safety Test was found to be completely accurate in selecting the children whom the ophthalmologist identified as needing visual care, although the latter was more effective than the former. Because of the high percentage of cases in which visual anomalies contributed to reading failure and because of the difficulties involved in identifying them, very careful attention should be given to visual examinations in the diagnosis of poor readers.

The advantage of clear visual impressions has long been recognized as a requisite to reading. This fact undoubtedly accounts for the numerous attempts to identify all interferences with visual impressions. Visual perception, however, involves far more than receiving clear impressions; but the knowledge of this fact has been ignored by many investigators, who have tried to explain reading failure on the basis of peripheral visual interferences. It follows that the full significance of visual difficulties can be appreciated only when studies of peripheral interferences and perception are combined.

Visual perception probably involves many of the higher mental processes and consequently may be associated with intelligence, previous experience, language facility, and bodily well-being. According to this view, most of the causes of reading failure are interrelated, so that the study of one necessitates consideration of others. While it is expedient to isolate them for measurement, the interpretation of such measurements must again consider related factors. It is evident, then, that the full import of visual interferences with reading necessitates a broader study than does one involving only peripheral interferences.

EMOTIONAL FINDINGS

The psychiatrist found significant emotional problems in 41 per cent of the 22 cases studied. However, emotional difficulties were found to be the causes of reading failure in only 32 per cent of them. The percentage of cases showing emotional problems is lower than reported by some investigators. Gates,[6] in particular, stated that about 75 per cent of retarded readers examined by him and his associates exhibited emotional difficulties. However, he believed that the emotional problem was a cause of reading failure in only one-fourth of these cases, or approximately 19 per cent. In the present investigation, however, emotional problems appeared to be a cause in 32 per cent of the cases examined.

A part of the discrepancy between the relative number of cases exhibiting emotional maladjustments in this and other studies may be due to the fact that the definition of emotional maladjustments adopted by the psychiatrist who participated was more rigid than that of the diagnostician in other studies. It may be due also to the fact that the psychiatrist in this study did not require the children to read during his interview with them. Some of the poor readers exhibit emotional problems only when required to read.

Although the literature concerning causes of reading disability contains many references to emotional problems, various reactions of each child have usually not been published. In this study, however, the examination of cases was carried forward by a psychiatrist, who carefully recorded specific reactions of his subjects as shown in chapter x. The reports of these reactions are very valuable both in understanding the cases studied and in suggesting items to look for in further studies of emotional disturbances among poor readers.

Of large importance is the fact that emotional reactions of children may be created by family problems or by attitudes within the home. In this connection, emotional and social factors are so closely related in some cases that they cannot be disentangled. Numerous emotional reactions unfavorable to learning are undoubtedly set up in young children before they enter school. The child who has been insecure at home may be so concerned over gaining security with his teacher and playmates that he cannot devote attention to learning to read. Children with fears and worries are ill fitted for the task of learning any subject matter. However, they are most likely to fail in reading, since it is taught early in the school program.

Unfortunately, emotional difficulties may also develop at school, and in a variety of ways. This study shows, for example, that whenever one child, who had a speech defect (Case 1), was called upon to read orally, his schoolmates were amused by the way he spoke, thus creating, on his part, fear of the reading situation. The teacher of another child reminded him that his sister and brother were her best readers and that she expected him to excel also. An unfavorable attitude toward reading was thus created. Probably no comprehensive list of such experiences has ever been compiled. One reason is that children seldom relate them unless they have a great deal of confidence in the person to whom they are told.

It should be added that emotional reactions may aid in learning to read as much as they may interfere with it. Some children become highly motivated when confronted with failure while others withdraw and are afraid to try to learn. The effects of emotional disturbances are so diverse and their manifestations so varied that they should never be overlooked during the examination of a poor reader.

SCHOOL METHODS

Inadequate adaptation of methods of teaching reading appeared to be a cause of reading failure in 18 per cent of the twenty-two cases. This incidence is lower than usually reported in the literature. Part of the discrepancy may be due to the fact that children with Binet I.Q.'s under 85 were not included in this investigation and that children with normal and superior intelligence are more likely to adapt themselves to teaching methods used with an average group of children. However, the discrepancy may also be due to the fact that the investigator could not obtain enough information on the previous methods of teaching used with the subjects of this study to make an adequate evaluation of them. Data on school methods, teachers' personalities, and various administrative policies, emphasized as important in previous investigations, were meager in this study, except in a few cases. Usually the only information available was the opinion of teachers who handled the child at the time he was examined.

Since a large number of these severely retarded readers improved, it seems logical to assume that better adaptation of methods of teaching reading to some of the deviating cases has greater value than the number of such cases reported in this study indicates. Such adaptations would be especially valuable if made early in the child's school life. Failure to make appropriate adaptations is due largely to the dearth of information concerning the pupils' needs and the method to apply when a given set of symptoms is exhibited. Even those teachers especially skilled in handling remedial cases in reading often have to resort to trial-and-error in order to select the method which will be most successful.

NEUROLOGICAL FINDINGS

Alexia or some other neurological difficulty was considered a cause of reading failure in 18 per cent of the twenty-two cases. Previous studies have not reported the proportion of seriously retarded readers so diagnosed. In fact, no previous study was found in which reading-disability cases with normal intelligence were examined by a neurologist before remedial training was started. In instances in which remedial training has been unsuccessful, the case has usually been assumed to be alexia. The present study shows that many pupils who had made little or no progress in learning to read before this diagnostic study, were not victims of alexia in the judgment of the neurologist. Moreover, a few cases diagnosed as alexia made progress beyond the level expected of a child with such a handicap.

These findings do not solve the controversial issue concerning alexia as a factor in reading disability. They do show that some cases diagnosed as alexia may learn to read satisfactorily if given sufficient time and if special remedial techniques are used. Perhaps all of them could be taught to read to some extent if enough were known about the relationship of various symptoms to causes, so that appropriate remedial methods could be applied. Further studies in this area may prove very valuable in revealing the extent to which neurological difficulties are responsible for reading disability and the possibility of promoting growth in reading among such cases.

SPEECH AND FUNCTIONAL AUDITORY FINDINGS

Speech and functional auditory factors were found to be contributing causes of reading disability in 18 per cent of the twenty-two cases; dyslalia was considered one of the causes in 14 per cent of them; and the remainder were accounted for by inadequate auditory discrimination and insufficient auditory memory span for sounds.

This finding agrees in general with those reported by most investigators, although the actual percentage of cases can be compared in only a few studies. It is higher, for example, than reported by Stulken[7] and by Hall.[8] Monroe[9] expressed the belief that speech difficulty might be considered a cause of reading failure or the result of a common cause. This agrees with the opinion of the speech specialist in this study concerning several cases, particularly Case 10, where both the dyslalia and the reading difficulty seemed to be caused by insufficient auditory memory span for sounds. Two cases of stuttering were reported, but neither was related to reading failure.

The percentage of cases of dyslalia in this group was larger than that usually found in the general school population of comparable age. This may mean that both reading and speech difficulties are deviations from the normal pattern, since the cause-and-effect relationship between the two has not been well established. On the other hand, it may mean, as Monroe said, that there are other basic factors of which speech and reading difficulty are symptoms. Two of these basic factors may be inadequate auditory discrimination and insufficient auditory memory span, as indicated by the few studies in the literature which are reinforced by the findings of the present investigation. Unfortunately, it is not possible to draw final conclusions concerning this phase of the study, because the standardized tests available are unsatisfactory and the norms for the tests constructed for this investigation are not thoroughly established.

ENDOCRINE FINDINGS

Mild hypothyroidism was the only endocrine disturbance found by the endocrinologist. Such a difficulty was found in about a third of the thirty children examined but was considered a cause of reading difficulty in only 9 per cent of the twenty-two cases studied in detail. This finding disagrees with the opinion of Mateer[10] that reduced function of the pituitary gland was a common cause of reading disability. However, the findings cannot be compared to those of Olson,[11] whose cases were studied continuously for a number of years. Therefore, this investigation shows, for the first time, the approximate number of severely retarded readers who exhibit endocrine deficiency.

Of particular importance is the fact that, when the endocrine disturbances were present, they not only retarded progress in learning to read but also had much wider significance. For example, in Case 16 this difficulty interfered with orthoptic treatment, social adjustment, and physical well-being. While this factor is less important than those referred to earlier, as measured by its frequency of occurrence, the influence it exerts on certain cases is indeed marked.

AUDITORY-ACUITY FINDINGS

Insufficient auditory acuity was found as a cause of poor reading in only 9 per cent of the cases. In each case the child and parents had been aware of the deficiency before this examination was made. The studies in the literature report that good readers tend to be somewhat better in auditory acuity than poor readers; but, as Jastak[12] pointed out, no case has been reported in which the reading deficiency is ascribed to insufficient auditory acuity alone. Thus the present study reinforces the general opinion that insufficient auditory acuity is relatively unimportant as a cause of severe reading retardation.

Attention should be directed to the fact that, although in relatively few cases was there significant loss of auditory acuity in the whole range of frequencies, several showed a loss of acuity only in the upper frequencies. This loss was considered unimportant by the co-operating otolaryngologist. However, a recent study by Kennedy[13] showed that a loss in these upper frequencies is conducive to poor reading in some cases. The significance of this finding cannot be determined until further study reveals more fully and accurately the effects of such auditory-acuity deficiencies.

GENERAL PHYSICAL FINDINGS

Among the various difficulties not included above but which might be classed as physical, malnutrition was the only one that proved to be a cause of reading failure, and it was present in only one case. Previous studies have listed poor dentition, infected tonsils and adenoids, asthmatic and allergic conditions, susceptibility to colds, disorders of the lymphatic system, circulatory disorders, gastrointestinal difficulties, and tuberculosis, none of which was exhibited by the cases included in this study.

The foregoing list provides another example of anomalies found in poor readers but not adequately evaluated as to their causal relationships. The results of the present investigation indicate that such anomalies be studied carefully before assuming that they are causes of severe reading retardation.

DOMINANCE FINDINGS

This study made no contribution to the evaluation of dominance as a cause of reading failure. Tests of dominance were given to each case, and the results are reported in chapter x. However, dominance was not included among the causes of reading disability because the group of specialists co-operating in this study were unable to interpret the test results. The importance of this factor, as emphasized by Orton,[14] Dearborn,[15] and Stanger and Donohue,[16] has not been ignored. However, the findings of Twitmeyer and Nathanson[17] to the effect that a consistent dominance does not exist, supplemented by significant differences in interpretation by other writers in this field, leave so many questions that the problem itself assumes major proportions and becomes so involved that it should be made the basis of a separate and intensive study.

INTELLIGENCE

Similarly, no contribution was made by this study to an understanding of the relationship between intelligence and reading failure. The cases in this study were purposely selected so that they would be sufficiently intelligent to indicate that there must be interferences in some other area, or reading progress would be normal.

The literature has shown that defective intelligence is a very close correlate of reading and also sets the limits of achievement in reading. Intellectually defective children, therefore, are poor readers, and little can be done to improve their reading markedly. The cases in this study were selected to avoid this factor as a cause.

UNIQUE CONTRIBUTIONS OF THIS INVESTIGATION

This study has shown that home and family relationships were a very important cause of severe reading retardation. This factor has not previously been given the emphasis which it appears to merit. Emotional maladjustments were also found to be important as a cause of reading disability and were closely related to family problems. Specific emotional reactions recorded by the psychiatrist in this study are especially helpful in understanding the problems presented by each case.

Visual difficulties, which have previously been the center of much controversy, were proved to be responsible for reading failure in a significant percentage of the cases in this study. Binocular incoordinations were found more frequently than were any other type of visual anomaly, and orthoptic treatment to correct these difficulties was shown to be highly beneficial.

Inappropriate school methods accounted for fewer cases of reading failure than was anticipated, but the full details concerning this factor were difficult to obtain from the group of children studied. Evidence that neurological difficulties caused reading failure in a number of the cases was secured. Doubt remains concerning the progress which certain pupils so affected might have made, if sufficient time had been allowed and more refined methods of treatment had been used.

Speech and functional auditory anomalies appeared to be causes of reading failure in a number of cases. Dyslalia was the most frequent cause, as stuttering was not operative as a cause in any case. Inadequate auditory memory span for sounds and insufficient auditory discrimination appeared to be causes of both reading and speech difficulty in some cases. Tests for these anomalies appear to be worthy of fuller standardization.

Endocrine disturbances were limited to cases of mild hypothyroidism. This anomaly was responsible for relatively few cases of reading failure but was a potent cause when it was operative. This difficulty has not been studied adequately in the literature on causes of severe reading retardation. General physical difficulties other than those just mentioned were also responsible for few cases of reading failure. Malnutrition was the only one of many general physical difficulties previously cited in the literature which was found important in the cases in this study. Insufficient auditory acuity operated as a cause of reading failure in only two cases, and they were taught to read in spite of this handicap. It is considered relatively unimportant as a cause, in agreement with the results of most previous research.

This study made no contribution to the understanding of the effects of dominance anomalies, because the group of specialists could not adequately interpret the results of tests. Likewise, it made no contribution to the effect of less-than-normal intelligence, since the cases were selected so as to eliminate those seriously retarded intellectually.

Furthermore, this study has revealed the need for further research as brought out in the section that follows.

PROBLEMS FOR FURTHER INVESTIGATION

This study is not unlike many others in that it has revealed more problems in need of further study than it has solved. Some of the more important problems brought to a focus are listed below.

First, an extension of the type of study reported here is urgently needed, since data based on thirty cases examined and twenty-two cases treated do not provide an adequate basis for valid conclusions concerning many of the issues considered. The comprehensive diagnostic procedure developed in this study offers promise of valuable returns and should be applied to a sufficient number of cases to justify valid conclusions. Such an extension of the study is desirable because further clarification concerning the causes of reading failure is greatly needed. This end can be achieved only by thorough investigation, with careful checking and evaluation of findings. Until more precise and accurate information is available, research workers, reading diagnosticians, and classroom teachers will not be certain concerning the relative importance of various probable causes of reading disability and may spend considerable time on unimportant factors.

Second, the disagreement concerning the potency of various causes reported by different investigators has been reinforced by the findings of this study. Such disagreement may be due, in part, to the use of different tests and varying norms. It is essential, therefore, that tests and examination procedures be critically evaluated and that norms of expectancy be established for all tests in which they do not now exist.

An example of this need grows out of the fact that the effect of various visual difficulties on learning to read is highly controversial. Some investigators have found significant positive relationships, while others have found none. The tests used varied from the Snellen chart and the Keystone Visual Safety Test to a careful refraction.

This study provides clear evidence of disagreement between the findings and interpretations of an ophthalmologist concerning the need for visual care and the results of the two tests just mentioned. Furthermore, when a refraction is completed, there is difference of opinion as to the importance of the findings. Specifically, in this study the ophthalmologist considered hyperopia less than $+1.50$ as insignificant and not worthy of correction. On the other hand, Eames[18] maintained that hyperopia between $+0.50$ and $+1.50$ needed correction. A large number of poor readers rated in this area. As pointed out earlier, detailed study is also needed to determine the relationship between peripheral visual anomalies and visual perception, so as to aid more fully in understanding the extent to which visual difficulties contribute to reading failure.

Another example is the need for valid tests of dominance and clarification of the relation of hand, foot, ear, and eye preferences to reading retardation. Various investigators, using similar tests, have obtained different results. The tests of preference in current use are so inadequate that the results secured could not be evaluated in the present investigation.

Furthermore, the controversial issue concerning alexia might also be solved if adequate tests of alexia were available for use by reading diagnosticians. At least, a case diagnosed as alexia could be given appropriate treatment, as was done in the present research, to see if he could be taught to read.

The foregoing examples emphasize the fact that a comprehensive study of causes of severe reading retardation is largely dependent upon the use of valid tests which have been standardized.

Third, since the services of competent specialists in each allied field cannot always be obtained as in this study and since adequate tests are not available for use in selecting cases in need of special examination, it would be advisable to know more fully and accurately than is known at present the symptoms of each causal factor. The number of symptoms of various causes of reading failure exceeds the number of causes. Furthermore, one symptom may indicate any one of several causes. A study in this area should aid in identifying a pattern of symptoms with a particular cause of reading disability. Such research was beyond the scope of this study, yet the evidence secured indicated that such sets of symptoms could be identified.

Children with serious emotional problems, for example, might be identified from some of the manifestations listed in Table 19 of chapter x. Attitudes toward success and failure, methods of explaining deficiency, reaction to loss of status, emotional and physical reactions, and evidence of mental conflict may be recorded as shown above. From such symptoms the most significant can be selected.

In other areas, such as the visual, symptoms of the various types of difficulties need to be determined. Such habits as holding a book too near the eyes or too far away or to one side of the line of vision may indicate visual disturbances. Frowning, tears in the eyes, attempts to wipe away a blur, and frequent glances at distance when reading may signify the presence of visual anomalies. Inability to use the eyes at near-point for a prolonged period, for example, was exhibited by a number of cases, who were found in this study to have binocular inco-ordinations. In addition, a more accurate visual screening test would be helpful.

Furthermore, the hypothyroid case who should be seen by the endocrinologist exhibits certain types of characteristics and reactions. He may be overweight, slow in physical and mental reactions, and easily fatigued. On the other hand, a few of the cases of hypothyroidism were thin and alert. Undoubtedly other symptoms in this type of case would aid in identification.

Again, more detailed information concerning the proper therapy for each cause or constellation of causes would be extremely valuable to both the remedial and the classroom teacher. Such information would aid in saving many pupils from continuous failure, as one cause after another is investigated and one method of treatment after another is tried.

Finally, when causes of reading failure have been identified, methods of prevention should be more fully determined. As pointed out above, this study has shown that many severely retarded readers learn to read after they have experienced years of failure. This supports the contention that, when causes of reading failure are known, preventive or corrective measures may be used as soon as symptoms are noted.

The need for more emphasis on prevention is evident from the number of severely retarded readers referred for clinical examination. The effect on the individual child of being a reading problem is often very great, as the case summaries in chapter xi show clearly. Consequently, preventive measures which avoid such disaster are extremely desirable. This study indicates that much more may be done than has previously been attempted in preventing the development of reading disability.

PRACTICAL IMPLICATIONS OF THE STUDY

The information secured from this investigation has wide implications for anyone concerned with diagnosis and remediation of deficient readers. Even prevention of reading disabilities cannot be adequately planned until more knowledge is gained concerning the reasons for this failure.

In many instances, teachers and diagnosticians search for a single anomaly to explain reading failure. This procedure often results in omission of many other causes of importance, with resulting waste of time in treating an anomaly which is only coincidental with poor reading. This study has shown that many anomalies were identified and only part of them appeared to be important to reading growth. In the cases in which treatment was directed toward coincidental anomalies, nothing was accomplished. Such a waste of time tends to discourage the child and results in greater difficulty in remedial instruction when real causes are identified.

The diagnostic examination of severely retarded readers should not end with an attempt to identify a wide number of possible causes. Evaluation of each factor in the light of all information available concerning the child should follow. An anomaly found with one child may be insignificant when all other findings are considered, whereas in another instance with a different constellation of causes, the same anomaly may take on much greater significance. Here is a challenge to the diagnostician to identify all anomalies associated with reading failure. Many may be closely related and interact to impair reading progress. Accurate evaluation of anomalies in order to identify them as causes calls for broad training and wide experience on the part of the diagnostician. Such care is essential to avoid inconsequential or incorrect remedial steps.

At present, identifying causes of poor reading is a difficult task. This study indicates that the pooled opinions of several experts in varied fields is more reliable than the opinion of a reading examiner alone. It is not always possible for the examiner to obtain the services of competent specialists in allied fields. This practical limitation emphasizes the need for a thorough search for symptoms of various causal factors in order that the advice of appropriate specialists may be sought only as particular groups of symptoms are exhibited.

An alternative, or perhaps an added, means of securing evidence of this need is to give tests for the purpose of selecting children who should be referred to specialists in allied fields. Some tests have already been constructed or adapted for this purpose. The few tests available must be used with caution, as they are still not completely reliable in identifying all children in need of attention.

The analysis of relative frequency of various causal factors shows that more attention should be given to home and family problems of severely retarded readers. In the group of children considered, this cause operated more frequently than visual and emotional difficulties, both of which have received wider attention in diagnostic routines. Such problems cannot be measured quantitatively and are relatively difficult to elicit in many cases; but persistent efforts on the part of reading examiners may be well repaid in understanding the reading problem. Appropriate treatment will then facilitate learning to read. Furthermore, this finding is highly suggestive to school people. It is possible that a better understanding of children's home relationships might be an excellent means of preventing cases of reading disability.

Many of the anomalies in allied fields may be discovered and remedied without appreciable growth in reading. This is because such remediation only prepares the child for learning to read and does not teach him the skill. A direct, vigorous reading program must follow correction of causal factors. For example, correcting a visual difficulty does not teach the child to read but enables him to learn with greater ease when he is given remedial instruction. Likewise, psychiatric treatment for an emotional problem results in no reading growth without teaching, but it may remove the emotional block so that the child is able to direct his attention toward learning. In many instances it is probable that an enthusiastic, capable teacher can motivate a child to learn to read, even though he has inhibiting difficulties, although much less time and effort might be needed if the inhibiting factors were corrected prior to learning.

Efficient and flexible techniques for teaching reading are extremely important, especially to children whose inhibiting difficulties cannot be readily corrected. Despite the use of methods currently employed, it is significant that a few of the retarded readers in this study did not improve appreciably, even after therapy in allied fields. This fact provides a real challenge to discover other means of teaching such children to read. For example, cases diagnosed as alexia made the least gains in reading in this study. Perhaps they, too, can be taught if more effective teaching methods are developed. Children with short memory span for sounds made less progress than others. Those cases with a permanent but partial loss of hearing in one ear required special adjustments. Since, at present, none of these defects mentioned can be corrected, more effective methods for teaching such children to read will need to be developed.

This study shows clearly that a large proportion of children who are considered "unteachable" may learn to read when adequate diagnostic and remedial steps are taken. The findings give promise of definite help for a much larger proportion of seriously retarded readers than has been achieved in the past.

NOTES

1. Mary I. Preston, "The Reaction of Parents to Reading Failure," *Child Development*, X, No. 3 (September, 1939), 173–79.

2. Margaret Ladd, *The Relation of Social, Economic, and Personal Characteristics to Reading Ability* ("Contributions to Education," No. 582 [New York: Bureau of Publications, Teachers College, Columbia University, 1933]).

3. See p. 132 of this study.

4. Charles A. Selzer, *Lateral Dominance and Visual Fusion: The Application to Difficulties in Reading, Writing, and Speech* ("Harvard Monographs in Education," No. 12 [Cambridge: Harvard University Press, 1933]).

5. Paul Witty and David Kopel, "Factors Associated with the Etiology of Reading Disability," *Journal of Educational Research*, XXIX (February, 1936), 449–59.

6. Arthur I. Gates, "The Role of Personality-Maladjustment in Reading Disability," *Journal of Genetic Psychology*, LIX (September, 1941), 77–83.

7. Edward H. Stulken, "Retardation in Reading and the Problem Boy in School," *Elementary English Review*, XIV, No. 5 (May, 1937), 179–82.

8. Margaret E. Hall, "Auditory Factors in Functional Articulatory Speech Defects," *Journal of Experimental Education*, VII, No. 2 (December, 1938), 110–32.

9. Marion Monroe, *Children Who Cannot Read* (Chicago: University of Chicago Press, 1932).

10. Florence Mateer, "A First Study of Pituitary Dysfunction," *Psychological Bulletin*, XXXII (1935), 736.

11. Willard C. Olson, "Reading as a Function of the Total Growth of the Child," in William S. Gray (comp. and ed.), *Reading and Pupil Development* ("Supplementary Educational Monographs," No. 51 [Chicago: University of Chicago, 1940]), pp. 233–37.

12. Joseph Jastak, "Interferences in Reading," *Psychological Bulletin*, XXXI (April, 1934), 244–72.

13. Helen Kennedy, "A Study of Children's Hearing as It Relates to Reading," *Journal of Experimental Education*, X (June, 1942), 238–51.

14. Samuel T. Orton, "Specific Reading Disability—Strephosymbolia," *Journal of the American Medical Association*, XC (April, 1928), 1095–99.

15. Walter F. Dearborn, "Structural Factors Which Condition Special Disability in Reading," *American Association on Mental Deficiency*, XXXVIII (June, 1932—June, 1933), 268–83.

16. Margaret A. Stanger and Ellen K. Donohue, *Prediction and Prevention of Reading Difficulties* (New York: Oxford University Press, 1937).

17. E. B. Twitmeyer and Y. Nathanson, "The Determination of Laterality," *Psychological Clinic*, XXII (1935), 141–49.

18. Thomas H. Eames, "The Ocular Conditions of 350 Poor Readers," *Journal of Educational Research*, XXXII (September, 1938), 10–13.

BIBLIOGRAPHY

BIBLIOGRAPHY

ADAMS, OLGA. "Implications of Language in Beginning Reading," *Childhood Education*, XII (January, 1936), 158–62.

ANDERSON, MARGARET, and KELLEY, MAE. "An Inquiry into Traits Associated with Reading Disability," *Smith College Studies in Social Work*, II (September, 1931), 46–63.

ANDERSON, V. A. "Auditory Memory Span as Tested by Speech Sounds," *American Journal of Psychology*, LII, No. 1 (January, 1939), 95–99.

ARTHUR, GRACE. "An Attempt To Sort Children with Specific Reading Disability from Other Non-readers," *Journal of Applied Psychology*, XI (August, 1927), 251–63.

———. *A Point Scale of Performance*. New York: Commonwealth Fund, Division of Publications, 1930.

BENNETT, CHESTER C. *An Inquiry into the Genesis of Poor Reading*. "Teachers College Contributions to Education," No. 755. New York: Bureau of Publications, Teachers College, Columbia University, 1938. Pp. viii+139.

BETTS, EMMETT A. "A Physiological Approach to the Analysis of Reading Disabilities," *Educational Research Bulletin* (Ohio State University), XIII (September and October, 1934), 135–40, 163–74.

———. *The Prevention and Correction of Reading Difficulties*. Evanston, Ill.: Row, Peterson & Co., 1936. Pp. xiv+402.

———. "Retardation in Reading," *The Role of Research in Educational Progress: Official Report of the American Educational Research Association* (Washington: American Educational Research Assoc. of N.E.A., 1937), pp. 186–91.

———. "Visual Aids in Remedial Reading," *Educational Screen*, XV (April, 1936), 108–10.

BIRD, GRACE E. "Personality Factors in Learning," *Personnel Journal*, VI (June, 1927), 56–59.

BLAKE, MABELLE B., and DEARBORN, WALTER F. "The Improvement of Reading Habits," *Journal of Higher Education*, VI (February, 1935), 83–88.

BLANCHARD, PHYLLIS. "Reading Disabilities in Relation to Difficulties of Personality and Emotional Development," *Mental Hygiene*, XX (July, 1936), 384–413.

———. "Reading Disability in Relation to Maladjustment," *Mental Hygiene*, XII (October, 1928), 772–88.

BLANKENSHIP, ALBERT B. "Memory Span: A Review of the Literature," *Psychological Bulletin*, XXXV (1938), 1–25.

BOND, GUY L. *The Auditory and Speech Characteristics of Poor Readers*. "Teachers College Contributions to Education," No. 657. New York: Teachers College, Columbia University, 1935. Pp. 48.

BOOTHBY, WALTER M.; BERKSON, JOSEPH; and DUNN, HALBERT L. "Studies of the Energy of Metabolism of Normal Individuals: A Standard for Basal

Metabolism, with a Nomogram for Clinical Application," *American Journal of Physiology,* CXVI (July, 1936), 468–94.

BROMBACH, T. A. "Blind Spot Measurements and Remedial Reading Problems," Southbridge, Mass.: American Optical Co., 1936. Pp. 26. Mimeographed.

BRONNER, AUGUSTA F. *The Psychology of Special Abilities and Disabilities.* Boston: Little, Brown & Co., 1917. Pp. vi+269.

BUSWELL, GUY T. *Fundamental Reading Habits: A Study of Their Development.* "Supplementary Educational Monographs," No. 21. Chicago: University of Chicago, 1922. Pp. xiv+150.

CARTER, HAROLD D. "Emotional Correlates of Errors in Learning," *Journal of Educational Psychology,* XXVII (January, 1936), 55–67.

CARTER, THOMAS MILTON. "A Study of Radiographs of the Bones of the Wrist as a Means of Determining Anatomical Age." Doctor's thesis, Department of Education, University of Chicago, 1934. Pp. 199.

CASTNER, B. M. "Prediction of Reading Disability Prior to First Grade Entrance," *American Journal of Orthopsychiatry,* V (October, 1935), 375–87.

CLARK, BRANT. "Additional Data on Binocular Imbalance and Reading," *Journal of Educational Psychology,* XXVII (September, 1936), 473–75.

CLOWES, HELEN. "The Reading Clinic," *Elementary English Review,* VII (April, 1930), 98–101, 111.

COLE, LUELLA. *The Improvement of Reading.* New York: Farrar & Rinehart, 1938. Pp. 338.

COLLINS, S. D. *Eyesight of the School Child as Determined by the Snellen Test.* "Public Health Reports," reprint No. 975. Washington: Government Printing Office, November, 1924. Pp. 37.

CRIDER, BLAKE. "Certain Visual Functions in Relation to Reading Disabilities," *Elementary School Journal,* XXXV (December, 1934), 295–97.

————. "The Lack of Cerebral Dominance as a Cause of Reading Disabilities." *Childhood Education,* X (February, 1934), 238–39, 270.

————. "Ocular Dominance: Its Nature, Measurement, and Development." Unpublished Doctor's dissertation, Department of Psychology, Western Reserve University, 1934.

CROSLAND, H. R. "Superior Elementary-School Readers Contrasted with Inferior Readers in Letter-Position, 'Range of Attention' Scores," *Journal of Educational Research,* XXXII (February, 1939), 410–27.

DAMEREAU, RUTH. "Influence of Treatment on the Reading Ability and Behavior Disorders of Reading Disability Cases," *Smith College Studies in Social Work,* V (December, 1934), 160–83.

DAVIDSON, HELEN P. *An Experimental Study of Bright, Average, and Dull Children at the Four Year Mental Level* ("Genetic Psychology Monographs," Vol. IX, Nos. 3 and 4 [Worcester, Mass.: Clark University Press, 1931]), pp. 119–289.

DAVIS, IRENE POOLE. "The Speech Aspects of Reading Readiness," *National Elementary Principal,* XVII, No. 7 (July, 1938), 282–88.

DAVIS, LOUISE FARWELL. "Visual Difficulties and Reading Disabilities," in GRAY, WILLIAM S. (ed.), *Recent Trends in Reading* ("Supplementary Educational Monographs," No. 49 [Chicago: University of Chicago, 1939]), pp. 135–43.

DEARBORN, WALTER F. "The Nature and Causation of Disabilities in Reading," in GRAY, WILLIAM S. (ed.), *Recent Trends in Reading* ("Supplementary Educational Monographs," No. 49 [Chicago: University of Chicago, 1939]), pp. 103–10.

————. "The Nature of Special Abilities and Disabilities," *School and Society*, XXXI (May 10, 1930), 632–36.

————. *The Psychology of Reading*. "Columbia University Contributions to Philosophy, Psychology, and Education," Vol. XIV, No. 1. New York: Columbia University Press, 1906. Pp. 135.

————. "Structural Factors Which Condition Special Disability in Reading," *Proceedings and Addresses of the Fifty-seventh Annual Session of the American Association on Mental Deficiency*, XXXVIII (June, 1932—June, 1933), 268–83.

DEARBORN, WALTER F., and ANDERSON, IRVING. "Aniseikonia as Related to Disability in Reading," *Journal of Experimental Psychology*, XXIII (December, 1938), 559–77.

DEARBORN, WALTER F., and COMFORT, FORREST D. "Differences in the Size and Shape of Ocular Images as Related to Defects in Reading," in EMMETT A. BETTS, "Reading Disabilities and Their Correction," *Elementary English Review*, XII (May, 1935), 131–41.

DOLCH, EDWARD W. *The Psychology and Teaching of Reading*. Boston: Ginn & Co., 1931. Pp. v+261.

DURRELL, DONALD DEWITT. "Confusions in Learning," *Education*, LII (February, 1932), 330–33.

————. *Durrell Analysis of Reading Difficulty*. Yonkers-on-Hudson, N.Y.: World Book Co., 1937.

————. *Improvement of Basic Reading Abilities*. Yonkers-on-Hudson, N.Y.: World Book Co., 1940. Pp. viii+407.

————. "The Effect of Special Disability in Reading on Performance on the Stanford Revision of the Binet-Simon Tests, Master's Thesis, College of Education, University of Iowa, August, 1927," in EMMETT A. BETTS, "Reading Disabilities and Their Correction," *Elementary English Review*, XII (May, 1935), 133–34.

Durrell-Sullivan Reading Capacity and Achievement Tests, Intermediate Test, Form A, for Grades 3–6. Yonkers-on-Hudson, N.Y.: World Book Co., 1937.

EAMES, THOMAS H. "The Anatomical Basis of Lateral Dominance Anomalies," *American Journal of Orthopsychiatry*, IV (October, 1934), 524–28.

————. "A Comparison of the Ocular Characteristics of Unselected and Reading Disability Groups," *Journal of Educational Research*, XXV (March, 1932), 211–15.

————. "A Frequency Study of Physical Handicaps in Reading Disability and Unselected Groups," *ibid.*, XXIX (September, 1935), 1–5.

————. "Improvement of School Eye Testing," *Education*, LVI (September, 1935), 14–17.

————. "The Ocular Conditions of 350 Poor Readers," *Journal of Educational Research*, XXXII (September, 1938), 10–16.

————. "Restrictions of the Visual Field as Handicaps to Learning," *ibid.*, XXIX (February, 1936), 460–65.

EAMES, THOMAS H. "A Study of the Speed of Word Recognition," *ibid.*, XXXI (November, 1937), 181–87.

FARRIS, L. P. "Visual Defects as Factors Influencing Achievement in Reading," *California Journal of Secondary Education*, X (October, 1934), 50–51.

———. "Visual Defects as Factors Influencing Achievement in Reading," *Journal of Experimental Education*, V (September, 1936), 58–60.

FENDRICK, PAUL. *Visual Characteristics of Poor Readers.* "Teachers College Contributions to Education," No. 656. New York: Teachers College, Columbia University, 1935. Pp. 54.

FENDRICK, PAUL, and BOND, GUY. "Delinquency and Reading," *Pedagogical Seminary and Journal of Genetic Psychology*, XLVIII (March, 1936), 236–43.

FERNALD, GRACE. *Remedial Techniques in Basic School Subjects.* New York: McGraw-Hill Book Co., 1943. Pp. xv+349.

FILDES, LUCY G. "A Psychological Inquiry into the Nature of the Condition Known as Congenital Word-Blindness," *Brain*, XLIV (1921), 286–307.

GATES, ARTHUR I. "Diagnosis and Treatment of Extreme Cases of Reading Disability," *Thirty-sixth Yearbook of the National Society for the Study of Education*, Part I: *The Teaching of Reading: A Second Report* (Bloomington, Ill.: Public School Pub. Co., 1937), pp. 391–416.

———. *Gates Reading Diagnosis Tests.* Rev. ed. New York: Bureau of Publications, Teachers College, Columbia University, 1933.

———. *Improvement of Reading.* New York: Macmillan Co., 1929. Pp. xii+440.

———. *Interest and Ability in Reading.* New York: Macmillan Co., 1930. Pp. xii+264.

———. "The Measurement and Evaluation of Achievement in Reading," *Thirty-sixth Yearbook of the National Society for the Study of Education*, Part I: *The Teaching of Reading: A Second Report* (Bloomington, Ill.: Public School Pub. Co., 1937), pp. 359–88.

———. "The Necessary Mental Age for Beginning Reading," *Elementary School Journal*, XXXVII (March, 1937), 497–508.

———. *The Psychology of Reading and Spelling with Special Reference to Disability.* "Columbia University Contributions to Education," No. 129. New York: Teachers College, Columbia University, 1922. Pp. vii+108.

———. "The Role of Personality Maladjustment in Reading Disability," *Journal of Genetic Psychology*, LIX (September, 1941), 77–83.

GATES, ARTHUR I., and BENNETT, CHESTER C. *Reversal Tendencies in Reading: Causes, Diagnosis, Prevention, and Correction.* New York: Bureau of Publications, Teachers College, Columbia University, 1933. Pp. i+33.

GATES, ARTHUR I. (with the assistance of GUY L. BOND). "Failure in Reading and Social Maladjustment," *Journal of the National Education Association*, XXV (October, 1936), 205–6.

GATES, ARTHUR I., and BOND, GUY L. "Reading Readiness: A Study of Factors Determining Success and Failure in Beginning Reading," *Teachers College Record*, XXXVII (May, 1936), 679–85.

———. "Relation of Handedness, Eye-sighting, and Acuity Dominance to Reading," *Journal of Educational Psychology*, XXVII (September, 1936), 450–56.

GILCREST, E. P. "The Extent to Which Praise and Blame Affect a Pupil's Work," *School and Society*, IV (December, 1916), 872–74.

GOOD, G. H. "Relationship of Fusion Weakness to Reading Disability," *Journal of Experimental Education*, VIII (September, 1939), 115–21.

GRAY, WILLIAM S. (ed.). *Reading in General Education*. Washington: American Council on Education, 1940. Pp. xiii+464.

———. *Standardized Oral Reading Paragraphs*. Bloomington, Ill.: Public School Pub. Co., 1916.

GRAY, WILLIAM S., with the co-operation of DURRELL, DONALD D.; GATES, ARTHUR I.; HORN, ERNEST; and MCKEE, PAUL. "Reading," *Review of Educational Research*, VII (December, 1937), 493–507.

GRAY, WILLIAM S.; KIBBE, DELIA; LUCAS, LAURA; and MILLER, LAWRENCE W. *Remedial Cases in Reading: Their Diagnosis and Treatment*. "Supplementary Educational Monographs," No. 22. Chicago: University of Chicago, 1922. Pp. viii+208.

HALL, MARGARET E. "Auditory Factors in Functional Articulatory Speech Defects," *Journal of Experimental Education*, VII, No. 2 (December, 1938), 110–32.

HARDWICK, ROSE S. "Types of Reading Disability," *Childhood Education*, VIII (April, 1932), 423–27.

HARRISON, M. LUCILLE. *Reading Readiness*. Boston, Mass.: Houghton Mifflin Co., 1936. Pp. vii+166.

HEAD, HENRY. *Aphasia and Kindred Disorders of Speech*, Vol. I. New York: Macmillan Co., 1926. Pp. xvi+549.

HERRICK, C. JUDSON. *An Introduction to Neurology*. 5th ed. Philadelphia and London: H. B. Saunders Co., 1931. Pp. 417.

HILDRETH, GERTRUDE. "Bilateral Manual Performance: Eye-Dominance and Reading Achievement," *Child Development*, XI (1940). 311–17.

———. "Reversals in Reading and Writing," *Journal of Educational Psychology*, XXV (January, 1934), 1–20.

HILDRETH, GERTRUDE H., and GRIFFITHS, NELLIE L. *Metropolitan Readiness Tests*. Yonkers-on-Hudson, N.Y.: World Book Co., 1933.

HINCKS, ELIZABETH M. *Disability in Reading and Its Relation to Personality*. "Harvard Monographs in Education," No. 7. Cambridge: Harvard University Press, 1926. Pp. 92.

HINSHELWOOD, JAMES. *Congenital Word-Blindness*. London: H. K. Lewis, Ltd., 1917. Pp. ix+112.

HOLLINGWORTH, LETA S. *Special Talents and Defects: Their Significance for Education*. New York: Macmillan Co., 1923. Pp. xix+216.

HOWES, ESTHER CORNELIA. "An Analysis of Some of the Determining Factors of Educational Achievement of Deaf Children." Unpublished Master's thesis, Department of Education, University of Chicago, 1936. Pp. 52.

IMUS, H. A.; ROTHNEY, J. W. M.; and BEAR, R. M. *An Evaluation of Visual Factors in Reading*. Hanover, N.H.: Dartmouth College Publication, 1938. Pp. viii+144.

JAMESON, AUGUSTA. "Methods and Devices for Remedial Reading," in GRAY, WILLIAM S. (ed.), *Recent Trends in Reading* ("Supplementary Educational Monographs," No. 49 [Chicago: University of Chicago, 1939]), pp. 170–78.

JASTAK, JOSEPH. "Interferences in Reading," *Psychological Bulletin*, XXXI (April, 1934), 244–72.

JENKINS, D. L.; BROWN, ANDREW W.; and ELMENDORF, LAURA. "Mixed Dominance and Reading Disability," *American Journal of Orthopsychiatry*, VII (January, 1937), 72–81.

JUDD, CHARLES H. "Photographic Records of Convergence and Divergence" ("Yale Psychological Studies," New Ser., Vol. I, No. 2), *Psychological Review Monograph Supplements*, VIII, No. 3 (1907), 370–423.

KANARIK, ROSELLA, and MANWILLER, C. E. "How a High School Attacks Its Learning Difficulties in Reading and Arithmetic," *Pittsburgh Schools*, XI (January, February, 1937), 94–116.

KENDREW, E. N. "A Note on the Persistence of Moods," *British Journal of Psychology*, XXVI (1935), 165–73.

KENNEDY, HELEN. "A Study of Children's Hearing as It Relates to Reading," *Journal of Experimental Education*, X (June, 1942), 238–51.

KIRK, SAMUEL A. "The Effects of Remedial Reading on the Educational Progress and Personality Adjustment of High-Grade Mentally Deficient Children," *Journal of Juvenile Research*, XVIII (July, 1934), 140–62.

———. *Teaching Reading to Slow-learning Children*. Boston: Houghton Mifflin Co., 1940. Pp. v+225.

LADD, MARGARET. *The Relation of Social, Economic, and Personal Characteristics to Reading Ability*. "Teachers College Contributions to Education," No. 582. New York: Bureau of Publications, Teachers College, Columbia University, 1933. Pp. vii+100.

LEAVELL, ULLIN W., and STERLING, HELEN. "A Comparison of Basic Factors in Reading Patterns with Intelligence," *Peabody Journal of Education*, XVI (November, 1938), 149–55.

LICHTENSTEIN, ARTHUR. "An Investigation of Reading Retardation," *Journal of Genetic Psychology*, LII (1938), 407–23.

LORD, ELIZABETH; CARMICHAEL, LEONARD; and DEARBORN, WALTER F. *Special Disabilities in Learning To Read and Write*. "Harvard Monographs in Education," Ser. I, Vol. II, No. 1. Cambridge: Harvard University Press, 1925. Pp. 76.

LOUTTIT, C. M. *Clinical Psychology: A Handbook of Children's Behavior Problems*. New York: Harper & Bros., 1936. Pp. xx+695.

LUCKIESH, MATTHEW, and MOSS, FRANK K. *Reading as a Visual Task*. New York: D. Van Nostrand Co., Inc., 1942. Pp. xv+428.

McALLISTER, C. N. "The Fixation of Points in the Visual Field," *Psychological Review Monograph Supplements*, VII (March, 1905), 17–53.

McCALL, WILLIAM A. *How To Measure in Education*. New York: Macmillan Co., 1922. Pp. xii+416.

MATEER, FLORENCE. "A First Study of Pituitary Dysfunction," *Psychological Bulletin*, XXXII (1935), 736.

MAY, CHARLES H., and PERERA, CHARLES A. *Manual of the Diseases of the Eye*. 18th ed. rev. New York: William Wood & Co., 1943.

MILLS, LLOYD. "Eyedness and Handedness," *American Journal of Ophthalmology*, VIII (December, 1925), 933–41.

MONROE, MARION. *Children Who Cannot Read*. Chicago: University of Chicago Press, 1932.

———. *Diagnostic Reading Examination: Manual of Directions*. Chicago: C H. Stoelting Co., 1930.

————. *Reading Aptitude Tests*. Boston: Houghton Mifflin Co., Riverside Press, 1935.

————. "Reading Aptitude Tests in Beginning Reading," *Education*, LVI (September, 1935), 7–14.

MONROE, MARION, and BACKUS, BERTIE. *Remedial Reading: A Monograph in Character Education*. Boston: Houghton Mifflin Co., 1937. Pp. xi+171.

MORGAN, W. P. "A Case of Congenital Word-Blindness," *British Medical Journal*, II (November 7, 1896), 1378.

MORPHETT, MABEL VOGEL, and WASHBURNE, CARLETON. "When Should Children Begin To Read?" *Elementary School Journal*, XXXI (March, 1931), 496–503.

NEWELL, NANCY. "For Non-readers in Distress," *Elementary School Journal*, XXXII (November, 1931), 183–95.

NOLAN, ESTHER GRACE. "Reading Difficulty versus Low Mentality," *California Journal of Secondary Education*, XVII (January, 1942), 34–39.

OLSON, WILLARD C. "Reading as a Function of the Total Growth of the Child," in GRAY, WILLIAM S. (comp. and ed.), *Reading and Pupil Development*. ("Supplementary Educational Monographs," No. 51 [Chicago: University of Chicago, 1940]), pp. 233–37.

The Ophthalmograph, the Metron-O-Scope: Manual for Controlled Reading. Southbridge, Mass.: Bureau of Visual Science, American Optical Co., 1937–38.

ORTON, SAMUEL T. *Reading, Writing, and Speech Problems in Children*. New York: W. W. Norton Co., 1937. Pp. 215.

————. "The 'Sight-reading' Method of Teaching Reading, as a Source of Reading Disability," *Journal of Educational Psychology*, XX (February, 1929), 135–43.

————. "Specific Reading Disability—Strephosymbolia," *Journal of American Medical Association*, XC (April, 1928), 1095–99.

PARKINS, GEORGE A. *The Diagnosis and Elimination of Visual Handicaps Preventing Efficient Reading*. Rutland, Vt.: Tuttle Pub. Co., 1941. Pp. 142.

PARR, F. W. "Factors Associated with Poor Reading Ability of Adults," *School and Society*, XXXV (May 7, 1932), 626.

PRESCOTT, DANIEL A. *Emotion and the Educative Process*. Washington: American Council on Education, 1938. Pp. xviii+323.

PRESTON, MARY I. "The Reaction of Parents to Reading Failures," *Child Development*, X, No. 3 (September, 1939), 173–79.

————. "Reading Failure and the Child's Security," *American Journal of Orthopsychiatry*, X (April, 1940), 239–52.

RIDENOUR, NINA. "The Treatment of Reading Disability," *Mental Hygiene*, XIX (1935), 387–97.

SANOHARA, T. "A Psychological Study of the Feeling of Shame," *Japanese Journal of Psychology*, IX (1934), 847–90.

SAUNDERS, MARY JANE. "The Short Auditory Span Disability," *Childhood Education*, VIII (October, 1931), 59–65.

SCHMITT, CLARA. "Developmental Alexia," *Elementary School Journal*, XVIII (May, 1918), 680–700 and 757–69.

SELZER, CHARLES A. *Lateral Dominance and Visual Fusion: The Application to*

Difficulties in Reading, Writing, Spelling, and Speech. "Harvard Monographs in Education," No. 12. Cambridge: Harvard University Press, 1933. Pp. 119.

SHERMAN, MANDEL. "Emotional Disturbances and Reading Disability," in GRAY, WILLIAM S. (ed.), *Recent Trends in Reading* ("Supplementary Educational Monographs," No. 49 [Chicago: University of Chicago, 1939]), pp. 126–34.

SHOCK, NATHAN W., and SOLEY, MAYO H. "Average Values for Basal Respiratory Functions in Adolescents and Adults," *Journal of Nutrition*, XVIII (August, 1939), 143–53.

SPACHE, GEORGE. "Eye Preference, Visual Acuity, and Reading Ability," *Elementary School Journal*, XLIII (May, 1943), 539–43.

———. "The Role of Visual Defects in Spelling and Reading Disabilities," *American Journal of Orthopsychiatry*, X (April, 1940), 229–38.

———. "Testing Vision," *Education*, LIX (June, 1939), 623–26.

STANGER, MARGARET A., and DONOHUE, ELLEN K. *Prediction and Prevention of Reading Difficulties.* New York: Oxford University Press, 1937. Pp. ix+191.

STROMBERG, ELEROY L. "The Relationship of Measures of Visual Acuity and Ametropia to Reading Speed," *Journal of Applied Psychology*, XII (February, 1938), 70–78.

STULLKEN, EDWARD H. "Retardation in Reading and the Problem Boy in School," *Elementary English Review*, XIV, No. 5 (May, 1937), 179–82.

SULLIVAN, ELLEN B. "Attitude in Relation to Learning," *Psychological Monographs*, XXXVI, No. 169 (1927), 1–149.

SWANSON, DONALD E., and TIFFIN, JOSEPH. "Betts' Physiological Approach to the Analysis of Reading Disabilities as Applied to the College Level," *Journal of Educational Research*, XXIX (February, 1936), 433–48.

TAYLOR, EARL A. *Controlled Reading.* Chicago: University of Chicago Press, 1937. Pp. xxviii+367.

TEEGARDEN, LORENE. "Clinical Identification of the Prospective Non-reader," *Child Development*, III (1932), 346–58.

TERMAN, LEWIS. *The Measurement of Intelligence.* Boston: Houghton Mifflin Co., 1916. Pp. xviii+362.

TERMAN, LEWIS, and MERRILL, MAUD. *Measuring Intelligence—a Guide to the Administration of the New Revised Stanford-Binet Tests of Intelligence.* Boston: Houghton Mifflin Co., 1937. Pp. x+460.

THORNDIKE, E. L., and WOODYARD, ELLA. "Influence of the Relative Frequency of Successes and Frustrations," *Journal of Educational Psychology*, XXV (April, 1934), 241–50.

TINKER, MILES A. "Diagnostic and Remedial Reading, II," *Elementary School Journal*, XXXIII (January, 1933), 346–57.

———. "Remedial Methods for Non-readers," *School and Society*, XL (October, 1934), 524–26.

———. "Trends in Diagnostic and Remedial Reading as Shown by Recent Publications in This Field," *Journal of Educational Research*, XXXII (December, 1938), 293–303.

TRAXLER, ARTHUR E. *Summary and Selected Bibliography of Research Relating to the Diagnosis and Teaching of Reading, 1930–1937.* New York: Educational Records Bureau, October, 1937. Pp. 60.

TULCHIN, SIMON H. "Emotional Factors in Reading Disabilities in School Children," *Journal of Educational Psychology*, XXVI (1935), 443–47.

TWITMYER, E. B., and NATHANSON, Y. "The Determination of Laterality," *Psychological Clinic*, XXII (1935), 141–48.

WAGNER, GUY W. "The Maturation of Certain Visual Functions and the Relationship between These Functions and Success in Reading and Arithmetic" ("Studies in Psychology of Reading," Vol. I; "University of Iowa Studies in Psychology," No. 21), *Psychological Monographs*, XLVIII, No. 3 (Princeton, N.J.: Psychological Review Co., 1937), 108–46.

WALLIN, J. E. W. "Congenital Word-Blindness: Some Analyses Cases," *Training School Bulletin* (Vineland, N.J.), March, 1920, pp. 76–84, 93–99.

WEISENBURG, THEODORE, and MCBRIDE, KATHERINE E. *Aphasia*. New York: Commonwealth Fund, 1935. Pp. xvi+634.

WELLS, DAVID W. *The Stereoscope in Ophthalmology*. Rev. ed. Boston: E. F. Mahady Co., 1926. Pp. viii+107.

WELLS, F. L. "A Glossary of Needless Reading Errors," *Journal of Experimental Education*, IV (September, 1935), 34–43.

WHIPPLE, GERTRUDE. "Causes of Retardation in Reading and Methods of Eliminating Them," *Peabody Journal of Education*, XVI (November, 1938), 191–200.

WHIPPLE, GUY MONTROSE. *Manual of Mental and Physical Tests*, Vol. I. Baltimore, Md.: Warwick & York, 1914. Pp. xvi+365.

WHITE, A., and POULL, L. E. *Reading Ability and Disability with Subnormal Children*. New York: Department of Public Welfare, 1921.

WITTY, PAUL, and KOPEL, DAVID. "Factors Associated with the Etiology of Reading Disability," *Journal of Educational Research*, XXIX (February, 1936), 449–59.

———. *Reading and the Educative Process*. Boston: Ginn & Co., 1939. Pp. x+374.

———. "Sinistrad and Mixed Manual-Ocular Behavior in Reading Disability," *Journal of Educational Psychology*, XXVII (February, 1936), 119–34.

WITTY, PAUL, and SKINNER, CHARLES E. *Mental Hygiene in Modern Education*. New York: Farrar & Rinehart, Inc., 1939. Pp. x+539.

WOLFE, LILLIAN S. "Differential Factors in Specific Reading Disability. I. Laterality of Function," *Journal of Genetic Psychology*, LVIII (1941), 45–56.

———. "Differential Factors in Specific Reading Disability. II. Audition, Vision, Verbal Association, and Adjustment," *ibid.*, pp. 57–70.

WOODY, CLIFFORD, and PHILLIPS, ALBERT J. "The Effects of Handedness on Reversals in Reading," *Journal of Educational Research*, XXVII (1934), 651–62.

WOOLEY, HELEN THOMPSON, and FERRIS, ELIZABETH. *Diagnosis and Treatment of Young School Failures*. Bureau of Education Bull. 1. Washington: Bureau of Education, 1923. Pp. vi+115.

INDEX

INDEX

Accommodation, 16, 24, 131
Accommodation-convergence reflex, 16
Adduction, 22
Aggressive reactions, 85
Alexia, 36, 39, 98, 99, 106, 115, 138, 165, 170, 171, 178, 179, 189, 190, 207, 208, 209, 227, 233, 237
   acquired, 36
   congenital, 1, 37, 98
   developmental, 35, 98
Alternating internal strabismus, 185
Alternating vision, 21, 46
Ametropia, 14, 18, 19, 134
Aniseikonia, 26–29, 98, 224
Anisometropia, 15
Antisocial children, 81
Anxieties, 79, 87
Articulation, inaccurate, 55
Articulatory defects, 99
Associations
   indifferent, 77
   pleasant, 77, 88
   unpleasant, 77
Astigmatic error, 180, 193
Astigmatism, 14–19, 98, 124, 127, 128, 136, 178, 185, 188, 189, 194
   hyperopic, 29, 206
   myopic, 17, 223
Attitudes, 93
Auditory acuity, 50–55, 99, 140, 165, 206, 209, 215, 221, 229, 231
Auditory defects, 183
Auditory difficulties, 211, 215, 221
Auditory discrimination, 50–53, 99, 106, 116, 144, 145, 164, 187, 191, 192, 193, 202, 228, 231
Auditory factor, 3
Auditory function, 50
Auditory fusion, 52
Auditory memory, 38, 72
Auditory memory span, 50, 53, 54, 80, 99, 116, 144, 145, 165, 178, 179, 180, 183, 185, 186, 202, 206, 207, 208, 228, 231
Auditory perception, 55
Auditory problems
   defective hearing, 60
   discrimination, 50, 52, 53, 99, 106, 116,

144, 145, 164, 187, 191, 192, 193, 202, 228, 231
   loss of hearing, 115, 141, 142, 144, 180, 189, 197, 199, 202, 203, 209, 237
   memory span, 50, 53, 54, 80, 99, 116, 144, 145, 165, 178, 179, 180, 183, 185, 186, 202, 206, 207, 208, 228, 231

Basal age, 69
Behavior
   aggressive, 100
   delinquent, 90
   difficulties in, 89
   maladjustment, 85
   problem of, 81
Betts Telebinocular, 18, 28
Betts tests of Visual Sensation and Perception, 14, 16, 19
Binocular co-ordination, 18, 19, 21, 22, 24, 25
Binocular fixations, 21
Binocular inco-ordination, 20, 29, 98, 223, 224, 231, 234
Binocular measurement, 13
Binocular vision, 12
Blind spots, 26, 115, 223
Blood pressure, 147
Bombastic child, 79
Brain injury, 174–75
Broken homes, 94

Compensatory mechanisms, 87
Conditions in the school, 98
Convergence, 8, 20, 131
Convergence insufficiency, 196, 197, 203
Co-operation between home and school, 95

Deceleration, 171
Defeatism, 87
Definition of reading disability, 11
Delinquency, 82, 89, 90, 100
Depth perception, 19
Descent of testicles, 60, 62
Developmental history, 106
Dextrad movements, 40, 41
Diplexia, 98

253